The Seer and The Sayer

Revelations of the New Earth

Victoria Hanchin

BALBOA.
PRESS

A DIVISION OF HAY HOUSE

ISBN: 978-1-4525-5727-4 (sc)
ISBN: 978-1-4525-5729-8 (hc)
ISBN: 978-1-4525-5728-1 (e)

Library of Congress Control Number: 2012915132

Balboa Press books may be ordered through booksellers or by contacting:

Balboa Press
A Division of Hay House
1663 Liberty Drive
Bloomington, IN 47403
www.balboapress.com
1-(877) 407-4847

Because of the dynamic nature of the Internet, any web addresses or links contained in this book may have changed since publication and may no longer be valid. The views expressed in this work are solely those of the author and do not necessarily reflect the views of the publisher, and the publisher hereby disclaims any responsibility for them.

The author of this book does not dispense medical advice or prescribe the use of any technique as a form of treatment for physical, emotional, or medical problems without the advice of a physician, either directly or indirectly. The intent of the author is only to offer information of a general nature to help you in your quest for emotional and spiritual well-being. In the event you use any of the information in this book for yourself, which is your constitutional right, the author and the publisher assume no responsibility for your actions.

Any people depicted in stock imagery provided by Thinkstock are models, and such images are being used for illustrative purposes only. Certain stock imagery © Thinkstock.

Printed in the United States of America
Balboa Press rev. date: 8/21/2012

Contents

Dedication

To the International Council of 13 Indigenous Grandmothers: global keepers of ancestral wisdom whose work lights the way to a future of unity for the next seven generations and beyond.

To the Younger Tribe: the awakening younger people of the next seven generations, into whose committed hands and loving hearts we entrust our future.

Foreword

I want to keep this foreword brief, because I'm eager for you to get into reading this book, *The Seer and The Sayer*. It is dynamite! It is a compelling true story that will ignite in you, as it did in me, an explosion of expanded consciousness. Before it does, I will introduce myself, so that you understand why I have such a profound basis for introducing Victoria's book to you.

I am a film and television producer, director and writer, and have received Emmys, a Peabody and lots of other awards for my work. I started in TV in 1969, partnered with my husband, as one of the original writers of *Sesame Street*. In the early 70's, with Marlo Thomas, I created *Free to Be... You and Me*, a record album, book and ABC-TV special. All of these works are still in circulation today, some 40 years later.

I grew up with my audience. My most recent work is a feature documentary, *For the Next 7 Generations*, about the International Council of 13 Indigenous Grandmothers from around the world who came together to heal our Mother Earth and all her inhabitants and to light our path to a peaceful and sustainable future, the kind of future that Victoria's story reveals for us.

Back in 2007, Victoria read that we were making the film, and called me in New York City to ask if she could do a fund-raiser. Surprisingly, I knew who Victoria was because someone had sent me an article that she'd written indicating a Mayan 2012 connection to the sacred three-rivers site in Pittsburgh, with its fourth underground river.

That fund-raiser connected us to Flordemayo, the Mayan Grandmother on the Council and in the movie. Through her, we got connected to her teacher, Mayan High Priest Don Alejandro Oxlaj, who is charged with interpreting the Mayan prophecies. Both came to Pittsburgh for the event. While there, Don Alejandro and Flordemayo blessed the sacred three-rivers site, with its underground fourth river. And Don Alejandro gave Victoria written confirmation of the three rivers' link to the ancient Mayan 2012 prophecies.

In 2010 Flordemayo introduced Victoria to Mohawk Grandmother Dona from Ohio. Both are major players in the book, whom I know you will immensely enjoy meeting.

Since the Pittsburgh fundraiser, Victoria and I have become close friends and soul supporters in all our efforts. I have had the privilege of seeing this book evolve from its earliest chapters to its glorious conclusion.

After reading each series of chapters, I would share with her with my spontaneous reactions, which are the best expressions of my thoughts about the book. They reflect the book's impact and my own expansion as I continued to read, so I will end this foreword by quoting from them.

Reading the initial chapters inspired what I wrote in my opening paragraph. It is worth repeating: "It's dynamite. Could ignite an explosion of consciousness." To assuage Victoria of her concerns that people might think she was off-the-wall, I added, "What saves it from seeming 'woo-woo' is its tone of informed innocence and deep receptiveness."

From the reading of the second batch of chapters:

"An amazingly compelling story with a strong ring of Truth—whose truth remains to be seen, giving it a real element of suspense. Just what every good story needs."

Third batch of chapters:

"Your book is the only thing that keeps me from being depressed about what I see happening all around me in the world. I use your book and its vision as an antidote. It tells the Big Story of the emerging New Earth, and gives us all the pieces that will help us to manifest it."

And finally:

"I finished your book and I am in awe. The ending is right where it should be. And it's not the ending. It really feels like it's a new beginning for the world."

Carole Hart
July 17, 2012

Author's Note

The Seer and The Sayer: Revelations of the New Earth is a true story, carefully documented as I lived it, over a period of two years. All the characters are real, and all have given me permission to use their actual names and identities. "It's time to be transparent," several of them informed me. "Visionaries are writing about the New Earth. You are showing how to live into it." I was moved, not to mention grateful for this solidarity, that they were willing to stand with me in communicating the revelations and miracles of this unusual story.

I learned from quantum physics that the future exists as a possibility. I learned from my Landmark Education Training to choose a future—a possibility—that moves me, and inspires me to be a bigger person than I think I am; a future that *wants* me; then to take a stand for the future that I am committed to creating.

This is what I have been summoned to do. I take my Divine Assignments seriously.

Most of the world longs for a better future. This story reveals an extraordinary version of what that future holds—if we choose.

Appreciation

The creation of this book and the experiences that formed it are so interwoven with the many Kindred Spirits in my life that I am in a continual state of appreciation.

First and foremost, to Grandmother Dona Greene, my primary co-adventurer in this story: Your heart, vision and knowledge have richly seeded this emerging New Earth. I am so privileged to have shared this journey with you. You are an inspiration.

To Grandmother Flordemayo, of the International Council of 13 Indigenous Grandmothers: Thank you for keeping after me to meet Grandmother Dona, and for sharing your Serpent wisdom. That kept me grounded in my own. Thank you for being a catalyst for me to discover the unusual puzzle pieces I carried for contributing to the New Earth.

To Carole Hart, dear friend, extraordinary ally and filmmaker for the 13 Grandmothers' movie: Thank you for seeing my essence, and for acknowledging my larger Self and highest vision even when I doubted myself. Thank you for being there with me from the beginning and throughout this unexpected journey.

To Ross Hamilton, inspiring collaborator, mentor, and authority on the Serpent Mound: Thank you for sharing an explicit vision of the Golden Age and for substantiating its connection to the Serpent. Thank you for all of your support.

To my community of unity, the *Transformational Alliance Peaceburgh*: for sharing what really matters, and especially to the Younger Tribe, for continually inspiring me. Special thanks to those of you who became characters in this story: Nance Stewart, Frank Valley, Kathy

Evans-Palmisano, Kimberly June, Tenanche Rose Golden, Miguel Sague, Douglas Harbst, Kellee Maize and Kevin May. Thank you for trusting me, for going public with me, and for helping me to define "the new normal." And to James and Mai Needham, and Ac Tah who are non-local honorary members of my community of unity.

To my SisterGoddess allies and persistent book-writing buddies, who helped me to get past my resistance to writing my story, and who gave me honest feedback, loving support and shared the wonder along the way: Lilan Laishley, Pat Fero, Kathy Evans-Palmisano, Regina Rivers, Tenanche Rose Golden, Kellee Maize, and Mai Needham. I could never have done this without you. You are awesome co-creators. And to Debbie Khumayyis: You are an original Seer and Sayer.

To my editor, Charlon Bobo: Thank you for your fierce stand for the highest pathway for my story, and for helping me to bring forth the best version I could generate. You are a gift. We made it GOOD, Honey!

To my vibrant, amazing mother, Beryl Hanchin: You are my first Goddess. Thank you for teaching me from the beginning that I am a multi-dimensional being.

To my brother, Ron Hanchin: Thank you for tuning in to catch the melody for the Sacred White Buffalo's second song, and recording it for me with that ancient flute. And to my sister Gail Hanchin MacLeish and my brother Russ Hanchin, for your unconditional love.

And last, but not least, to my two sons, who are my wonder and delight. Adam Willard Lyons and Jacob Matthew Lyons: You dance in my heart. It is for your highest and best future that I write this book.

My Confession to You, Dear Reader

I begin this amazing true story with a confession: I initially refused to write it. Even though I succeeded in opening myself to being "a mouthpiece for Mother Earth" so that my adventure and these experiences became possible at all, I was too uneasy about sharing them publicly.

What stopped me was that I was still too vested in being acceptable within the prevailing old paradigm of consensual reality. That version of reality is based on a materialistic, literal-thinking consciousness where judgmentalism prevails—and where I risked being judged as crazy. After all, my training and work has been as a mental health specialist; a psychotherapist in private practice for over 25 years. Some of the experiences I share could be seen by some of my professional peers (and possibly even some clients) as evidence of delusional psychosis. And I was supposed to be a representative and advocate of mental stability.

Yet as I grappled with this anxiety, I realized that the real psychosis of our times is our insistence on a reality that is exclusively material: materially concrete, limited to three dimensions and that excludes from reality anything that science cannot prove. This materialism-based, literalistic consciousness fuels our desire to acquire money and what it can buy as our basis for security and our highest goal. It promotes the consciousness of greed, scarcity and fear, and the belief that we are separate from each other and from the rest of creation. And it even has us resist the accumulating scientific evidence of an interconnected, multi-dimensional reality—a reality known by the ancients and Indigenous peoples.

Quantum science continues to demonstrate what the ancients knew: that this perception of our separation from one another is erroneous. We are in fact interconnected—what the Indigenous, the ancients, and spiritually awakened people call "oneness." My experiences were uncanny, even miraculous, verifications of just such interconnection. Yet I still struggled: If the public does not want to believe quantum science, why would they want to believe me and my story?

In the midst of my struggle about writing this book, Steve Jobs of Apple, Inc. died. Various media quotes about his character, his essence and his most profound life wisdom that he shared before he died became a grounding force for me. His words became a structure of support for me to stand upon, propelling me on, to speak my truth, and even clarifying why it was so important for me to do so.

I actually carried his words around in my purse. I referenced them daily, along with visits to my Altar of Surrender (which you will hear about in my story), in an ongoing commitment to get out of my ego-based fears and my habit of holding myself back.

Steve Jobs said:

> "Your time is limited, so don't waste it living someone else's life. Don't be trapped by dogma—which is living the results of other people's thinking. Don't let the noise of others' opinions drown out your own inner voice. And most important, have the courage to follow your own heart and intuition—they somehow already know what you truly want to become. Everything else is secondary."

And, most comfortingly, he spoke these words, which always move me to tears:

> "Here's to the crazy ones, the misfits, the rebels, the troublemakers, the round pegs in square holes—the ones who

see things differently. They push the human race forward, and while some may see them as the crazy ones, we see genius, because the ones who are crazy enough to think that they can change the world, are the ones who do."

After quenching my thirst for these affirming words yet again, and drying my "Tears of Truth," I chuckle. I remember the little magnet I carry in my pendulum pouch, right next to my collapsible dowsing rods. It reads, "Those who say it cannot be done shouldn't interrupt the people doing it." And now I feel ready to take the leap.

So here, dear Reader, is my story of the extraordinary and the impossible, with peeks, glimpses, and outright revelations from the Earth herself, of how this New Earth consciousness looks and feels.

Here is my story of how together we can co-create the New Earth of unity, joy and peace, rebirthing humanity beyond 2012 into the predicted Golden Age.

Victoria A. Hanchin
July 17, 2012

TRUST

"You have been consecrated, Victoria. You have been given a specific journey—a specific mission and message. Stay centered in your Serpent Medicine. Walk with it. You have been prepared for this for some time… Trust."

~ Grandmother Flordemayo
of The International Council
of 13 Indigenous Grandmothers

Chapter 1 - The Adventure Begins

· ·

"ECSTATIC!"

Loudly, almost commandingly, this spoken word penetrated my sleep state and awakened me. My eyes flew wide open at rapt attention, my heart pounding, as the face of my alarm clock came into focus: it was 7:32 a.m. Then my alarm went off.

No dream, no visuals… just this commanding, loud word, from an unseen speaker, waking me just moments before the alarm.

"What an odd way to be awakened," I mused, still staring at my alarm clock. I lay there gathering myself from the impact of this abrubt awakening, gradually remembering that today was the day of my inaugural trip to the ancient sacred site of the Serpent Mound in Ohio. And I would finally meet in person Grandmother Dona, an elder of Mohawk lineage. She and I had discovered a deep kindred-spirit connection through our frequent telephone conversations over the past month.

"Well, that mysterious voice from the Dreamtime certainly got my attention, I muttered aloud. " I will definitely keep this word in mind—and this numerology. Ecstatic. 7:32. Okay, then!"

I got out of bed, continuing to follow this sense of a clear imperative to operate on high-alert, paying attention to synchronicities, and listening for inner guidance. With this heightened awareness, I began packing for my weekend adventure.

While scanning my bedroom sanctuary, my breathing shifted to heart-centered as my eyes melted into a soft focus. My gaze landed on the collection of medicinal-grade essential oils, and my body registered an expansive YES! I felt directed to bring three oils: *Present Time, Into the Future, Joy.* I paused for a sense of confirmation. Yes, those were the only ones. I pulled them out of the box of essential oils and put them into my backpack without a second thought.

I continued scanning my bedroom, viewing my personal altars that I had created over the previous months. They were operating as 3-D vision boards, representing and energizing my various intentions and projects. I felt a strong *YES* to pack up the entire Serpent Altar, which I also called my Altar of Surrender.

The Serpent Altar served a deeply significant purpose for me. It symbolized my intention to shed, like a snake, the outgrown skin of my habitual, limited self and to surrender into the highest vision of who I came here to be, and the highest vision of what I came here to contribute. It was my daily reminder to embody and to live from my Highest Self and my Highest Purpose.

I felt that this Serpent Mound trip would leave me deeply transformed. So I took a moment to surrender now, into my Highest Self and my Highest Purpose, before I packed up each symbolic element of this altar.

"If the love letters you keep sending me are true, Dear God, I surrender to who You keep saying I am." I re-read that poem by Hafiz from my altar. It always shifted me into my Larger Self, and out of my fear-based, small ego. It expressed the exact way that I needed to surrender: out of limitation and into Infinite Oneness. Then I packed the altar poem.

Next, I tenderly held the central item of the Serpent Altar: a perfectly-preserved taxidermy specimen of a baby rattlesnake, poised to strike. I recalled the way it had been gifted to me—in a magical and unexpected manner—the day before my phone introduction to Grandmother Dona. This museum-quality serpent was the original inspiration to create this magnificent Altar of Surrender. As I surrendered to my Highest Self and Highest Purpose once again, I felt my deep kinship with the Serpent. I had loved snakes for years. They had populated my dreams and meditations, sometimes appearing as flying, winged serpents.

I recalled that during my Indigenous studies with the Seneca Grandmother Twyla Nitsch and her assistant, Grandmother Spider, I learned that the Serpent was my core power animal, my "within" power animal, according to their tradition of discerning power animals that accompany our human journeys. As I continued my studies with Grandmothers Twyla and Spider, I was astonished to learn that the Indigenous peoples respected "snake medicine" as teaching about transmutation, transformation, death/rebirth, creation, alchemy, ascension, healing, and wholeness. Wow. Powerful medicine! And each of these themes were near-and-dear to my heart.

My inner journey with the serpent over the years had been mirrored outwardly by continuous discoveries of its cosmological, mythical, spiritual and symbolic significance.

I had already discovered and practiced the Hindu teachings of Kundalini Yoga for several years. In that spiritual tradition, the Life Force, or "Kundalini," is described as serpent energy, coiled at the base of the spine in the body that arises within as we awaken to higher consciousness. I had learned that this same Life Force existed as a serpentine force in the Earth as well, demonstrating the principle "as above, so below; as within, so without."

I had also discovered that the Serpent and the spiral were interchangeable as the earliest prehistoric symbols for the ancient

Great Mother Goddess; the first embodiment of divinity for most original cultures on this planet. I deeply resonated with the Mother aspect of Creator—the Feminine Face of God. And I had chosen subsequently to follow that path of devotion and service, committing myself to be a "mouthpiece" for Divine Mother and Mother Earth.

Even though patriarchal religions for the past 5,125 years have demonized the serpent and eliminated the Great Goddess which it symbolized for the prior 500,000 years, I knew the original truth of the serpent: Life Force. Not "evil."

Years later, I was amazed to learn that the Mayan deity, Quetzalcoatl, was depicted as the Feathered Serpent; a snake-bird. I was stunned to recall those flying serpent images appearing in my personal meditations and dreams.

A few years after my studies with Grandmothers Twyla and Spider, other synchronicities arose to offer me additional personal experiences with Indigenous wisdom teachers: Mayan Elders Grandmother Flordemayo from Nicaragua and Don Alejandro Oxlaj from Guatemala, whom we brought to Pittsburgh; Pittsburgh-based Taino Elder Miguel Sague; and Ac Tah, a Mayan spiritual teacher from the Yucatan whom we also brought to Pittsburgh. Each taught me their authentic Indigenous prophetic messages of "2012" and beyond. These messages were a call for transformation, not media-hyped messages of doom.

The unity message that I was taught by each of these Indigenous teachers was that December 21, 2012 was the conclusion of a repeating 26,000-year cycle—tracked by the ancient Mayan Calendar—that most all the Indigenous peoples acknowledge and respect. The corresponding astrological alignments occurring at the conclusion of this cycle are interpreted by their ancient wisdom as offering celestial support for humanity's transformation, if we are aware enough to choose it. "2012" was operating as a code for recognizing an opportunity for humanity's transformation, a time of choice, for a spiritual rebirth.

This 26,000-year cycle is now known to modern science as the "Precession of the Equinoxes." *How did the ancient Mayan sky-watchers first know about that?* I wondered.

This huge cycle is tracked by the Maya by counting smaller 5,125-year Ages called "Long Counts." This final Age, called "the Fifth Sun" by the Maya ends at the same 2012 timeframe as the 26,000-year "Precession" which it is tracking.

The Indigenous message being lost in all the media-hype and doom-mongering is that a momentous transformational choice is being presented to humanity; one that can become a pathway to co-create a New Earth of unity and greater good.

I was so moved to have the great privilege of receiving these Indigenous teachings firsthand, and being a mouthpiece for them, as I was for Mother Earth. These Indigenous messages carried the ancient memory of Mother Earth and humanity's highest future path. They all taught about interconnection and unity. And our most current quantum science now verifies in modern language many aspects of their ancient wisdom.

I recalled now that even African and Chinese Indigenous teachings were part of my Divine Assignments over the years. In 2003 I had brought to Pittsburgh Sobonfu Some's wisdom, of spirit and unity through ceremony, from her Burkina Faso, West African culture. And in 2009 I had published my interviews with Huang Xiang, expressing his poetic Chinese wisdom about unity consciousness, and his experience with the four rivers of Pittsburgh.

Everything I had been taught from Indigenous wisdom traditions of all the races was converging, like the flow of oneness of my beloved three converging Pittsburgh rivers. And their hidden fourth underground river was representing the unifying heart of all the ancient Indigenous wisdom-streams.

I looked once more at my baby rattlesnake specimen before packing it to bring to Grandmother Dona. Yes, the Serpent and I were very, very close allies. And now, I would be going to the Serpent Mound, and meeting "the Spirit of the Serpent" there, as Grandmother Dona had foreseen.

I recalled one of my early phone conversations with the Mohawk Grandmother: "I have been told that I am a Seer," Grandmother Dona explained.

Despite her retirement from Kent State University as an instructor and researcher, Grandmother Dona continued her ongoing informal research on the Serpent Mound, with several Indigenous collaborators and a well-known psychic. Then, after she and Nicaraguan-Mayan Grandmother Flordemayo did a Summer Solstice Ceremony together at the Serpent Mound, Grandmother Flordemayo immediately contacted me and urged me to call Grandmother Dona, and connect with her.

I somehow lost Grandmother Dona's phone number, and never called her. Then with perfect synchonicity, the day after I created my Serpent Altar and surrendered to my Highest Self and Highest Purpose, Grandmother Flordemayo contacted me again, urging me to make the call.

Once I called Grandmother Dona, she repeatedly told me she could sense that the "Spirit of the Serpent" at the Serpent Mound was waiting to meet me. She said, "The Serpent has waited a long time for you to come. It is time. There is important work to do there. I saw that the Serpent has a gift for you. If it is still there when we arrive, then it has been protected, and is being held for you."

I continued my visual scanning and packing, guided by my body-signals' confirmations. Yes, I need to bring all my sacred ceremonial objects that I had created from my 13-month-long vision quest training with Grandmother Spider in 1992: my snake rattle, my snake shield, and my serpentine-shaped, feather-decorated branch that was my ceremonial "Listening Stick." (That was the time when my vision quest ceremonial work had humorously shown me that I did not need the traditional talking stick since I already talked quite enough. My deeper training would be that of "Sacred Listening.") And I packed a gift to offer the "Spirit of the Serpent," of a snakeskin from my Serpent Altar.

I packed those sacred ceremonial objects, and added the gifts that I was bringing to honor Grandmother Dona when we would finally meet later that evening in Ohio.

As I packed my little Toyota, I mulled over my phone conversations with Grandmother Dona from the prior month. She had shared stories about her life as a researcher of Cultural Studies and teacher of Child Development at Kent State University, and many of her adventures as an activist with Indigenous communities. She had told me stories about developing programs to teach young children about Nature and about Indigenous wisdom stories. I had shared information about my "serpent medicine" and my Indigenous studies. I had shared about developing women's workshops for restoring the wisdom of the Sacred Feminine, and my psychotherapeutic counseling work to restore individuals to their sense of wholeness and purpose.

Grandmother Dona and I connected deeply and immediately, as we realized that our individual expressions of personal life-mission were so finely matched: to restore a sacred world; a world where humans remember their divine essence and co-create a New Earth of unity, joy and peace that works for all; a world that honors Mother Earth, the sacred feminine, and the Heart.

So many Grandmothers, I mused. How perfect it was that these various opportunities for personal connections with Indigenous Grandmothers had simply shown up in my world over the past 20 years, beginning with my 1992 studies with Seneca Grandmother Twyla Nitsch and her authorized assistant teacher, Grandmother

Spider. Then connecting in 2007 with Grandmother Flordemayo and the other Grandmothers of the International Council of 13 Indigenous Grandmothers through their filmmaker, Carole Hart (who is herself a wise Grandmother and who became a powerful ally for me). And now, Grandmother Dona.

All these Grandmothers. I recalled hearing an Indigenous prophecy: "When the Grandmothers gather, peace will come to the Earth." I prayed now that this peace would become manifest, visibly and unequivocally.

I knew quite well by now, how to recognize the movement and presence of these life-directing synchronicities. They appeared as correlations, messages, prods, prompts, events, omens and alerts arising in the outer world, that continually validated inner world experiences. They typically emerged within a profoundly meaningful timeframe, irresistibly catching my attention, as if orchestrated from a Higher Consciousness; from Source; from Creation Itself. I had learned to honor these synchronicities, and to track them as vivid prompts to follow the Trail of Guidance in the service of my highest purpose.

And I had learned to trust this process. These synchronicities were usually confirmed in multiple ways. And they never failed to unfold something quite profound, even transformative.

I felt I was being trained by the Universe in sacred listening and in radical trust to collaborate with a vast, intelligent Life Force that was taking me beyond my usual pragmatic and limited perceptions. I laughed when I learned that Albert Einstein had described his experience of this process as "spooky action at a distance!" I wondered if Einstein, too, had experienced body chills as inner confirmation of this mysterious process.

Driving toward Ohio with my updated GPS, I thought, *Well, what a perfect way for today to begin: "ECSTATIC! 7:32!" An alert that is already signaling me from this vast, intelligent Life Force the day that I am to travel to Ohio, to this ancient sacred site of the Serpent Mound, finally to meet Grandmother Dona in person. We will see what wants to unfold from all the synchronicities that have already emerged to bring the two of us together.*

We had no specific plans once I got there, other than to follow the Trail of Guidance.

Of course, I was curious whether the Spirit of the Serpent had protected that mysterious gift for me these three months since Grandmother Dona had spotted it there with Grandmother Flordemayo. And Grandmother Dona confided her glimpse of Sacred Seeing, that "once you are here, we will somehow be shown a water source at the Serpent, which connects the Serpent Mound site to the three converging Rivers and the fourth Underground River there in Pittsburgh."

My whole body covered with goosebumps as Grandmother Dona told me about an underground water source connecting the two sites. That seemed vital, necessary, though I was not yet sure why.

I had just begun to fill her in about the extraordinary visit by Mayan Elders in 2007, confirming that Pittsburgh's three rivers were connected to their 2012 Mayan prophecies of the "promised time of a return to unity." They explained that our three rivers, uniting to return to the source (represented by the ocean), were a geographic reminder put here by Creator of humanity's Oneness with all of Life.

In addition, Pittsburgh's converging three rivers and the underground fourth river had been written about as a "Universal Portal" by local planetary stewards Nance Stewart and Frank Keller, who had become my collaborative consultants. Their meditative transmission work identified the four rivers as a perfect earthly "geographic mirror" of the heavenly portal seen in our Milky Way Galaxy with its converging three rivers of stars and the starless Dark Rift. It was this portal at the Dark Rift with which the Earth and sun would align at the conclusion of 2012, in a rare 26,000-year cosmic alignment. Our converging four rivers portal was one of 12 such geographic portals on Earth, downloading evolutionary impulses from the center of our Milky Way to assist the necessary planetary Shift and rebirth heralded for this timeframe and beyond.

Something big wants to be noticed about water, and stars too, in connection with the Great Serpent Mound, and Pittsburgh, I realized.

I would definitely stay tuned in. Life had trained me in Sacred Listening. I had already served as the inadvertent catalyst for the Mayan Elders' visit and became a mouthpiece, a spokesperson for the sacred rivers and for these authentic Mayan messages of planetary transformation. My visit to the Serpent Mound was already being linked in with these previous Divine Assignments.

This was beginning to feel epic. In my Larger Self, I felt expansive and joyful. From my smaller ego self, I squirmed. I still felt an undercurrent of concern.

My ego self chimed in with its comments: *I am still working as a licensed Clinical Social Worker. I do mental health counseling. Even though I brand my work as "Wholistic Psychotherapy," could the authorities strip me of my license for this sort of "woo-woo" involvement?* I breathed deeply and commanded: "Surrender, surrender!" I recommitted myself to my Highest Self and Highest Purpose.

Grandmother Agnes—another one of the International Council of 13 Indigenous Grandmothers—taught me that the longest, hardest journey for modern humans is the "18-inch journey from the head to the heart."

Surrender, surrender. Breathe through my heart, I repeated relentlessly.

I was discovering that the journey from the head to the heart must be traveled many times before a permanent residence in the heart was possible... at least for *my* ego.

Chapter 2 - Meeting Grandmother Dona

. . . .

AFTER FIVE HOURS OF DRIVING, I arrived at the farm where Grandmother Dona lived. Her cozy farm home was situated atop an ancient Earthwork mound—one of the hundreds of ancient Native American burial and ceremonial mounds punctuating the town of Circleville and surrounding areas. The Serpent Mound, as part of this ancient complex of mounds, was about an hour drive from her home.

Even though these ancient Earthwork mounds had been taken from their Indigenous inhabitants centuries ago by successive parades of colonists, farmers, and developers, they still radiated an energetic presence of mystery. It was as if they held untold stories that wanted to be heard. It seemed that the highways, communities, malls and penitentiaries sprawling over the land were suffocating the memory-voices of the land. Perhaps there were still hidden openings for these ancient land-memories to escape, and to be discerned by ears that could hear.

My initial meeting with Grandmother Dona was joyful; so natural and light-hearted. We immediately felt like old friends. I offered her my gifts, honoring her. First I gave her a framed image of an ancient Mayan oracle-speaker, depicted as emerging from the mouth of a serpent which was arising out of the undulations of sacred copal smoke. Then I gave her an ornament I had crafted from three feathers: the yellow of the Yellow-Shafted Flicker Woodpecker, representing overcoming obstacles with love; the red of the Cardinal, representing awakening, transformation, and sacred-partnership; and the blue of the Blue Jay, representing right use of power. I had researched these colors and birds' attributes through various Indigenous animal medicine resources. Their attributes expressed the common ground that connected my sacred life purpose with Grandmother Dona's.

Grandmother Dona received these gifts with delight and laughter, as she presented me with her gifts, to honor me. She, too, had a similar feather ornament for me, out of feathers with the three same colors, but from South American birds, rather than from my North American ones, also representing these same attributes! This degree of alignment and synchronicity typified many of our long-distance daily phone reports and discoveries, and now it was happening in our face-time. Her other gift to me was a walking staff, with a serpentine-like petrified vine coiling along its length. She told me, "An Indigenous Cherokee Grandmother gifted me with this serpent staff, which clearly must now go to you." I was stunned, moved, and deeply honored.

Together we set up the Serpent Altar of Surrender, and did a simple, heartfelt spontaneous ceremony. We each spoke of surrendering to the Highest Path of what wanted to happen from our coming together. We committed to our process of collaborative sacred listening. Grandmother Dona showed me my room. I spotted a grasshopper on the bed pillow. We carefully scooped it off, gave it a blessing, a placed it outside where it would be happier.

We retired to bed after a light dinner. I unpacked my ceremonial objects and placed them around the bedroom. As I lay in the cozy bed settling into sleep, I heard a clear inner message, *Your whole life has prepared you for this work that will unfold.* My skin prickled in acknowledgement of a deep sense of truth.

I trusted that voice, and sent out a prayer to receive continuous and clear sacred listening, so that we would accurately follow the Trail of Guidance, as I like to call the process. Through this process, Grandmother Dona and I would be discerning the Big Picture of why we were being called to the Serpent Mound and what needed to occur there through our collaboration. I also had a sense that there was something important for me to integrate about this thing called my serpent medicine.

I recalled that I had received an intuitive reading from a gifted psychic consultant, Debbie, who had foreseen that I would experience what she called a shamanic opening, that would arise effortlessly. I wondered whether this sort of experience might occur here at the Serpent Mound.

Then sleep overtook me. Throughout the early morning hours I kept rousing from sleep with the sense that I was doing multi-dimensional work during my Dreamtime, which had to do with my being coached about how to assist humanity to shift from ego-based to essence-based ways of living.

Chapter 3 - Receiving Our Divine Assignment

· ·

THE NEXT MORNING AS I WAS drying off after my shower, I was surprised by being caught in a nearly invisible spider web with the tiniest, barely-visible baby spider connected to it. The tiny spider was so newborn that it was almost transparent. It must have steered its way to my body through this delicate web, and now had made a landing on my body. I smiled. I was the landing-ground for this baby spider's birthing-arrival on Earth!

I sensed that this was a good omen; a demonstration that humans could function as supportive allies to the Natural world. In the Seneca Animal Medicine teachings, the spider represented the Web of Life; life as interconnected. An affirming warmth spread through my body, and I realized that this was a synchronistic tip-off for the day.

I joined Grandmother Dona for breakfast with the news of the baby spider and its messages. I sat at the kitchen table as she cooked our breakfast, and we continued tuning in to the spider theme. It turned out that Grandmother Dona's "within" power animal is the spider, like mine is the serpent.

She began telling me about a family of crab spiders that inhabit her kitchen. I laughed, noticing this synchronistically-evolving theme of spiders, and pulled out my camera. I showed her my digital photo of a large crab spider that had created an enormous web on the side of my house. I had photographed it at night. The web filaments in the photos showed up as stunningly rainbow-colored.

Suddenly my attention was interrupted by the dramatic experience of my eyes being penetrated by an intense beam of light projecting from the heart-shaped prism hanging in the window across the kitchen from me. I stopped talking and became captivated by it, staring into its light-beam, even though it felt a bit blinding. The beam of light was refracting all the colors of the rainbow as it projected directly into my eyes, and it seemed that it was searing through my eyes into my brain, as if re-wiring me. I realized that I had just been speaking about the rainbow-colored spider web, and observed with heightened attention.

I continued to focus on the experience, describing it to Grandmother Dona. "The core of light coming through this prism is now surrounded by a visual pulsing web that is expanding and contracting, like a heartbeat. The web is itself rainbow-colored. It's a pulsing rainbow spider web. Around its perimeter, rays of golden-colored light are actually radiating out. Wow, we were just discussing the baby spider landing on me, and the crab spiders and my photo of their rainbow web. Now this prism is showing us these same rainbow web images! How cool is this?"

Grandmother Dona was intrigued now, and wanted a turn to experience the phenomenon. Reluctantly but kindly, I relinquished my seat to her. Grandmother Dona squealed, "Oh my! I see the rainbow web, too. Now I see an image of a butterfly in the center of the heart prism. It is also pulsing, like a living heart. Now there are white crosses on the butterfly wings and they are radiating light!"

She graciously returned the chair to me. I positioned myself back into the intense beam of light again. As I focused, I also saw the pulsing butterfly. "Wow, the butterfly is now turning into a woman with wings. It's like she is dancing in the pulsing light!" I moved out of the seat to allow Grandmother Dona to check it out.

"I see her, too!"

We never stopped to marvel that each of us could simply move in and out of position and continue to witness the same continuing phenomenon emanating from the light beams of this prism.

I watched again. The winged female shifted into a heart shape and continued her pulsing. "Oh my goodness… now the heart looks like a red flame surrounded and held by a blue field of light, like the feminine being supported and held by the masculine. Wow! Now the blue light field has turned into a downward-pointing triangle, holding the pulsing red flame as an upward pointing triangle interconnecting with it. It looks like a pulsing Star of David now. That is the symbol for the union of the masculine and the feminine, and in many spiritual traditions it also represents the union of Heaven and Earth."

I became aware that these themes would be relevant to the unfolding purpose of our work together at this ancient sacred site of the Serpent.

The rainbow beam of light emanating from the heart prism now shifted its angle. Instead of penetrating into my eyes, it was now landing on my lips. It shifted again to land on my throat.

"Grandmother Dona, I am getting the sense that we are being instructed by these images, and next the light wants to bless us!" I stood up so that the beam of light could now infuse my heart, then my navel at my solar plexus. I re-positioned myself again so that its light beam could infuse as many of my chakras as possible. Then I gave Grandmother Dona her turn to be blessed in this amazing manner. She stood in the path of the beam of light and moved her body to align her chakras with the rainbow beam as well.

Then Grandmother Dona told me, "You know, earlier this morning before you came out from your shower, I saw that rainbow beam project all the way across the kitchen onto the living room wall. So I went and got the serpent staff that I gave you last night, and I held it in the rainbow light to bless it! Then do you know what happened? That rainbow light shifted and landed next on the center of my ceremonial drum that I am bringing to the Serpent Mound today. Spirit is also blessing our ceremonial tools with this rainbow light."

Now we finally looked at each other in amazement.

"I left the serpent staff outside last night," she continued, "so that it would be re-energized by the drizzling rain. We have been in a drought here, so there hasn't been rain for a month. That rain seemed like a gift confirming and fertilizing our collaboration. I also wanted the staff to be re-energized by the simultaneous energy of the sun and moon that were both visible this morning on opposite sides of the sky—male and female energy."

We stared at each other with our jaws dropping and laughed simultaneously. We understood that the elements of the Natural world were actively involving themselves—weighing in—both to bless our adventure and to inform it: the Sun; the Moon; the rain; the Light; the rainbows. Amazing. And we were able to slow down, pay close attention, and listen within to our inner prompts opening up.

Grandmother Dona twinkled. "The sunlight coming through that heart prism certainly gave us a detailed visual and experiential tutorial. I guess we have officially begun our transformational work, even though we aren't at the Serpent Mound yet." We marveled at this in silence for a few moments. These very clear synchronistic images were indeed quite directive.

"Yes," I mused, "it seems we are being shown many aspects of the Great Shift of consciousness predicted for 2012 and beyond, into the emerging New Earth consciousness. For me, this confirms that the transformation already in process on this planet must continue to be heart-based, from the right-brain, not from left-brained logic, because everything we just witnessed emanated from the *heart* prism. And this Shift is clearly about becoming respectful of the interconnecting Web of Life, and learning to be instructed by it. We are being clearly shown that the Web of Life is a living, pulsing, Web emanating from pure Light that conveys information and guidance, if we will pay attention."

"Yes," injected Grandmother Dona, "and the rainbow shows that all 'colors' of life, all varieties of species and races, are important and are to be unified as an interconnected whole. And this reminds me of the Indigenous prophecy of the coming of the "Rainbow Warriors" predicted for this timeframe, who will appear from all races, respecting the wisdom teachings of the Indigenous about restoring the Web of Life—the Sacred Hoop."

"Whew, that is right!" I exclaimed, "and the butterfly is a universal symbol for transformation. Anodea Judith writes about the butterfly's transformational process as resembling humanity's. She observes that the caterpillar voraciously consumes everything in sight before it goes into its cocoon; its transformational stage. Then its 'imaginal cells' actually dissolve the caterpillar inside the cocoon, into a soup-like substance that is unrecognizable. But then it re-configures into this beautifully-colored winged creature, and emerges with a whole new identity, able to fly. She points this out in her book, *Awakening the Global Heart* and notes that humanity is still in the voracious consumption stage. But she is convinced that transformation is imminent."

"Absolutely," Grandmother Dona agreed. "Now what about the winged female? Was that a fairy? Are we to connect with those elemental Nature Spirits? Or was that about women transforming?"

"Well," I mused, "I suspect we are being shown that the predicted planetary transformation intensified by the 2012 alignments needs be led by women to a significant degree—or at least that it emphasizes the restoration of the Sacred Feminine and right-brain consciousness. But I do like the Fairy idea. I was shown in my 13-month long vision quest process with Grandmother Spider that I also have 'Fairy Medicine,' a natural and instinctual connection with Nature Spirits. I have never witnessed any, though. I recall that mythic stories tell that all the various Nature Spirits asked Great Spirit to become invisible to humans because humans became so predatory. I would be thrilled if we could experience a mutual communication with them."

"Well, we will have to see what wants to unfold."

"Exactly." I continued, "Then we saw that pulsing Star of David with the intersecting colors of the blue masculine and the red feminine. We are being shown the integration of these dual aspects of creation, the Yin/Yang Life Force, the God/Goddess. This visual reminds us of the integration needed within humans of our masculine/feminine polarity, as well as the needed integration of our Divine/Human polarity so we can co-create Heaven on Earth. We are getting information about what is necessary for integration and wholeness. Big-time stuff here!"

Grandmother Dona laughed. "All in a days work! Or maybe a weekend or two! We had better see what we need to do next. Let's continue in this spontaneous ceremony that is so beautifully unfolding. Why don't we each pull a *Sacred Path* card? I find that working with such wisdom-infused cards allows a structure for more synchronistic guidance to find me. Let's open to guidance about how we are to accomplish whatever will support this extraordinary revelation; of *how* things are to change down here on this planet." Her 70-something face was radiant.

A woman after my own heart! I nodded and pushed "play" to start the Jennifer Berezan CD, of a supportively mesmerizing song, "Returning to the Mother of Us All." I noticed the time; it was 12:12 PM.

I commented on that powerful numerology to Grandmother Dona. She nodded her head in agreement. "Twelve is the number of the 12 disciples of the Christ, and the 12 planets that circle around the sun, as well as the 12 signs of the zodiac that our Earth travels through in the 'Precession of the Equinoxes' that the ancient Maya were tracking for their sacred Calendar, ending the long count in 2012," she observed. "I also remember reading that during this ascension process, humanity will activate all 12 strands of our DNA that have appeared to be dormant."

Before I could answer her, I heard my inner voice distinctly declare the ancient Hawaiian Lomi Priestess teaching that I had recently been taught: "The world is what I SAY it is!" That startled me. But before I could question it, I next heard an inner musical rendition of the Hindu Kundalini chant, the "Ajai Alai," that I had been prompted to play on repeat mode as I fell asleep every night this past week. My skin activated goosebumps, recognizing the similarity of the intent of this powerful chant: "whoever masters this chant, chanting it in the purity of service to the Light, whatever they say must be, must be." Both of these inner instructions were about the power of spiritually-aligned authority to declare how things are to manifest. I made note of this instruction. It seemed vital, if a bit daunting.

Now my hair was prickling. But before I could ponder that new body signal any further, I heard a voice so loud and distinct that I thought it was spoken from a person standing next to me. In a voice that sounded distinctly similar to Maya Angelou's, I now heard spoken, "And make it GOOD, Honey!" I began laughing at these alternately intense and lighthearted directives arriving so successively and distinctly. I felt a deep and clear understanding now of all of these related messages. I shook my head in amazement.

Grandmother Dona looked at me with curiosity. I filled her in on what I had just experienced. I grinned and told her, "It appears that we have been instructed, sanctioned, blessed, and now empowered to serve an amazing Divine Assignment." I felt awed, reverent, happy... in fact, I felt ECSTATIC!

"What?" Grandmother Dona queried, studying my face.

I took a deep breath to backtrack and summarize. "Okay, as I am tracking these multiple synchronistic messages, my discernment is this: through our Hearts aligned with the Divine Light of Creation, and with the Web of Life—through the power of what has already been revealed, as well as through our highest imaginations—we are to call forth this New Earth of unity and peace. We are to do this at the ancient ceremonial site of the Serpent Mound."

I continued, feeling deeply moved. "We are being given the privilege and the responsibility of Sacred Seeing and Sacred Saying; of calling forth and anchoring into physical expression the New Earth vision revealed to us this morning; of a world fulfilling these balanced and interconnected ways of being."

I looked into Grandmother Dona's eyes that were big with tears as she took in the impact of my words. I reached out to take her hand. "Do you see how clearly we are being shown this? Just as we have been tracking it so far, through our process of seeing, speaking and ceremony? That appears to be the method and the purpose for which we have been brought here to collaborate at this ancient sacred site of the Serpent Mound; to do acts of Sacred Seeing and Sacred Saying in collaborative ceremony, to anchor in this New Earth, and to energetically activate the predicted Golden

Age consciousness of unity and peace beyond 2012. And we will continue to be guided explicitly."

Grandmother Dona exclaimed, "I do get it. That makes perfect sense. It is so clearly revealed. This is so perfect. I am so moved, and so honored to be part of this."

As if to verify the accuracy of my interpretation, at that moment I looked down and spotted and another grasshopper that had just appeared at our feet on the carpet. This time, we caught the synchronistic importance of its presence, emphasized by its second appearance. We had missed that it was speaking to us last night on my bed pillow. Grandmother Dona made a gesture, blessing the little grasshopper, then consulted the Ted Andrews *Animal Speak* reference book from the table, looking up the grasshopper's medicine.

"Hmmm. It says here that, related to its ancient ancestor the cricket, the grasshopper represents "uncanny leaps forward." It looks like we will be making some 'uncanny leaps forward' into the future to help establish a future that fulfills the prophecies of unity and harmony, all in our weekend together. And it teaches to listen on the subtle level within, and to trust your inner voice."

She continued, "Well then, let's get on with this Divine Assignment! So, now we know WHAT purpose we are serving, and HOW this process is to unfold, let's see if there is specific guidance as to our NEXT STEPS." Grandmother Dona picked up the *Sacred Path Cards*. She prayerfully picked a card then silently offered the deck to me. I pulled my card in a prayerful, reverent manner as well.

I noticed that the *Sacred Path Cards* book and its card deck were by Jamie Sams, the Granddaughter of Grandmother Twyla, Medicine Woman of the Wolf Clan of the Seneca Tribe, with whom I had studied. Another reference book and card set was on Grandmother Dona's table, *Medicine Cards*. That book and card set—also by Jamie

Sams (with David Carson)—likewise taught Indigenous wisdom; about ways the animal world instructs humans to live in harmony with Mother Earth. I knew immediately that we were in good hands.

Grandmother Dona pulled the Cradleboard card. That card described "birthing the future through a process of responding to each moment creatively and lovingly, with deep relatedness and listening." This is exactly what we were doing. We saw this as another direct confirmation of our process. The card also described the Indigenous prophecy of the "Cradleboard of Creation." That prophecy was the one Grandmother Dona had referred to just moments ago... yet more confirmation. The card detailed the emergence of thousands of "Rainbow Warriors," of both genders, who will usher in the dream of the era of Peace. This was to occur during the timeframe of the appearance of the White Buffalo, which is the current generation.

I immediately recalled the local birth in Western Pennsylvania in 2006, of our Sacred White Buffalo, Kenahkihinen (a Lenape name, meaning "Watch Over Us"). There were also other White Buffalo births during this timeframe in other locations of the United States, all ceremonially verified and honored by the Lakota and other tribes. Their births represented a summons to pay attention. The White Buffalo's message is that humanity is now at the crossroads, and must choose unity and peace over material greed, before the ways of domination and greed destroy us.

I returned my focus to Jamie Sams' teaching from her book. I summarized the information. "The Cradleboard prophecy teaches that these Warriors of the Rainbow will remember what they are here for: to create a legacy of greater good; a world that works for all aligned with Indigenous wisdom. Jamie Sams quotes Chief Two Trees of the Cherokee as saying that these people, 'may be white on the outside, but are red on the inside.' She interprets this as meaning that these Rainbow Warriors 'are our Red Ancestors returning… as Guardians of Mother Earth… to assist All Our Relations' to make this shift into the New Earth of Unity." This guidance seemed like another exclamation point on the purpose of our collaboration.

I looked at Grandmother Dona. She nodded and beamed.

I looked at my card. I read aloud the information. "Power Place: Earth Connection/Empowerment." My skin prickled as I immediately thought of our intention to go to the Power Place of the Serpent Mound. I looked up at Grandmother Dona as she said, "Yep, the Serpent Mound."

More of the card's explanation jumped off the page at me. "Every internal thought of the seeker will be recorded by the rocks and Earth around that Power Place." And next, the lines, "Our Mother Earth has energy lines that are equal to the energy meridians of the human body."

Instantly I got a clear understanding that I was being instructed to use intention to connect the energy meridians of my body with the energy lines of the Earth when we arrived at the Serpent Mound. Through that "surrogate" connection—of my body as a microcosmic mirror of the macrocosm of the Earth—I was to do energy tapping on my own meridians on behalf of the Earth. I was to use my body as a mini-Earth to energetically anchor the qualities of this New Earth to facilitate the expression of this New Earth consciousness. And the Earth would record my every thought.

These instructions made perfect sense to me, since I had been learning meridian tapping in my psychotherapeutic work through the Emotional Freedom Technique. And I also had experience in surrogate testing, using my body as a stand-in on behalf of another through my 15 years of working with the Perelandra Flower Essence material. I recalled my inner message of last night, "Your whole life has prepared you for this work that will unfold."

I continued reading aloud, "The energy lines that feed all areas of Mother Earth's surface can be drawn to a specific area simply by calling the energy to the place where it is needed, via ceremony." This information was important, timely, and new to me. I made note of it. Jamie Sams had certainly recorded a legacy of amazing wisdom from generations of Indigenous practices. I felt in awe.

Then, these next words seemed like more confirmation and empowerment, "Great Mystery gave humans the legacy of *using our gifts to redirect the forces of Nature to catalyze the elements [earth, air, fire and water] in order to change planetary conditions. This reconnection process must be done with joy and celebration.*" As I looked at Grandmother Dona, we simultaneously broke into smiles, then laughter.

"WOW! ECSTATIC!" I exclaimed. I could barely continue reading! But there was more…

"The ability to infinitely create is one of our gifts as Catalyzers. When this gift is discovered and used properly, we become givers and receivers simultaneously, living antenna or bridges that conduct energy between Mother Earth and the Sky Nation."

Then my mouth fell open as I read this next line, *"Individual Power Places become the teachers that instruct us in our catalyzing abilities."*

My head was spinning. On my WholePersonWholePlanet.com website, I already described myself as "a catalyst for personal and planetary transformation." And now I would receive direct teaching about this from a Power Place called the Serpent Mound that I was being called to, in connection with my personal "medicine," my "within" medicine animal of the serpent!

A sense of the magnitude of our Earth connection steamed through these next lines, *"As we heal, Mother Earth feels our joy. We are like cells in and on her body."* How profound was that?

I continued reading: "The true meaning of power needs clarification (which is not about domination and control). The power of love, the power of healing, the power of compassion, the power of unity, and the power of knowing are our abilities. These are the gifts our Earth Mother seeks to share with us at this time."

The shift from the love of power to the power of Love. YES.

We looked at each other and simultaneously exclaimed, "ECSTATIC!" and laughed, jumping up to hug each other.

"What an amazing mission. What FUN!" Grandmother Dona laughed. Then she glanced at the clock. All this preparation, blessing, instruction and empowerment had taken us to 3 PM and the Serpent was more than an hour away. "I think we are quite well-briefed and ready. We had better get going."

I agreed, and playfully added, "And make it GOOD, Honey!"

With chuckles we gathered up our ceremonial objects and some food and water, heading out. I remembered to grab my journal to continue documenting every detail of this amazing adventure. We said farewell to the little grasshopper, still lingering with us on the carpet.

We took off to the Serpent Mound.

Chapter 4 - Tracing the Future
Back into the Present

· ·

As we drove to the Serpent Mound, I played a healing chant I had brought from my Kundalini Yoga practice. It was the Hindu mantra, "RA-MA-DA-SA, SA-SAY-SO-HUNG," which translates, "SUN-MOON-EARTH-INFINITY, INFINITY-THOU-I-AM." The intention of this mantra was perfectly aligned with all the unity-related information we just received about our Divine Assignment—another confirmation that we were on track. Not to mention that "Kundalini" translates as "the Life-Force expressed as a serpent-energy within the human body and the Earth."

We laughed about the unexpected process of our day, spending so much time receiving guidance about what was to occur and how we were to proceed, that we would have much less time at the Serpent than we had anticipated.

We acknowledged "the power of the small," of two ordinary women willing to step up, follow guidance and do extra-ordinary acts as Seers and Sayers, calling forth the New Earth consciousness that wants to emerge from unity. We sang the chant as we drove.

We arrived at the Serpent Mound a bit before 5 PM, before they officially closed the site to visitors. However, Grandmother Dona assured me that once we were admitted, they would not make us leave. We would have to keep in mind that once the sun set, it would be quite dark there, since the site was not commercially developed with lighting and visitors buildings. They did have a small gift shop and a roofed building with enclosed latrines with doors for privacy. That was it, besides a lookout tower and a covered shelter with some picnic tables.

As we walked up the pathway, a modest sign appeared. It simply showed an arrow with the words, "The Serpent." I loved it. My heart was already singing.

Grandmother Dona spotted a small group of people gathered next to the picnic shelter area, seated in a circle. She recognized someone she knew, and approached her to find out their purpose. Returning to me, she smiled, saying, "We have been invited to join this group as they listen to their invited speaker, the world's leading expert on the Serpent Mound, Ross Hamilton." We looked at each other with big grins, and I exclaimed, "Ecstatic!"

What profoundly supportive synchronicity! My hairs and skin prickled. I had been told by another psychic that I would meet Ross Hamilton. I had given up on that idea, since I had declined attending a field trip to the Serpent a few months prior where he was scheduled to appear with several other speakers. Today Ross was the only speaker! And this prediction was being fulfilled.

We listened eagerly as Ross Hamilton spoke extensively about the research he had been compiling about the Serpent Mound over a period of many years. He explained that the Serpent Mound is an effigy built on Earth to mirror the constellation "Draco," the dragon, or celestial serpent in the heavens.

This serpentine effigy mound in Peebles, Ohio is about 1330 feet in length as it coils through the area, and rises up from the ground about 3 feet. It is the largest effigy mound in the world. One can only see its full image from a highly-elevated position overhead. Similar to the Stonehenge, the Great Serpent Mound is situated to align to the Sun at the summer and winter solstices and equinoxes. The undulating Serpent effigy was built with an egg, or possibly a sun disc, in its open mouth.

The ancient Indigenous peoples were fairly universal in cultivating an aware connection with the "Star Nation," their term for the cosmic display of planets and constellations. Many Indigenous peoples' creation stories attribute their origins as deriving from the stars. The Mayans were the most adept of the ancient starwatchers, tracking the cycles of our celestial neighbors and their influence on Earth with their complex calendars. The Maya are still tracking human evolution in connection with the celestial influence day-by-day, with their sacred Tzolkin Long Count Calendar of 5,125 years, ending December 21, 2012.

Ross Hamilton shared information he obtained from the native people— particularly the Cherokee—that the builders of the Serpent Mound had an ancient technology whereby they could harness lightning from the sky, and ground it into the Earth, to fertilize the soil as well as to create atmospheric conditions conducive to health. The ancient builders of the Serpent Mound were called by the archaeologists, "the Adena people" which translated as "the people who wanted nothing." They were able to create all they needed to thrive from their technology of an Earth and Sky Union.

Ross shared his inspiring vision of working to crack the code of this ancient wisdom and technology to restore the knowledge of the ancient medicine days of the Serpent Mound. He described their knowledge as a "medicine of the union of Earth and Sky, capable of re-creating a Golden Age for humanity."

Ecstatic! There we were, with another conscious and skilled Lightworker, whose work also addressed creating the predicted return of the Golden Age of humanity. And he just happened to be the world's leading expert on the Serpent Mound. *Clearly, this Power Place has volumes to teach us about our catalyzing abilities,* I thought, recalling our guidance card.

At the conclusion of his talk, I introduced myself to Ross shaking his hand. I told him that I deeply resonated with his vision of restoring the great Serpent Mound to its original medicine, that I shared his commitment to find ways to live in harmony with Mother Earth, and to reconnect humanity with the ancient wisdom that the Indigenous peoples so beautifully expressed, of "right-relationship" with all of creation. He acknowledged me, and returned my handshake warmly. We looked deeply into each other for a moment. I told him, "We have joined with you in that great work today." He thanked me with a hug.

Grandmother Dona and I left the group and proceeded along the pathway toward the Serpent Mound. I was very attentive to the sensation of walking with the serpent staff that Grandmother Dona had gifted to me, tapping a steady rhythm into the Earth as we walked.

We became aware of a flock of Blue Birds singing joyously in the treetops overhead. We looked up and joined them, chanting, "Ancient Mother, I hear you calling, Ancient Mother, I hear your song..." It was like they were already celebrating the fulfillment of our purpose today—to create a ceremony that would activate and anchor the flourishing of the New Earth of Unity.

Speaking aloud, I recounted our guidance, and we set the intention accordingly: "We are calling forth our highest vision of the New Earth, seeing it completely fulfilled, and tracing it backwards from that fulfilled future into the present. We are Seeing it and Saying it in a sacred manner, feeling the fullness of it in our hearts, and the truth of it in our spirits."

"And we are making it GOOD, Honey!" Grandmother Dona reminded me.

We laughed and seated ourselves at a picnic table in the open area before entering the zone of the effigy mound. Once we entered the area of the Serpent, there would likely be too many others around. We wanted to do the speaking of the intention in relative privacy, then walk the length of the Serpent in a reverent process of feeling and grounding that new reality.

I took out my essential oils, *Into the Future* and *Joy*. I anointed Grandmother Dona with the oils on her hands, and she did the same with me. We inhaled their pure fragrance. After a moment of tuning in, we began taking turns describing what we saw and felt. I simultaneously tapped the meridians of my body, as a microcosm representing the meridians in Mother Earth's body—her ley lines:

"I see a world where we shift from the love of power to the power of love, in the service of Life."

"I see a world where compassion, understanding and acceptance replace blame, negative judgment, and intolerance."

"I see a world where generosity, integrity, sharing and kindness replace greed, domination, hoarding, and arrogance."

"I see a world where there is a commitment to find workable win-win solutions based in cooperation instead of win-lose competitive-based outcomes."

"I see a world where every person's unique gifts and talents are nurtured and welcomed; and making a contribution to the greater good is the motivating force."

"I see a world operating from the Heart—where the intuitive, interconnecting, creative right brain is supported by the logical, hierarchical, separation-based, left brain."

"I see a world where there is deep respect, honoring and sacred partnership between men and women based on deep reciprocal listening."

"I see a world of balance, where *being* is as valued as doing; *creating* is as valued as producing; and the *inner world* is as valued as the outer world."

"I see a world where quality of life, purpose and meaning are more important than quantity, accumulation and status."

"I see a world where we relate to all of creation as our family—the animals, trees, waters, insects, stones, sky, ancestors—remembering all life as our relatives."

"I see a world where joy, peace, sharing, kindness, creative self-expression, freedom and unity are the most prevalent feelings and conditions."

"I see a world where we are always connected with our High Self and Spirit, and we easily receive aligned guidance from Source, accepting challenges as means to growth."

"I see a world where each person knows how to be a Sacred Seer and a Sacred Sayer, and we know that we are each divine co-creators of Heaven on Earth."

We spoke like this, in turns, until neither of us had anything left to say. At that moment, I looked up to the sky. "Look, Grandmother Dona: three Turkey Vultures!"

"We call them Peace Eagles." She watched, smiling.

I laughed, calling up to them: "Okay, Peace Eagles, please come and eat up the rotten scraps of the Old World of war, violence, greed, and distorted power!" Grandmother Dona joined me in laughing.

I looked back up and gasped. "Grandmother Dona, look!"

As we gazed up to the section of sky where the vultures had been, they were nowhere in sight, but much higher up in the same sector of the sky were three Bald Eagles. The eagles looked like three circling dots. It was hard to grasp that eagles could fly so high. *And where had those three Peace Eagles disappeared to?* They were nowhere in sight.

Three. The number three seemed powerfully significant. The presence of three vultures, then three eagles, was a reminder to me of the three Rivers in Pittsburgh and their connection with the Mayan 2012 prophetic teachings of unity. Don Alejandro's ancient "Statement of Revelations and Prophecies" described the three rivers in Pittsburgh as representing the predicted unity of humanity, through the "people of the Eagle" (North America), joining with the "people of the Condor" (South America) connected by the "people of the Quetzal bird" (the Central American Maya).

The number three was also symbolic of the union of the Earth, the Human, and the Heavens. What a profound affirmation of this ceremonial process. I explained all this to Grandmother Dona.

Grandmother Dona's eyes brimmed with tears. "We really ARE making it GOOD, Honey!" She reached out and squeezed my hands. I nodded silently. I placed drops of the oil blends, *Present Time* and more of the *Joy* into her hands and she returned the act. We rejoined hands, to trace this fulfilled Future of Joy back to the Present.

I spoke with a deep feeling of awe, now aware that the vultures and eagles were participating in this momentous ceremony right along with us. "We thank the vultures for eating up the scraps of the Old World of Separation. We thank the eagles, messengers of the Great Spirit, for affirming the New World of Unity. And we now trace the fulfilled vision of the New Earth of peace and unity back from the Future, and we anchor it into the Present Time, established in joy." We held the feeling of this declaration in the silence of our unified hearts for a few moments, until it felt complete.

"Now let's anchor this new reality into the Serpent with walking," Grandmother Dona suggested. "I know from the research I have done here that the Serpent Mound was an ancient ceremonial healing site. Whatever ceremony was done here at the Serpent was then energetically disseminated underground to all the sacred sites around the world. We will set the intention that our ceremony today will go out worldwide, as well."

Now my eyes were filling with tears. I was so moved. Before I could utter the word, Grandmother Dona winked and exclaimed, "Ecstatic!" I smiled back.

We walked together in silence, with the soft thumping of my serpent staff the only sound. As the effigy mound became visible, I had to stop and allow tears to flow freely, accompanied by a feeling of waves of energy washing through my body. I had learned to recognize such tears as my Tears of Truth, an inner confirmation of the experience of a larger Presence of Truth. Grandmother Dona instinctually understood, and embraced me supportively.

We continued walking the path surrounding the Great Serpent, stopping at the old Cedar Tree at the heart of the Serpent, near its midpoint. We stood there together, and recapped the intention of our ceremony to this "Mother Tree." We asked that the Cedar send out the fulfilled vision of the New Earth that we had spoken into being, down through its roots, underground, to all the ancient sacred sites of the world in honor of our instructions, "Because we SAY so! And make it GOOD, Honey!" We were feeling joyful now, celebratory, and quite comfortable in our roles as Seers and Sayers of the New Earth.

As we continued walking, Grandmother Dona spotted the Serpent's gift for me. "See over there, up in the branches of that tree? It is a large shed snakeskin hanging there, just as it was three months ago when Grandmother Flordemayo was here at the Solstice. The Serpent has protected it, and saved it for you just as I sensed it would."

We walked to the tree. The branch was too high for us to remove the snakeskin. Grandmother Dona smiled. "The Serpent wants you to receive its gift of this snakeskin by reaching to retrieve it with your serpent staff." I easily guided my staff to the branch and pulled off the snakeskin onto the staff, as if it were an extension of my hand. I gave thanks to the Spirit of the Serpent.

Holding its gift, I laughed, "I too brought a gift of snakeskin for the Spirit of the Serpent, and it is from the same kind of snake." My skin prickled in goose bumps of confirmation. "We are exchanging snakeskins!" I offered my snakeskin in a return gesture.

We continued walking the path around the Serpent, to the head of the Serpent holding the egg, or sun disk, in her mouth. Here we had the inspiration to call in the energetic connection of Pittsburgh's underground fourth river, and the three converging rivers—the Allegheny, the Monongahela, and the Ohio. We visualized their converging flow connecting with us here at the egg of the Serpent.

We completed the ceremony walking the length of the Serpent, tapping the serpent staff, as we sang Mz. Imani's song lyrics, "We have a New Way to Walk on the Earth..." and calling out the beautiful attributes of the New Earth that we had detailed in our earlier ceremonial time with the eagles. We arrived at the tail of the Serpent, and sat down together in meditation, as we watched the gathering splendor of the sky as it shifted into the clouds and colors of the sunset.

Grandmother Dona broke the silence. "Do you see that?" she exclaimed. She was gazing directly at the Sun. I had to shelter my eyes from the intensity a bit, and refocus. But then I could see it too. Just to the right of the setting Sun was a vertical purplish cloud formation that looked like an uprising, undulating serpent.

"As above, so below; as below, so above," Grandmother whispered in awe.

I understood immediately. "We are sitting here, below, at the Serpent on Earth with the Sun disk in its mouth, doing ceremony to call in the New Earth of Unity. The Heavens are now mirroring

35

above, this same configuration of the Sun with the Serpent," I marveled.

"Yes. The Indigenous call this Sky Language," Grandmother Dona explained as we continued gazing in awe and gratitude. "Even the Cloud People are participating in our ceremony today." We resumed meditating in a state of reverence.

Our silent meditation was soon distracted by a young woman from the Ross Hamilton group, carrying a large blue bottle. She approached us quite naturally, as if interrupting a meditation was not a disruptive act.

She was smiling, and as she stood next to us she offered us the bottle and said, "Here, have some of this amazing local water. The locals claim it is very healthy. It is from an artesian well fed by an underground stream at a nearby property, close to where the crop circle appeared a few years ago. It flows 24/7/365, even when there is a drought like the one we have been having for several weeks. I suggest that you go there and get some more." And she proceeded to give us explicit directions for how to get there.

Grandmother Dona began laughing and explained to our new ally, "I was told in meditative guidance that the Serpent had a connection with Pittsburgh's underground 4th river, and that this actual connection would be revealed at the Serpent Mound today, through Vikki's presence. Our time was running out, and I was wondering how that guidance would be revealed. So here it is! How easy is this? It is being revealed by your walking up to us as if on cue, so naturally, and literally giving us directions for finding this water source connection!"

Now I was laughing too, and as Grandmother Dona and I looked at each other we exclaimed in unison, "Ecstatic!"

We briefly filled in the young woman about the converging three rivers of Pittsburgh and its fourth underground river, and their confirmed connection with the Mayan's ancient 2012 prophetic teachings of unity. Her eyes got big. "I have heard of those converging rivers. Now you are giving ME goosebumps!" She ceremoniously offered us a second bottle of the Serpent Water, and we promised we would return tomorrow to seek out the artesian well that was its source. It was getting dark quickly now.

We hugged her goodbye, then hugged each other. We closed our ceremony in gratitude and awe, once again declaring that "We made it GOOD, Honey!" We made our farewells to the Spirit of the Serpent and headed to Grandmother Dona's vehicle.

"Let's drive the road that completely encircles the Great Serpent Mound before we head home," Grandmother suggested as she began steering toward the exit.

"Great. I will put this CD back in to play the RA-MA-DA-SA healing chant, so it can seal in the energy of our magnificent ceremonial work."

As I pushed the "play" button and the chant began, I noticed the clock on the vehicle dashboard.

It was 7:32 PM.

I gasped.

I reminded Grandmother Dona of its significance, as I was awakened yesterday by the voice exclaiming "Ecstatic" just before my alarm went off at 7:32 AM. "Now it is exactly 7:32 PM!"

We drove in the silence of awe, listening to the chant intone the unity of all life—Earth and Heavens—as we circled around the sacred site and for the entire 90-minute drive home.

When we arrived at Grandmother Dona's and entered her home, the sound of a cricket was so loud inside the house that it sounded like a little machine. We recalled that the cricket was the more ancient ancestor of the grasshopper that had visited us before we had left today, reinforcing an ancient connection to its earlier message for us, "uncanny leaps forward."

We took off our jackets and walked into the living room to pay respects to our Serpent Altar of Surrender. There we made another synchronistic discovery. Our grasshopper ally from this morning had made its own uncanny leap. Somehow, it had leaped from the floor where we encountered it before our departure, up onto the Serpent Altar on the table! There it sat, as if congratulating us on our uncanny leaps forward.

Yes, we had made it GOOD, Honey!

As I drifted off to sleep, I couldn't help but wonder, *why 7:32?*

Chapter 5 - The Serpent Well and the Three Seeds

. . . .

I AWOKE TO THE SOUND OF Grandmother Dona drumming and singing her Indigenous songs, greeting the bright morning sun. I sleepily recalled the events of yesterday. They all seemed embedded within a feeling of communion with the elemental and natural world as we were guided through our day: the sun and moon, the beams of light, the insects and birds, even the clouds, all weighing in, all participating in the unfolding of explicit guidance, confirmed by so many other synchronistic events along the way. It felt so magical.

It felt like the way life was meant to be lived. No one would ever feel lonely or disconnected if they lived like this, I mused. THIS is what it feels like to live in the New Earth consciousness.

I wondered what process was in store for us today, as we continued to follow the trail of guidance. I smiled, recalling that this time we had very literal guidance—actual written directions—to the underground water source which connected the sacred site of the Serpent Mound to the sacred site of my beloved "Peaceburgh," as I liked to call Pittsburgh, and its four converging rivers.

But why that number, 7:32?

The same question that I had pondered as I fell asleep was still on my mind as I awakened.

I got dressed and emerged to the smells of coffee and cinnamon oatmeal. I hugged Grandmother Dona, who indicated that I should sit. I was grateful to do so, since I still wanted to finish recording all the amazing details of yesterday's adventure in my journal.

As I sat writing at the kitchen table, my concentration was interrupted by the distinct sound of something dropping onto the floor. It had the sound quality of a seed, like a hard kernel of popping corn, dropping and bouncing. I looked up and asked Grandmother Dona if she had heard that sound.

"Yes," she answered. "Did you drop a bead? You will never find it on the pattern of this floor." We both got down on the dark swirly-patterned floor to find what had dropped.

I explained that whatever it was had precipitated out of thin air in the space between us. Grandmother Dona snapped her head up and asked me to repeat what I had said.

"I was writing and all of a sudden, in the space between you over there and me over here, something fell to the floor and bounced a couple of times. It sounded to me like a seed, like a kernel of popcorn."

"That's what I heard too." She squinted her doe-like eyes at me. We got up from the floor without our evidence. We sat down to eat our oatmeal and fruit, shaking our heads in wonder.

In the silence of our eating and musing, we heard the sound of a second seed dropping next to us from mid-air onto the floor.

This time Grandmother Dona said, "You heard that, right?"

"Yep."

We both got down onto the floor again scouring it with our bare hands. No seed; only a few crumbs.

"Okay, so what is that supposed to mean?" I asked.

"I was just going to ask you that. I have no clue," she answered.

"So, we will put the "two seeds dropping out of the air" in the unsolved mystery file with the 7:32 phenomenon," I reasoned.

"Good idea," she nodded. "And we'll just let it be. An answer will show up when the time is ripe. Let's clean up and pick our Sacred Path guidance cards, so we can open our listening to guidance, and peek into what is up for the day."

Grandmother Dona pulled her card and read from the *Sacred Path Cards* book: "Medicine Bundle represents allies and support. It looks like today will feature the support of allies in the service of bringing forth good medicine for healing and transformation."

I took my turn. My was Shawl. As I read, an electrical wave of energy moved through my body and I felt quite moved. "It represents Returning Home, as in returning home to a *forgotten state of wholeness that we all used to know before we became separated from our Indigenous roots.* Wow. I will definitely vote for that! It speaks of returning home as remembering how to live in harmony and reverence with Mother Earth and with one another, and says that this wisdom is preserved and expressed by the 380-some surviving Native tribes in North America." I looked up from the pages of the book and added, "… not to mention the Indigenous African, Australian, Tibetan and Chinese and Celtic systems of ancient wisdom that teach these same ways of harmony and wholeness."

I concluded, "And it says, 'You may also be returning home to the magic you once believed in.' Well, yesterday we sure got a glimpse of that magic."

"Beautiful guidance," Grandmother Dona nodded. "Yes, I sure felt that magic when I was witnessing the 'sky-language' at the Serpent yesterday. I actually felt like I was seeing the Face of God in that cloud formation of the serpent cloud arising next to the Sun. It seemed like it was an image up there in the Heavens, mirroring the

Serpent Mound with its sun-disk egg down below where we were sitting looking up at it. That is why I had to get up early today, and do a Peruvian "Despacho" ceremony of gratitude.

I squeezed her hand. "Dayenu."

"What does that mean?" Grandmother Dona asked.

"It is a Hebrew word from their Seder service at Passover that translates as "that would have been enough! But God did even more—Dayenu!" It is repeated after each miracle told in the story of the Jews' exodus from bondage in Egypt to the freedom of the Promised Land. It sure expresses how I feel today. It's as if we are being escorted out of the prison of the Old Earth of separation consciousness, and into the promised New Earth of oneness. All that happened yesterday would have been enough, but there is even more that will unfold today. Dayenu."

At that moment we heard a bird calling out its song brightly, like a punctuation mark of agreement. "What kind of bird is that?" I asked, remembering that Grandmother Dona is an accomplished Naturalist.

"That is a Yellow-Shafted Flicker Woodpecker, a fearless little bird whose rhythmic pecking teaches 'new rhythms of growth,' especially spiritually. And the red and black markings on its throat and head signify the activation of latent talents and deep intuition. Those red and black markings are the traditional colors of the shaman. Yellow-Shafted Flickers are seen as catalysts for major change. Another clue for today's adventure, I suspect."

"Perfect. And I recall being taught that the color yellow represents 'overcoming obstacles with love,' in the Seneca tradition," I added. "That was the reason I included one of their feathers in that ornament I gave you."

Grandmother Dona paused to admire the feathered ornament once more, as we quickly packed our food and sacred items for the day's adventure. I added my journal to my backpack so I could record the morning's mysterious events and guidance as we drove back to the Serpent.

It was a beautiful day. As we navigated down the long driveway away from the farm, the Flicker appeared once again, escorting us. We felt so connected and supported by the Earth, Nature and the Universe as we proceeded.

A couple of miles before we arrived at the designated private property near the Serpent Mound, I received a hit of guidance. I heard clear inner instructions that once we found this artesian well—whose waters connected underground to the rivers in Pittsburgh—I was to "tune into my 'inner rivers.'" The inner rivers of my body's arteries, vessels and veins would become a body-based surrogate-map, representing Pittsburgh's three rivers system for whatever was to happen when we got to the well. In addition, I was to specifically connect in my heart to the underground interconnecting fourth river. These instructions all arrived clearly, along with a calm sense of knowing.

Just as I was receiving the last bit of this guidance, Grandmother Dona asked, "If you get any guidance about what we are supposed to do when we find this underground water source connecting Serpent Mound and Pittsburgh, please let me know."

I giggled, and told her that guidance had just arrived. "However, it doesn't tell me WHAT is to occur, yet, but it is only telling me HOW I will need to proceed. I guess we only get to see the very next step on the Trail of Guidance; only one step at a time."

Grandmother Dona shrugged, "Well, that is all we really need, because we are journeying in trust."

"Yep. I have learned to call it 'Radical Trust.'"

We arrived at the designated private property and drove through the gate which was always left partially open by the owners, despite the *No Trespassing* sign posted on the closed half of the gate. We were told that the owners did this to allow the many economically impoverished community members who were without running water to have access to the well water which flowed 24/7/365.

As we entered, we looked to the left, where we had been instructed that we would see the artesian well, near the bottom of the long uphill driveway. We both scrutinized the property there, and saw nothing in the open grassy field. I double-checked the instructions dictated by our ally at the Serpent Mound, as Grandmother Dona drove slowly further up the driveway, scanning both sides. We saw nothing but clear, grassy fields.

Suddenly I became aware that we were at the top of the driveway, up at the big farmhouse, where private cars and trucks were parked. "Oh, Grandmother Dona, now we really are trespassing! Let's just leave! This must be the wrong place." We saw nothing that looked like an artesian well. She grimaced, and swung her sacred chariot around and started her way back down the long hill of the driveway.

As we approached the bottom of the driveway, I spotted something that had not been visible to either of us on the drive up. "Look, Grandmother Dona, could that be the well? It looks just like a miniature version of the round, concrete artesian well in Pittsburgh at Point Park where the three rivers converge. And its little spout in the center is pouring forth the water, like ours in Pittsburgh has the central fountain that is fed by the underground fourth river."

"It sure looks like the artesian well to me, but how in the world was it so invisible to both of us as we came in? It is completely compelling in its full-view location. Nothing about it is hidden. It is right there in the middle of this cleared, grassy field, where we were told it would be."

I was wondering exactly the same question. She parked the vehicle, and we both exited in silence, making a becline for the well with no further discussion.

I was a bit concerned that our appearance at the top of the winding driveway may have announced our intrusion to the owners, but as we arrived at the well, all my usual inner chatter went blank. No more thoughts arose for commentary on the process. I was completely riveted into a level of attentiveness that was pure, empty of personality and ego-based concerns, cleared and completely free from the familiar inner conversations.

Grandmother Dona arrived at the well first. Without a word, she held her cupped hands under the water flowing from the down-turned spout, and washed her face in its pure waters. Then she turned away from the well, lifting her hands up to the sun, as if in silent ceremony.

As she stepped away from the spout, I stepped forward in silence, without hesitation and without thoughts or inner instructions appearing. I looked at the water flowing from the spout for a brief moment. Without any warning or volition on my part, my hands went under the spout to catch the water and my face followed immediately after my hands, submerging my mouth into the water running through my cupped hands. And I began toning a song into the waters.

A Big Voice was simply coming through me, toning a melody into the water that was flowing through my hands. Although this was occurring quite effortlessly, it was not a voice I recognized as my own.

As a remote part of me witnessed all this, nothing in me resisted or judged. I simply surrendered, merged into the experience, and allowed this magnificent song to come through me. It was a beautiful, wordless melodic aria of tones, reverberating into the waters, from a Big, compelling, sacred voice, using me as its mouthpiece.

This voice felt as if it was ancient, deep. It seemed to be arising from the depths of the Earth herself, coming up through my feet, up through my bones, up through my arteries, vessels and veins, and out of my mouth. It felt so vibrant and big that it reverberated through my bones, literally rattling my skeletal system with the power of its sound frequencies. This voice sounded commanding, and at the same time utterly beautiful. I felt a total, peaceful surrender to this magnificent voice, as I merged into it in full support from my heart.

Through my heart, I tuned into the presence of the underground fourth river, then immediately felt an intensified energetic engagement with it, feeling its flow spanning the two locations underground—here at the Serpent and there in Peaceburgh.

I felt the vast energy of Creation flowing through me, through the waters of the arteries, vessels and veins of my "inner three rivers," which I saw were now connecting to the three converging Pittsburgh rivers.

Then I had a vivid visual image of the Kundalini Life-force moving through the underground waters as a magnificent, huge swimming rattlesnake, undulating towards the three converging rivers in Pittsburgh, propelled by the sacred sounds of this Big Voice that was still toning its melodic aria through me, as I stood bending over this well. I saw and sensed an intensified linking of these two sacred sites.

The rattlesnake Life-force entered the three rivers, then turned and swam back down through the interconnecting fourth river; back down to the Serpent Mound well waters. It then began winding its way downward to the waters of the Mississippi River. It continued swimming through that river all the way down to the waters of the Gulf of Mexico. There, the Kundalini-activated waters bathed the Yucatan Peninsula with its serpentine force, where the Rattlesnake-carved Pyramid at Chichen Itza is located; a sacred Mayan site.

As I witnessed the rattlesnake image of the Kundalini Life-force tracing its pathway through these waters of the Earth, I continued toning into the waters in my cupped hands. This went on for 10 or more minutes. Then the Big Voice abruptly shifted from melodic toning to speaking words.

Still directed into the waters flowing through my hands, this Voice resounded in commanding authority, its intensity rattling through my bones even more profoundly than the toning. The Voice was distinctly articulating each word underwater into my cupped hands, in a Declaration:

"We are HOME. We are home, NOW. We are HOME, because I SAY SO!

It is BEAUTIFUL. It is beautiful NOW. It is BEAUTIFUL, because I SAY SO!

It is COMPLETE. It is complete NOW. It is COMPLETE, because I SAY SO!"

Suddenly, my body arose into a fully upright position, just as abruptly as my body had originally been moved into position with my mouth submerged under the waters. There were tears flowing from my closed eyes—more sacred waters. But my eyes remained tightly closed. This mysterious process was not over.

Once I stood upright, my arms opened and lifted into an outstretched position at my sides, with my hands open. The Big Voice repeated its Declaration, now into the element of the air, commanding once again:

"We are HOME. We are home, NOW. We are HOME, because I SAY SO!

It is BEAUTIFUL. It is beautiful NOW. It is BEAUTIFUL, because I SAY SO!

It is COMPLETE. It is complete NOW. It is COMPLETE, because I SAY SO!

BECAUSE I SAY SO!"

My uplifted hands were throbbing and pulsing with a pounding energy and they felt huge, as if they were five times bigger than their usual size. Everything became quiet. Then my heartbeat and bones began to settle into a more normal feeling. It was over. The big energy in my hands also began to settle. I remained with my eyes closed, motionless, allowing my breathing to ground me.

As I continued to reground myself, I realized that my recent offer to become a mouthpiece for Divine Mother and Mother Earth had been fully accepted—quite literally. My body was being used in a shamanic process; an ancient process of union, of human with Spirit.

My body was a holy vessel, connecting the energies of Spirit (the "Big Voice" of Divine Mother activating the Kundalini energies of Creation), through the energies of the human (me), with the energies of the Earth (the rivers and underground waterflow). I was functioning as a sacred human bridge between Heaven and Earth, as shamans have served throughout the ages. I recalled the omen of the Flicker's message this morning.

Everything continued to settle within me, feeling complete, right, and peaceful. I was still standing with my eyes closed and my arms and hands outstretched. Tears were still streaming from my eyes as I finally opened them.

As my vision focused through the tears, I was shocked to see an unfamiliar man, appearing to be in his fifties, standing directly across the well from Grandmother Dona and me.

The realization that he had been standing there and witnessing this mysterious, intimate and profound process jolted me out of the altered state I had been in. I flipped from feeling expansive and peaceful to feeling exposed and vulnerable, as I realized this was probably the property owner, alerted by our intrusive search for the well. I remained frozen in my arms-open position.

No one moved. No one said anything. Then I looked to my right, to see that Grandmother Dona was standing with her arms still outstretched also, an exact mirror of mine. She was looking across the well at this stranger. I looked back across the well at the stranger, and noticed that his arms were also outstretched, in the same position of ceremonial enactment that Grandmother Dona and I were still holding. I realized in that moment that he had actually stood with us, participating in support of whatever had been happening. He actually appeared reverent, and rather priestly.

As I was processing this realization, the freeze-frame of the scene broke, and the man ran over to our side of the well, introducing himself as the son of the elderly woman who owned this property. He didn't wait for us to introduce ourselves. Instead, he began sharing all kinds of personal information, pouring his heart out to us about his and his mother's lives. Suddenly he interrupted himself and said, "Why am I telling you all this personal information? I am a very private person. I don't share such information, especially with strangers. If I had witnessed what you two were doing 10 years ago, I would have run you off my property with a gun!"

Grandmother Dona bluntly asked what I was wondering, but was still unable to articulate: "So why didn't you run us off your property today?"

He shook his head and answered, "Well, when I first came down here, that actually was my intention—minus the gun. But when I arrived, and experienced what was occurring, it all felt so holy. Yes, 'Holy' is the right word. I felt something shift inside me, and then I just wanted to hold my arms out like yours and somehow support whatever was happening."

The three of us spoke together for over two hours as we stood at the well. Grandmother Dona shared the story of how we were introduced to each other by telephone through the persistence of Grandmother Flordemayo of the International Council of 13 Indigenous Grandmothers, after the two of them had collaborated in offering a public Solstice ceremony at the Serpent Mound. She shared how, after connecting with me, guidance had come to her about the Serpent Mound having an underwater source that connected this sacred site to Pittsburgh's convergence of rivers at The Point State Park location. She also shared her guidance that once I arrived to join her at the Serpent, the underground water connection would be revealed. And then we were directed to the well here at this property. He had witnessed the rest.

I shared the information about Pittsburgh's three (four) rivers connection with the Mayan 2012 prophetic teachings of unity, and the visit in 2007 by Mayan Elders Don Alejandro Oxlaj and Grandmother Flordemayo, confirming that connection. I explained about my vision for the upcoming Pittsburgh Celebration of Unity, a public ceremony of reconciliation and reunion to honor the Indigenous Elders as Keepers of Wisdom for how to live into this predicted time of unity. I explained my understanding that the Celebration of Unity performance in Pittsburgh needed to be energetically connected to the Serpent Mound, through this amplified connection established today. That way, the transformational, healing energy of the Celebration of Unity would be transmitted to the entire planet, through its connection with the Serpent Mound.

I was amazed that our listener took all this in stride, nodding and commenting affirmingly. He shared that his family had discovered that they, too, had Indigenous roots. He felt quite attuned to Native Indigenous traditions. He also felt connected to the Divine Feminine, especially through Mother Mary. It even made sense to him that the hidden fourth river in Pittsburgh had been identified by Grandmother Flordemayo during her visit there as a Sacred Feminine flow of Life-force.

What a welcome ally this man was.

He proceeded to inform us that their artesian well was supplied by an underwater source that was itself fed by three other underground tributaries that were also on the property, as if a mirror to the three rivers and fourth underground river in Pittsburgh. The waters ran 24/7/365 at the rate of one gallon per minute.

He said, "This is the only spring in the area that never runs dry. Heck, it doesn't even slow down—not even in a drought like the one Ohio has had this whole month. These waters come up through a volcanic upthrust over there on the property, where there was a crop circle a few years ago. Researchers came, and my mother gave them permission to check out whether it was real or a hoax. She surprised me by giving them permission—something she would typically not do. She has turned away developers and researchers for years. She is fiercely protective of our property, and I am, too. The researchers determined that the crop circle was the real deal."

Grandmother Dona and I exchanged looks. She had been telling me about this crop circle on the drive up.

He continued, "Around 60 neighbors without running water come each day to collect water from the well. My mother allows this, because they cannot afford running water. The economy is so bad around here, and the poverty is unbelievable. Most of these families are also without electricity. The locals say the water is very healthy. Some of them even call it holy water. But that doesn't mean we allow just anyone on our property. We watch things carefully. That is why I came down to run you two off the property, until I felt the holy energy of whatever you were doing. Ummm, what were you doing, exactly?"

Grandmother Dona and I exchanged looks again. I took a big breath of air.

"I was allowing myself to be used as a mouthpiece for the Kundalini Life-force of Divine Mother. It came through Mother Earth into me, through the toning, moving through the sacred sounds into the waters. The song was carried through the interconnecting waters, and amplified the connection between the sacred sites of the Serpent Mound and The Point—the site of the converging four rivers in Pittsburgh. The connection between the two sites is now greatly magnified and activated."

There. That sounded matter-of-fact and normal enough, didn't it? I was feeling flushed.

This gentle soul responded in a completely disarming way. "When I arrived at the well I could hear you toning into the waters in your hands as you bent over the well. It sounded eerie but beautiful. I felt something deep inside me that was so compelling. I just had to go with it. I knew what was happening was not just a woo-woo, temporary shot of well-intended, but dippy wanna-be ceremony. I suddenly felt in awe, and protective of what was happening, and my arms went up to mirror the postures that you and Grandmother Dona were holding. I was riveted. It just felt holy."

"Thank you," we both said in unison.

We noticed the time. Once again, it was approaching closing time at the Serpent. "We must get going. We want to get to the Serpent before closing," Grandmother Dona said.

Our new ally gave us each a bear hug and told us, "I personally give you both permanent and cart-blanche permission to come here to our property any time you want, to continue your holy work. I will support you in any way I can."

We returned the bear hugs and settled into our vehicle, heading to the sacred site.

As we drove off, Grandmother Dona said, "Well, those *Sacred Path Cards* were spot-on for today: my Medicine Bundle guidance card about finding allies was sure confirmed. And your Shawl card, about returning Home was, too... big time. We sure made it GOOD, Honey!"

I was shaking my head, and pinching myself. "ECSTATIC!" I agreed.

"Yep," Grandmother Dona continued, "and we haven't even made it to the Serpent Mound today yet. Dayenu. This would be enough, but there will be even more. It is so amazing."

When we pulled into the parking lot of the Serpent effigy, we each brought out our "sacreds," as Grandmother Dona called them. I carried my serpent staff that Grandmother Dona had given me, as well as my serpentine-shaped Listening Stick and the serpent spirit rattle that I had made years ago in ceremony with Grandmother Spider and other Native teachers. I also brought my carved box of frankincense resin and lavender flowers, as gifts to express my gratitude and blessing and to honor the Spirit of the Serpent Mound. I left my serpent-painted shield in the car.

We arrived at the heart of the Serpent Mound, where the ancient Cedar Tree was growing at the turn of one of the Serpent's undulations. I asked Grandmother Dona for time alone there. She agreed, taking off toward the tail of the Serpent, singing, "I walk in beauty."

I placed all my sacred serpent medicine objects at the base of the Cedar Tree, arranging them upon its roots. I silently connected to my "within" power animal, the serpent, as I stood for a moment, viewing this amazing array of sacreds. I had never for a moment imagined that there would come a time 18 years into the future when I would be called to bring them all together at an ancient serpent effigy sacred site mirroring a constellation of a celestial serpent in the Heavens, neither of which I had even heard of at the time that I was creating the sacred serpentine tools.

"Your whole life has prepared you for this work that will unfold," echoed the inner voice that sent me into sleep the first night at Grandmother Dona's. Now I remembered the guidance from my recent psychic consultation, "You will have a shamanic opening soon. It will be effortless. You have deep past-life roots as a shaman."

I again recalled this morning's omen of the Flicker, signifying the activation of latent talents and deep intuition; catalysts for major change; its red and black markings representing the colors of the shaman. I stared at the perfection, that these colors were also on my serpent shield, rattle, and Listening Stick.

I sat at the Cedar's roots, instinctually touching these sacred tools. I silently called to the sacred seven directions and to my own Soul essence. I inwardly asked to be connected with the spirit of this Elder Cedar Tree, and with the spirit of the Serpent. I waited a moment until I sensed an energetic connection. I asked for their blessings on my sacred snake medicine objects. I felt flooded with gratitude, as if it was done.

I then requested the spirit of the Cedar Tree to energetically connect with the spirit of my beloved Weeping Elm, my personal Power Tree in my own sacred site in Pittsburgh. I imagined this occurring underground through the vast, interconnecting root system. That, too, felt done immediately, and I expressed gratitude. Now my personal power place in Pittsburgh would always be connected with this sacred Serpent site in Ohio. I chuckled. *Because I SAY so.*

Then I requested a personal message from the spirit of the Serpent of this magnificent Serpent Mound, remembering that the Serpent was the original symbol for the ancient Great Goddess; Creator; Life-Force. Immediately and distinctly, I heard inwardly a profound and loving message:

"I am in you. You are in me. We belong to each other."

I was moved to tears. I allowed myself to weep quietly at all that was happening. I felt the deep love and truth expressed within this message. Along with this message I felt flooded with a sense of appreciative acknowledgement from the spirit of the Serpent: for all my radical trust, for following the guidance, and for surrendering into service as a mouthpiece for Divine Mother and Mother Earth.

I returned my appreciation and acknowledgement to the spirit of the Serpent, with an offering of frankincense and lavender flowers.

I sat pondering the Serpent's words. I realized that, in addition to this being a profound personal message to me—affirming my deep connection with the Serpent Mound—it also described the consciousness of Oneness that humanity is moving into, in the coming Golden Age of this New Earth. How perfect... a totally intimate message for me, and simultaneously a message for humanity and all life forms: "I am in you. You are in me. We belong to each other."

I then felt prompted to go to the egg at the head of the Serpent, for further instruction. I again gave thanks, gathered up my sacreds, and headed there on high alert, deeply listening within.

When I arrived at the egg, I felt compelled to ask about my vision for the Celebration of Unity that had been tentatively scheduled to coincide with the upcoming National ACEP Energy Psychology conference next summer, "Portals to a Transformed World: Integrating Indigenous Wisdom and Modern Practice."

I intuitively felt guided now to ask: *What is the highest purpose of this Celebration of Unity ceremonial enactment?* Although I was being assisted by a group of kindred-spirit friends in my Peaceburgh Community of Unity and we had worked on the original inspiration for creating the event, we had not yet fleshed out the details.

I immediately heard the clear answer within:

In addition to honoring the Indigenous as the Wisdom Keepers, this Celebration of Unity will be a spirit-infused, symbolic occasion. It will support humanity's emergence into an awakened consciousness of remembering its divinity and unity. Count 260 days forward from this date, as you now are seeding this intention into the egg of the Serpent. Count forward 260 days from today and hold the event on that date.

I recalled that 260 days is the sacred numerical basis for the Mayan Calendar, derived from honoring the 260-day human gestational period, from conception to birth.

I thanked the spirit of the Serpent, and spoke aloud this highest purpose of the Celebration of Unity, seeding that intention into the egg at the head of the Serpent. The seed of my intention would be given birth in 260 days—a full human gestational period—for a rebirth into remembering our divinity and unity. Tears streamed again from my eyes. *What perfection*, I marveled. *What profound cosmic support.*

I offered my gifts of frankincense and lavender flowers, tossing them into the Serpent's egg. Then I turned and walked the entire length of the Serpent, tapping the ground with my serpent staff as I walked, speaking aloud the various visions of the fulfilled New Earth as Grandmother Dona and I had done yesterday, feeling bathed in gratitude.

When I completed the walk and arrived at the tail of the effigy, I saw Grandmother Dona who sat in meditation. I sat to join her. I took out my camera for sunset photographs, as that time was quickly approaching.

As I focused through my digital camera viewer, an inexplicable and remarkable phenomenon occurred. Piercing the sun through its midline was a solid-looking column of Light, shooting all the way upwards into the Heavens and all the way downwards into the earth, into the ground of the coils of the Serpent's tail. It looked so solid that it appeared as if it was splitting the camera in half and the sun with it.

I showed Grandmother Dona this solid-looking shaft of light in my camera viewer that was not captured in my photos of it. It was so unusual that I asked Grandmother Dona to see if it showed up on her camera as well, which she was now pulling out of her backpack.

Sure enough, her camera showed this phenomenon as well. But it didn't register in any of the photographs that she took either.

We gave up, and instead committed the heavenly image to memory. I commented on how it seemed to portray the ancient concept of the "axis-mundi"—the world axis; a symbol of the Divine Light of Creation interconnecting the Heavens with the Earth.

Grandmother Dona shook her head in awe. "There it is again. 'As above so below.'"

The sunset was fading. I told her quickly about the seeding of my intentions at the Serpent's egg, and of my messages from the spirit of the Serpent. She stared at me and grabbed my shoulders: "Those seeds dropping out of thin air today! Your *seed*ing of the intention of the Celebration of Unity into the Serpent's *egg* here. The awesome guidance about a 260-day gestation time for the seed to mature and be born."

My mouth fell open as I stared back. We hugged each other. We quickly gathered up our sacreds and headed back to her vehicle.

Back home, while our stew was heating on the stove, we got out a calendar to count the 260 days. I had no idea where that would land us for the specified date that was meant to be the date of this Celebration of Unity. As Grandmother Dona counted, I prayed that it would not land on a weekday, which would make attendance logistics challenging.

"Okay," she announced. "Two hundred and sixty days from today takes us to Sunday, June 12, 2011. That is to be the date for this Celebration of Unity ceremonial enactment."

I was relieved. A Sunday. That was perfect. And that was the week following the ACEP conference. So, the Celebration was to be separate from that event, for some reason.

As we ate our dinner, I suddenly heard another seed dropping out of thin air and bouncing on the floor. Incredulous, I looked at Grandmother Dona. "Did you hear that?"

"No, what?" she asked.

I just heard a THIRD seed dropping to the floor and bouncing."

We both searched the floor a third time, again coming up empty-handed. "Why THREE seeds?" I asked. Is there more to this seed message?

She shook her head in amazement and shrugged, "We will just have to see. Maybe this is another Dayenu moment. This would have been enough already today, but more?"

We gave thanks together for the miracles of the day's guidance and process, and for the perfect flow of the entire weekend. Tomorrow I would be heading home to Pittsburgh, and Grandmother Dona would be traveling to North Carolina to visit family.

As we went to bed, we heard a steady, substantial rain falling, breaking the 30-day drought.

Chapter 6 - 7:32 Revisited

· ·

I RECEIVED A PHONE CALL FROM Grandmother Dona late in the evening the day after we parted company at the Serpent Mound. She was calling from North Carolina, where she was taking care of her daughter's home and animals while they were out of town.

"Hi, Grandmother Dona, what's up?"

"The strangest thing, Victoria. I am here at my daughter's, as you know. I was just putzing around, tending to things here with the animals. I noticed that their great, beautiful pendulum clock had stopped. I went over to it and guess what time it had stopped at?"

"Ummm… 7:32?"

"7:32."

"Really?"

"Really."

"Really! Why? What is the significance of those numbers?" I asked yet again.

"They are definitely important; definitely meant to get our attention. And it's working!"

"That's the third 7:32," I observed.

"Dayenu already." Grandmother Dona laughed.

Grandmother Dona changed the subject. "I hope now that you have had some time to digest things, you can see that your experience at the artesian well was a for-real shamanic phenomenon. It was completely legit. You must acknowledge your shamanic gifts. I am honoring you for this."

"Thank you for acknowledging me," I said awkwardly. I took a deep breath and changed the subject. "Well, it was amazing that we were led to a miniature version at the Serpent Mound, of the larger artesian well at the converging rivers of Pittsburgh's Point State Park. It was a visual link, as well as an underground water link."

I paused, and allowed myself to consider more fully Grandmother Dona's deep acknowledgement of me. "Thank you for inviting me to see this shamanic process for what it is. It means so much that you are honoring me. I want to take that in more fully. And I have to say that I am deeply grateful for the psychic readings I had from my intuitive consultant, Debbie, before coming to collaborate with you. She was explicit about a shamanic process opening up for me at some future time; 'effortlessly,' she had said. And that is sure how it was. I think that having that message from her helped me to keep my reactive ego out of the way, and surrender into allowing it all to unfold. I was just an empty receptive vessel."

"It was magnificent. You were clear, and wide open," Grandmother Dona affirmed. Then she chuckled. "That was some big cosmic voice coming through you! At first I didn't know what to think. Then I felt the deep healing power of it all, returning us Home, like that Shawl card described."

"Every part of this process is so magnificent and sacred. I trust how wide open and clear you are, too, Grandmother Dona. Well, let's keep listening for why these numbers keep showing up."

"Definitely. I can't seem to get 7:32 off my brain," she responded, with a committed curiosity.

Chapter 7 - Three Seeds Fulfilled:
The Celebration of Unity

• •

AROUND FOUR MONTHS LATER, WE WERE approximately mid-way into the gestation process of co-creating the Celebration of Unity for honoring the Indigenous as Keepers of Wisdom. I had shared with my creative team about the instructions from the Serpent, that this event would also support humanity's rebirth into remembering our divinity. We had set the date to reflect the 260-day gestation count revealed by the Serpent. Then, finally, I was led to discover the answer to the mystery of why a third seed dropped out of thin air.

I was introduced to a creative, awakened, inspiring 19-year-old Pittsburgh native, Kevin May, by a mutual friend who knew we both shared a passion for honoring Indigenous wisdom. After he and I chatted a bit, he handed me a printed copy of an online story by Charles Eisenstein, taken from the Evolver website. It was called, *The Three Seeds*.

Really.

The Three Seeds tells the story of humanity's long, 26,000-year journey into Separation. It explains that humanity took this journey by choice, as a way to explore all the perils, lessons and gifts that we needed to experience—about abuse of power, greed, alienation, destruction and disconnection—that arise from separation consciousness. This experience would equip us to make a fully conscious return into a new age of Reunion.

The story continues, explaining that we knew at the outset that there was a definite risk that humanity would become so lost in Separation that we might never return. So we planted three seeds at the beginning of the journey that would sprout at the final extreme moment to show us the way back Home to unity. These three seeds were: the wisdom lineages of *esoteric knowledge*, hidden deep within the world religions and Mystery Schools; the *sacred stories*, encoding ancient wisdom symbolically, by way of legends, myths, folklore and fairy tales; and the third seed was the *Indigenous Tribes*.

This story reveals that the Indigenous Tribes opted out of the deepest stages of separation, preserving the wisdom of living in a sacred manner on Earth, in right relation with all of Life and our Ancestors. Despite near-annihilation, they preserved as best as they could, how to return to an original memory of Wholeness, harmony and deep relatedness with Mother Earth and Creation. They had to hide most of the deeper knowledge, protecting it from total destruction, until it was safe and necessary to reveal it again. That time is now.

And now their ancient Indigenous wisdom was being offered again, to light our way Home.

When I read this story, I was speechless; in total awe. The story described everything about humanity's long perilous journey and the Shift-of-the-Ages, this transition period we are experiencing at the close of 2012. And it was exactly what we needed as a way to open the Celebration of Unity. I could imagine The Three Seeds story being enacted through movement and chant, accompanying its narration. This story would allow us to focus on honoring the Indigenous Elders as the third seed, without ignoring the contributions of the other two seeds of the other religious traditions and sacred teachings—a dilemma that I had been grappling with and didn't know how to resolve in a creative, non-lecturing manner.

Kevin became part of the Celebration of Unity ceremonial performance. We applied and were accepted to be an official part of the annual Pittsburgh Three Rivers Arts Festival, which allowed us to reach a larger audience, and receive support from the Festival's resources. And we were given a date that coincided exactly with our 260-day gestation count: Sunday June 12, 2011. We were even given funding to finance the perfect staging venue downtown, including lighting, sound and publicity. Our performance location was central to the Festival, and timed for the final celebratory day of their two-week series of events.

Our Celebration honored three local Indigenous Elders who became part of the event's creative planning. During the process, we discovered that they represented three Tribes—three seeds—that were key at the historic timeframe of the early colonists' arrival to America.

Miguel Sague is a Spiritual Elder from the Taino Tribe. The Taino were the first Natives that Christopher Columbus encountered when arriving in the New World along the Florida peninsula. Tenanche Rose Golden carried a combined history of African American, Taino and Powatan lineages. The Powatan Indians were the first Natives that the original Virginia colonists encountered at Jamestown. And Douglas Harbst is a European who carried Cherokee, Shawnee and Lenape lineages. The Lenape Indians were among the Natives the colonists encountered when they came to the Three Rivers region in Western Pennsylvania. We were moved by the perfection of those connections between early history and the people of our current ceremonial enactment event.

The Celebration of Unity ceremonial performance was rich, moving and creative. The event opened with a reading of Indigenous prophecies, followed by our local InterPlay troupe enacting The *Three Seeds* story to movement and chant. A ceremonial gift-offering honored each of these Elders and their Tribal traditions' wisdom, and was accompanied by a request to receive a wisdom-teaching from each of them. Each Elder responded with a profound Indigenous teaching, critical to humanity's return to unity.

The event ended with a Taino chant, led by Taino Elder Miguel Sague: "Powerful Spirit, oh hear our prayers." Everyone in the audience joined in the chanting and leaped up to join the InterPlay performers as they tossed rainbow streamers and danced a spiral dance of celebration. The audience expressed such joy and connection that they would not stop chanting and dancing. After three attempts by Miguel to finish the ceremony, they finally wound down enough so the celebration could conclude. The feeling of shared joy and unity was profound. A sense of our divine essence permeated the gathering. People lingered, reluctant to leave.

The Celebration of Unity was a beautiful reunion of Indigenous Elders and the prophesied Rainbow Warriors, all honoring the Indigenous wisdom of unity and respect for All Our Relations.

The next day—still basking in our extraordinary expression of unity and divine remembering—I received an email forwarded by a friend. It originated from Patricia Cota-Robles, a Planetary Lightworker from Arizona who has led many years of spiritually-oriented activity for evolving humanity's awakening. It told of the extraordinary timing of several cosmic and spiritual events surrounding the timeframe of our Celebration of Unity.

As it turns out, our Celebration of Unity event was embedded between the Heavenly events of a June 1st, 2011 New Moon and Solar Eclipse and a June 15, 2011 Full Moon and Lunar Eclipse. The day of the Celebration itself, June 12, was what the Christian churches recognize as the Pentecost, when they celebrate the Baptism of the Holy Spirit, understood by many as the energy of the

Divine Mother aspect of the Trinity. Our Unity event was infused with these extraordinary frequencies of Light and Love.

Here is what my dear friend Lilan Laishley, a PhD and an accomplished astrologer, had to say about the impact of this particular Lunar Eclipse in her Full Moon Newsletter around that date. She said that this was a "rare eclipse" where the moon traveled through the shadow of the center of the Earth, "with the Sun, Moon, and Earth *in perfect union*" (italics are mine). This eclipse was showing that the Heavens ("as above") were assisting the humans ("so below") to move into "perfect union" in the "pivotal point between spirit and matter—aligned in oneness—entering into the point from which all things are possible." (www.Laishley.com)

We really made it GOOD, Honey!

Then I received more confirmation.

June 12, 2011 was also the date when an extraordinary release of spirit-assisted music was sent out freely over the internet, called *Musical Rapture: A Healing Gift to Humanity.* The mystical and moving events around the creation and release of this music are miraculous in and of themselves. An email reported the process of celestial music being transmitted by Patricia Cota-Robles's son, Joao, who had suddenly died several months prior, and whose music "from the other side" was consciously received by a spiritually guided musician, Frederic Delarue. The intent of the son's musical transmission was to "make available to the world a greatly amplified influx of Mother God's Divine Love, *to accelerate humanity's ascension into Divine Love and Unity Consciousness.*" (Italics mine.) And in Pittsburgh, our Celebration of Unity was aligned—in timing and intention—with this release of heavenly music, guided by the instructions from the Serpent as to the exact date.

I was speechless. *How much awe is even possible?* I wondered.

Patricia Cota-Robles also summarized: "2011 is the eleventh year of the New Millennium. Eleven is the master number that reflects the transformation of the physical into the Divine."

Yep, that was our inspiration and intention.

Weee! We ALL made it GOOD, Honey!

Chapter 8 - Discovering the
New Earth Puzzle Pieces

. . . .

I CONTINUED TO REVISIT THE MEMORIES of my inaugural visit to the
Great Serpent. I devoured information about the ancient Serpent
Mound from Ross Hamilton's books and publications.

I was astonished by his accumulating evidence that even though
the effigy of the Serpent that currently exists was constructed
1,000 to 3,000 years ago, there are strong indications that its design
timeline was far more ancient. The effigy's design is based upon the
constellation Draconis—the Celestial Serpent or Dragon—and the
pole star was a part of Draconis some 5,120 years ago. That North
star was central to the design of the effigy mound, according to
the Cherokee tradition. This information makes it likely that the
Serpent Mound was a re-creation of an even older version of this
effigy that existed there between 5,000 and 6,000 years ago. Ross
Hamilton noted this information in his most recent book, *Star
Mounds: Legacy of a Native American Mystery.*

Interestingly, Ross's more ancient timeframe for the Great
Serpent's age matched the intuitive guidance that Grandmother
Dona had received, in reference to the sacred Serpent Mound pipe

artifact that had come into her keeping. Then additional confirmation of that older timeline arrived.

A Mayan spiritual teacher from the Yucatan, Ac Tah, that I had sponsored in Pittsburgh, also confirmed that the Serpent Mound's age was around 5,000 years. He had advised Grandmother Dona about this when he visited the Serpent Mound to do ceremony there on his inaugural 13-city American teaching tour of 2011, just after his visit to Pittsburgh. Grandmother Dona had shown him her Serpent Mound pipe at that time. Ac Tah confirmed, through his own ancestral-connected guidance, that both the pipe and the Mound site dated back 5,000 years.

Ross Hamilton's research revealed that there were 10,000 original mounds and related mound-works in the Ohio area—"an earth-star-connected effigy landscape of many hundred square miles." Many of these mounds were star-oriented spirit-animal lodges that were called "manitous." In his publication, "The Great Serpent Mound: Book of Wonders and Mysteries," Ross discusses evidence that the mound culture represented a Golden Age where the ancient Indigenous peoples utilized "a natural science incomprehensible today involving the attraction and conversion of lightning into a powerful force of life and growth so effective as to leave the people literally wanting nothing."

Ross is passionate about reclaiming this ancient science of nature, whereby the separation between Heaven and Earth can be dissolved, and we can again live in unified relationship with the Cosmos. He is convinced that if we recover this ancient knowledge, and live in alignment with it, humanity can recreate a Golden Age on Earth where there is such flourishing that we too will "want for nothing," like the ancient mound-builders.

I felt shivers of resonant agreement as I read his information.

Even the earlier archeologists studying the Serpent Mound were so impressed by evidence of their abundance, that they called the mound-builders, "the Adena," or "they who require nothing." Hamilton's research indicates that the Lenape Tribe, who apparently absorbed the Allegheny Tribes, may have been the progenitors of the mound-building Adena people. And these extinct mound-builders may have been related to or absorbed by the Cherokee. The Cherokee still retain significant knowledge about the Serpent Mound to this day. And they are among those rare remaining keepers of the nearly lost knowledge of the "ancient science of nature."

Since the Serpent Mound has twelve astronomical alignments—including True North, lunar and solar alignments, and alignment with the constellation Draconis—it is clear that this site functioned in a manner complementary to that of Stonehenge in England. And like the Maya, its builders seemed to have knowledge of the 26,000 year "Precession of the Equinox" period, which was fundamental to the prophetic time-tracking done by the Mayan Calendar Day Keepers.

Ross Hamilton had spoken about the ancient mound-builders as using these star-oriented effigy mounds as sites from which to be in direct communication with their "star ancestors." I already knew that many Indigenous tribes across the globe attributed their origins to specific stars or constellations, so this made sense to me.

Honestly, I thought, *we are all from the stars. Big Bang R US! How sad that we ever came to believe that we are somehow separate from those cosmic origins.*

But the Indigenous peoples still honor their connections to the stars. And I was so inspired by the ancient Indigenous technologies and worldview Ross Hamilton was uncovering: effigy mounds built as star-lodges; their locations as maps indicating earthly correlations with heavenly constellations of stars. This ancient achievement demonstrated an aware, culturally-embodied expression of the perennial wisdom, "as above, so below." Such aware interconnection expressed a way of living that honored the remembrance of the heavenly origins of our original essence, intimately expressed in daily life. It is this interconnected consciousness that humanity almost completely lost as we have journeyed deeper and deeper into separation; into "the superstition of material literalism," as Deepok Chopra calls it.

What would our modern lives be like if we had continued to cultivate the memory of our universal origins, instead of relegating it to the level of "myth"? And then further distancing ourselves by degrading myth to mean "a lie or untruth," instead of myth's more accurate meaning: "stories that encode and preserve memories of deep truths."

Fortunately, modern science is shifting to actually confirm this ancient understanding. Modern day research like Brian Swimme's *Canticle to the Cosmos* is eloquent and moving in demonstrating the science behind such ancient wisdom. We are from the stars. We are made from stardust that continues in its evolving, through us.

Reflecting on all this, I realized that knowledge of the ancient earth-star sites was not only being uncovered in Ohio. Simultaneously, right here in Pittsburgh, we too were discovering the knowledge brought to us by Mayan Elders of our own local "earth-star-connected landscape." Don Alejandro's "Statement of Revelations and Prophecies" had given Pittsburgh the Mayan prophetic link: our converging rivers had been confirmed to be "a geographic reminder" put here by Creator. They showed humanity a visual story in our landscape of the promised return to unity, as the flow of three rivers converge and return to the source, represented by the ocean.

And our converging "Point" of three rivers with the fourth underground river was also recognized (by Nance Stewart and Frank Keller's work) as an earthly map to the section of the Milky Way's Starless Dark Rift that is part of the 26,000-year cyclical alignment, occurring at the ending of the Long Count of the Mayan calendar.

I wondered how many other ancient *and modern* earth-star connected landscapes were yet to be discovered? And how inspiring to be living in a modern city connected with such a significant one!

What a profoundly necessary piece of the puzzle Ross Hamilton was carrying, with his work of reclaiming the ancient earth-star connected science, to assist bringing forth this Great Shift of the Ages into the New Earth. And what a surprise it had been for me to learn that I was a "Divine Dot Connector," who would help to bring forth such profound puzzle pieces as the Mayan 2012/Three Rivers prophetic connection, and the subsequent connection between the Serpent Mound site and the Three Rivers site with the underground Fourth River.

I knew that many awakening Souls were experiencing incredible "Divine Dot Connecting" downloads and discovering that they carried important puzzle pieces too, once they became committed to serve this transformational process on Earth. I was already being linked up with several such transformers, in Pittsburgh and beyond, with whom I was glad to be sharing this extraordinary journey. It made me so curious about the multitudes of awakening Lightworkers that I had no knowledge of, who were still far enough below the radar with me that we had not discovered one another yet.

It was becoming clear that anyone committed to higher consciousness is very likely carrying profoundly necessary pieces of the puzzle to discover and bring forth this New Earth and the predicted return of a 1000-year Golden Age. After all, we are living in the most pivotal time in history since the last 26,000-year cycle of the Precession of the Equinoxes completed. Only, that earlier "Shift" occurred *before* recorded history, so we don't know what it was like for humanity then.

Interestingly, according to Taino Elder Miguel Sague's anthropological research (mayatainoprophecy.webs.com), humanity at that time did have their breakthrough to higher consciousness that emerged at the completion of the previous 26,000-year cycle. That breakthrough was humanity's cultural shift into new abilities for sharing personal spiritual experiences through cave art and community-based shamanic ceremony.

Now it is our turn in this Great Cycle of spiritual evolution. How would we come together at this next completion of the 26,000 year Precession of the Equinoxes, to co-create the highest and best Shift for our timeframe?

As if in response to this question, I flashed internally with another Divine Dot Connection alert: I suddenly recalled a poem that was downloaded to me in 1998—as if it was being dictated— that perfectly addressed this compelling idea of each person carrying a puzzle piece of the predicted shift into Wholeness:

The Mandala's Great Song*

"And in each of the villages, the
Great Council was convened.
And all the people gathered to tell of their journeys.
And as each story was told,
And deeply heard by the people,
Each person's treasure of wisdom was received.
And each person's wisdom was brought
to the Great Mandala.
And as each piece of the Great Mandala
was restored,
Its Truth and Beauty began to vibrate.
And this Great Vibration,
The Mandala's Great Song,
Vibrated in the people
And there was harmony."

(*Mandala: from Sanskrit, a circular design symbolizing completion, used as a guide in meditation, to guide the seeker into the "diamond world" or the "varja-dhatu," "from the many to the One.")

Now 14 years later, I can better understand this poem as a descriptive prediction of this current timeframe of the Shift of the Ages, and how it is that we will co-create this New Earth together. Everyone's journey needs to be heard, and each person has treasures of experience and wisdom to contribute. Indigenous traditions call these inner gifts our "Original Medicine." It is time for each person to offer that essence-based Soul-gift.

My musings moved me to recall how Nance Stewart magnificently offered her Original Medicine and contributed essential Divine Dot Connecting, when she chronicled her own spiritual journey with her spiritual collaborator Frank Keller in her books, Ancient Landscapes/ Distant Music (twinmiracle.com). It was her story with Frank Keller that originally revealed to me the sacred four rivers portal of Pittsburgh, as well as the predicted future of Pittsburgh and the New Earth for my catalytic 2006 *Point of Light* article.

Nance's unique puzzle pieces provided very deep ballast for my own sacred journey. I realized that is what we end up doing for one another as we fulfill our own higher purposes. I recalled Nance saying to me that on the highest path, all sites on Earth would become sacred. That idea fueled my own deepest sense of purpose, which is to reclaim a sacred world.

As my dear friend and transformational ally, Pat Fero says, "Everyone who is willing to serve this Great Shift will be used— and to the fullest extent possible—by the Universe." And to birth the transformational process we must listen deeply to one another, in order to bring forth and receive those treasures of personal wisdom, so that none are lost. Every person is a reflection of The

One, the interwoven Wholeness of the Web of Life. All gifts are unique and all are needed.

This memory of our original unity, our Oneness, is being unveiled day-by-day. As the Spirit of the Serpent communed to me at my initial visit to the Serpent Mound, "I am in you. You are in me. We belong to each other." We are discovering how to live into this great truth of our interconnection.

A vital puzzle piece of the New Earth consciousness is remembering that we are multi-dimensional beings; not just material beings, but energy-based spiritual beings. Ross Hamilton's vast research on the ancient sacred sites of the Ohio Valley, centered on the Serpent Mound, assists this remembering that we are multi-dimensional beings. As he resurrects ancient generations of preserved Indigenous wisdom of our Earth connections correlated to our Star connections, he reminds us. As Hamilton reclaims this knowledge, he makes possible humanity's reconstruction of "this ancient science of nature, whereby the separation between Heaven and Earth can be dissolved, where we can again live in unified relationship with the Cosmos."

That is a vision of unity that I resonate with; that I intend to stand for; to become a part of; to help co-create. That is a vision which expands the sense of unity that is a fundamental part of the emerging New Earth. True unity would not be limited to unity within Earth alone, but would be connected to all of Creation, including the vast Cosmos from which we all have our origins.

That cosmic linking seems to be a HUGE puzzle piece toward our wholeness, for which humanity can be in gratitude to Ross Hamilton and the original Indigenous Keepers of this wisdom. I can't help but smile as I realize that their work is LITERAL Divine Dot Connecting... just view any sky-map of star-linked constellations.

Chapter 9 - An Illuminating Phone Call with Grandmother Flordemayo

. . . .

I FOUND MYSELF MENTALLY REVIEWING THE Trail of Guidance so far in my unusual and unexpected adventure.

In a short timeframe, the process of Divine Dot Connecting had linked me to Grandmother Dona, then linked both of us with the Serpent Mound, with the Serpent Mound's underground water source connected to Peaceburgh's four rivers portal, and to the Serpent Mound's most knowledgeable researcher, Ross Hamilton—and his amazing work there of resurrecting ancient Indigenous knowledge of our Earth-Star connections. Many extraordinary peeks and glimpses of the New Earth of oneness, peace and joy had been revealed.

All this was clearly in service to a larger extraordinary process: that of uncovering key puzzle pieces to illuminate how to consciously co-create the New Earth and the predicted Golden Age of 1,000 years of peace. I was breathless from the magnitude of all that had been revealed so far. And, Dayenu! I knew there would be more.

Suddenly I felt an impulse to call Mayan Grandmother Flordemayo, and thank her for introducing me to Grandmother Dona.

I caught her on a rare occasion when she was at home from her travels with the International Council of 13 Indigenous Grandmothers. She greeted me warmly. I thanked her profusely for keeping after me to contact Grandmother Dona, and I shared with her the story of our collaborative adventures at the Serpent Mound so far.

Grandmother Flordemayo responded to my report by telling me: "You have been prepared for all this, for some time. There is nothing to question here. You are being guided as to what to do next. Leave it in the hands of the Great Mystery. Trust."

She went on to teach me more about the significance of the Serpent from her Mayan lineage. "The Serpent taught the Maya about movement in time, and mathematics—movement, time, space, velocity. The snake represented all that knowledge. The Serpent represents a new time; a new Creation; a New Earth; a new way of living in harmony. The Serpent moving through the waters, as you witnessed it at that sacred well, shows renewal, because the Serpent is knowledge, and water is Life."

Then Grandmother Flordemayo shared her personal experience of revelation at the Serpent Mound. This experience occurred during her trip to the Serpent, at the invitation from Grandmother Dona, to host an on-site Summer Solstice ceremony. And I didn't know it initially, but her personal Serpent Mound experience was part of the impetus for Grandmother Flordemayo to contact me and urge me to call Grandmother Dona and to meet her.

Grandmother Flordemayo told me:

"I had been feeling a strong desire to make a journey to the Serpent Mound when Grandmother Dona's invitation came for creating the Summer Solstice Ceremony there. I arrived at

Grandmother Dona's and was staying overnight at a retreat center with her and several others, before going to the Serpent the following day. Shortly after going to sleep, I was awakened by the appearance of my Grandmother—my Mother's Mother.

Her presence was so vivid, and so loving. She held me and stroked my hair, telling me, "Child, you are part of the Serpent Mound people. I want you to know that your Mother's people have traveled back and forth to this snake mound... back and forth over many, many years. This Serpent Mound is also your home, and these are your people! It is so good for you to return here, again and again."

Grandmother Flordemayo paused to allow me to absorb the impact of such a nocturnal visitation. I had the feeling that Flordemayo herself was re-living its impact as she related the experience to me, gathering her focus once again to continue:

"So I felt that I needed to have the experience of sleeping overnight at the Serpent, on the land there. We got permission from the Park staff to sleep out on the land, and then more was shown to me. That night I experienced seven huge balls of blue Light—each six feet in diameter—moving over the length of the Serpent effigy. I recognized those blue balls of Light as an aspect of my Spirit Teachers that were revealing themselves. It was very sacred."

Grandmother Flordemayo concluded emphatically:

"To me, when my Ancestors show up like that, and Spirit shows up like that, and they speak to me, that is more 'real' than anything else. That is my priority. I want people to know they have a really ancient Cosmic-lineage plan. You know, one that goes way beyond that other kind... what do you call it? That geno-gram thing?"

I had to laugh with her, and agree. "Yes, I agree. Our definition of 'reality' MUST expand! Our Ancestors and Spirit want to assist us, if we allow. And your point is well-taken. Our more complete lineage goes back too far to trace, yet it is an accessible part of us, if we tune in. Collaborating with Spirit is my top priority also. I wish more people could have these experiences, and know first-hand the reality that we are multi-dimensional beings."

Grandmother Flordemayo ended our call with a deep blessing. She said: "You have been consecrated, Victoria. You have been given a specific journey; a specific mission and message. Stay centered in your Serpent medicine. Walk with it. Keep in prayer and guidance. You must not defer to anyone else… it is between you and your Beloved."

I recognized the truth of this, deep in my bones. I thanked her profusely.

After I hung up from this extraordinary and affirming phone call, I recalled the compelling Trail of Guidance that had led me to connect with Grandmother Flordemayo in the first place. The memory began surfacing vividly. *Whoa*, I realized, *now I see why Spirit was sending me a huge head's up!*

I began integrating the memory.

I had first reported on the visionary work of the International Council of 13 Indigenous Grandmothers in my 2006 *Point of Light* article about the Mayan Calendar and the Shift of the Ages, where I had included the claim of a Pittsburgh three rivers/Mayan 2012 connection. Surprisingly, that article had gone viral online. Then I got the newly-published book about the 13 Grandmothers, *Grandmother Council the World,* and I was eager to learn more about them.

Looking at the photos of each Indigenous Grandmother in that book, I came to the image of Grandmother Flordemayo. Suddenly I experienced one of the most intense and unusual experiences of my life. Not once, but three times, as I looked directly at Flordemayo's photo, an electrical energy shot through my body, and I burst into tears. One time would have been unnerving enough. But it happened again. And then, *again.*

I recalled that I was able to stay present to what was happening in my body. I was still teary-eyed. I sensed that I needed to meet this Grandmother. That is when I realized that she was the only Mayan Grandmother of the 13 on the Council. I sensed that there might be a direct connection between the report in my article about the claimed Pittsburgh three rivers/Mayan 2012 connection and this Mayan Grandmother. I felt strongly that I needed to meet her in person.

I gazed intently again at her photo, this time with dry eyes. It felt like my Soul was communing, through the photo, with Grandmother Flordemayo's Soul. It felt like Flordemayo's gaze, through the anchor-point of the book's photo, was engaging me in a multi-dimensional process of remembering something; perhaps a Soul-contract to complete some work together with her in this lifetime. However, I kept this impression to myself. I had never experienced anything like this.

That unusual experience prompted me to call Carole Hart, the filmmaker of the Grandmothers' movie, *For the Next 7 Generations*, whose contact information was on the back cover of the book. To my surprise, a live voice answered. Carole Hart herself greeted me pleasantly from New York City.

She told me that the movie was not yet completed—they did not have sufficient funds to finish the documentary about the Grandmothers' story. I replied that I thought I could interest Pittsburghers to host a fundraiser for the Grandmothers' movie, since my local article suggesting that that there was a Mayan prophetic link with our three rivers had generated quite substantial interest and response locally, and had gone viral online as well.

I remember being stunned by Carole Hart's reply to me, "Now I know why your name sounds familiar to me. I have read your article! I was given a copy of that *Point of Light* magazine featuring your "We Are the Ones..." article by someone from Pennsylvania, who is also following the 13 Grandmothers' story. You did a really great job explaining complex spiritual topics, the Mayan Calendar, the sacred feminine, and the Grandmothers' work. Now I know why I recognize your name."

You could have knocked me over with a feather!

Carole helped me organize the Pittsburgh fundraiser. Grandmother Flordemayo committed to participate in the event. After sharing with her my article about the claimed three rivers link to the Mayan 2012 prophecies, Grandmother Flordemayo communicated with her Mayan teacher, the High Priest Don Alejandro, inquiring about the validity of the claim. His response was to join Grandmother Flordemayo in the visit to Pittsburgh, bringing the confirming Mayan 2012 prophetic information with him: the "Statement of Revelations and Prophecies."

Together they blessed the three rivers and its underground fourth river in a sacred ceremony with us.

I could finally see the big Dot Connecting picture: Grandmother Flordemayo had been my link to confirming the Pittsburgh three rivers/Mayan 2012 prophetic connection then, and was now serving as my link to Grandmother Dona and the Serpent Mound/New Earth connection.

So that is what the premonition experience with Grandmother Flordemayo's photo was all about. Now I understand what premonitions really are. I was glad that I had gotten better since then, at tuning in to the subtle realm of guiding synchronistic signals, so that subsequent messages from the Universe did not have to knock me over with such melodrama to get my attention.

Not only did Grandmother Flordemayo become a major catalyst for me to discover key puzzle pieces that I didn't know I was carrying, but Carole Hart became my steady ally and deep soul-friend on the journey.

Ecstatic.

Chapter 10 - A Halloween
Return to the Serpent

· ·

GRANDMOTHER DONA AND I HAD EACH independently received guidance through dreams and meditations that we had more work to do together at the Serpent Mound. Our guidance was also in agreement as to when. We were to go there again for ceremony on Halloween weekend. We were happy to tune in again to the Trail of Guidance, to see what other details would be revealed.

A few days before departing Pittsburgh to make the several-hours drive to Ohio, beautiful omens, synchronicities and messages began to appear.

First, I witnessed an incredible double rainbow around the nearly-full October moon, in the night sky. *A rainbow in the night sky!* I did not even know such a phenomenon was possible.

I had already seen a double rainbow around the sun while visiting my personal power place a couple of days earlier. Now the double rainbow was being mirrored at night around the moon. Only this time, as I watched the parade of puffy white clouds sail across the waxing moon where they reflected the double rainbow surrounding it, another shape began appearing in the clouds. It was a vertical purple cloud formation arising in an undulating upward movement to the right of the moon. It looked like a purple serpent arising. I gasped as I realized that this was the nighttime duplicate of the sky phenomenon Grandmother Dona and I had witnessed at sunset at the Serpent Mound the first time we were there together.

I sensed that this phenomenon was conveying that there was a complimentary process, mirroring what we had done so far at the Serpent Mound, that would need attention when Grandmother Dona and I returned at Halloween. Because of the sky-language's association with nighttime and the moon, the possible themes needing attention might be related to healing the shadow side of humanity, or bringing the depths of the unconscious more fully into the light, or exploring the Feminine consciousness represented by the Moon. Or, all of the above. We would have to see what wanted to happen.

Then, two days before I was to leave, I witnessed flying overhead a stream of thousands of crows—miles and miles of crows—flying toward my personal power place. I immediately thought of the song, "There's a river of birds in migration, a nation of women with wings!" So, Feminine energy was definitely to be a part of our next Serpent Mound work. I recalled that according to Jamie Sams' and David Carson's Indigenous teaching in their *Medicine Cards* book, crow is the Keeper of Sacred Law; and part of this sacred law is that, "all things are born of women." Crow also represents the ability to shape-shift reality as well as signaling an omen of change. And here was an airborne river of crows, thousands of them. Hmmm… BIG change coming to our limited ideas about reality. So, perhaps this big shape-shift to our notions of reality would come through women, or the reclaiming of the so-called "feminine" right-brain.

I had also been led through synchronicity to the page in Ted Andrews' *Animal Speak* book which showed a song that can be used to call power animals: "Riu, Riu Chiu." It is a Spanish Renaissance song about protecting the Feminine from the predators. Its words translate, "Riu, Riu Chiu/Who guards the river?/God [and the power animals as God's guardians] guards the wolf [predator] from our Ewes [the Feminine]."

It is a song about the end of predatory consciousness. Indeed, that would be big change coming. That would express the Great Shift from the love of power to the power of Love.

I knew that we would be singing this song at some point in our ceremonial work, which would be revealed when the time was right. How interesting, that a song from the Spaniards, who historically had been responsible for so much destruction of Indigenous wisdom, would now be used to represent the end of predatory consciousness.

The final piece of guidance Grandmother Dona and I received before I departed was that our ceremony at the Serpent Mound on October 31st was to be a part of a larger online global meditation, organized by Tom Kenyon, also scheduled to occur on Halloween. With a synchronistic affirmation, his instructions for this internet-organized meditation arrived with a description that its purpose was to shift people out of exploitive, predatory consciousness toward Earth, and to reconnect us to our essence of Divinity and Unity. We were excited that this global meditation, facilitated online by such a respected Lightworker as Tom Kenyon, was so completely aligned with our current guidance and with the purpose of the Celebration of Unity (which you read about in previous chapters).

Once I arrived at Grandmother Dona's, we took time to review and to practice together the elements of Tom Kenyon's global Halloween meditation and ceremony that we would be enacting at the Serpent Mound. Then we set out driving in her sacred vehicle, Beauty. We paid great attention to the landscape in the area as we drove.

We were amazed by the number of penitentiaries along the route to the Serpent Mound. Not only did these jails seem to symbolize the sorrow of the land and the people held hostage to devaluation and domination during centuries of power abuse, they also represented those convicted of even more extreme predatory activity. Grandmother Dona pointed out how many brand new detention facilities had been constructed just for juveniles. She also pointed out that the same architect that designed the penitentiaries and detention facilities had also been hired to design the public schools in the area—and they looked nearly indistinguishable.

"What were the architects thinking?" I asked in dismay.

Grandmother Dona sadly noted, "The adolescent males in this poverty-plagued part of Ohio have a saying, that they are headed either to the military or to the penitentiaries. Those are their prevalent options."

We were filled with sadness on behalf of males in Ohio being prescribed such limiting, detrimental futures that funneled them into tracks of predatory training, impairing their ability to connect with their hearts. We were moved to sing our Riu, Riu Chiu song on behalf of *all* males and the limiting socialization that constricts their hearts and spirits. We sang our song to shift the predatory consciousness of *all* misuse of power. We sang it over and over as we drove past these penitentiaries.

When we arrived at the Serpent effigy, this time Grandmother Dona took me on a path—Brush Creek Trail—that led to the area below the mound outcropping. Our first stop there was to visit the huge Dolomite altar stone that at some point in history, had been heaved over the cliff and landed at the bottom where we now stood inspecting it. According to a local Algonquin Indian, this massive stone had been the horizontal stone of an altar and had served as a tonal emitter. When struck, it would emit its tone for up to 10 miles away, within range of another ancient mound called Fort Hill. It had served as a long-distance ceremonial communication device.

We each took turns lying on it, to tune in for more sacred listening. I went first and Grandmother Dona walked off toward some trees to give me privacy. As I lay on this ancient stone, I heard internally the chant, "The earth, the air, the fire, the water/ Return, Return, Return, Return." I had a deep feeling—it felt like a memory—that as humanity moves into this approaching timeframe of unity, we will experience unity with even the most basic elements of Life: earth, air, fire and water. I found myself recalling Ross Hamilton's vision of the "Return" of the Medicine Days. I felt the deep wash of energy moving through my body, signaling confirmation of this impression.

As Grandmother Dona rejoined me for her turn to lie upon the Dolomite stone, she reported that she had just been paying a visit to a nearby Elder Tree. While honoring that tree, inwardly she heard a song. That song was "The earth, the air, the fire, the water/Return, Return, Return, Return."

I shared with her that I had received the same song as I lay on the stone. Grandmother Dona marveled at this. It was as if the ancient Dolomite stone and surrounding landscape held that memory of unity at this location for us both to tap into, giving it to us at this moment as a poignant message.

I walked off a bit to give Grandmother Dona her private time with the ancient stone. I wandered down a trail and Grandmother joined me after a bit, pointing out the eagle's nest in a nearby tree. We sent the eagle blessings and gratitude.

She guided my vision back around to the stone outcropping that supported the head of the Serpent Mound effigy above us. "See in the ledge there, the face of a serpent on the edge of the cliff formation?"

I could clearly see the distinct profile of a serpent face there in the facets of the stone ledge of the cliff overhead. I felt a deep thrill of familiarity and sense of belonging that was nearly overwhelming.

As we continued walking the trail below the Mound, I received a strong hit of guidance that the Spirit of the Serpent had an additional gift for me on this visit. I had the feeling that the gift would be brought to my attention along our walk. I sent out a quick prayer: "Thank you, and make it unmistakably clear to me how to find it." And my attention cranked up to high-alert.

Just a bit further along our walk, beneath the tail of the Serpent effigy, I spotted a pile of stones lining a downhill trench that joined into our trail. I felt my attention heighten and my vision soften as I scanned the tumble of stones. I inwardly asked to be shown whether there was something there for me.

I immediately spotted a stone that looked completely distinct from those surrounding it. It stood out in my vision from all the rest. It appeared yellowish, while all the others appeared grey. I picked up this stone from the rubble pile.

Turning the yellowish stone over in my hand, I inspected its facets. My hair stood on end and a rush of energy coursed through my body as I saw a distinct serpentine face in the stone's profile. It looked like a miniature of the serpentine face above us in the cliff ledge that Grandmother Dona had just pointed out to me. The snake profile in this stone looked very old and wise. On the top surface of the serpent's head, I saw a milky-colored vein. The vein was shaped somewhat like a wide "M" and looked like a river meandering through the stone.

I showed the stone to Grandmother Dona, and told her about being guided that it was another gift to me from the Serpent. She inspected it with great care and respect, noticing how heavy it was for its small size. She immediately recognized the serpent's profile in it.

Grandmother Dona observed, "I am familiar with this kind of stone. I was told by local geology researchers at the Mound that this is the kind of stone that the middle layer of the Serpent Mound was constructed with, although they also determined that it did not originate from this area. From what the researchers were able to figure out, this kind of stone was brought into the area by the original Mound Builders to construct the effigy mound. But from where, who knows?" After admiring the serpent's profile, she also noticed the unusual river-like veining on its top surface.

We gave blessings and gratitude, and walked the trail back up to the Serpent effigy. We had hoped to do our fire-based Peruvian Despacho ceremonial offering of gratitude. But we noticed that the winds were picking up, gusting to 25 miles per hour—not safe conditions for a fire.

Instead, we felt prompted to keep listening. As I did so, I heard the clear inner word, "Perfection." Although for me, this word would have typically made me uncomfortable, in this moment it felt apt; accurate; true.

As we watched the sunset together, we both witnessed a purple, serpentine cloud arising as it had previously, but this time to the left of the setting sun, and then, amazingly, *another* purple serpentine cloud forming to the right of the sun, as a mirror of the other one. I recalled our other serpentine cloud-language experiences. As we stared, transfixed, witnessing the awe-inspiring parade of these and other cloud formations being generated by the spectacular sunset, suddenly Grandmother Dona began sobbing.

She could barely speak through her tears, "I am seeing a vast, sparkling, emerald green river pouring forth right from the sun, going directly into my heart. It is healing all the heartbreak I have carried as a woman for over seven decades. I feel my heart healing completely. It is the most beautiful, most magnificent thing I have ever experienced. It is beyond words. I feel that, as this green river of healing love heals my heart, it is also healing the hearts of all of the women in all of patriarchal history who have been devalued and dominated and heartbroken."

She turned to me with her tear-streaked, luminous face, and I hugged her, moved to tears myself. We laughed as we hugged. We danced together, then began singing. Our joy was an outpouring explosion of healing energy on behalf of all females, and on behalf of the wounded feminine within males. In the back of my mind, I saw the nighttime double rainbow around the moon and the river of crows flooding the sky. I was speechless. I felt so connected to Life beyond the capacity for words.

The sun was now growing dim. We knew the groundwork had been laid for an extraordinary ceremony tomorrow. We would unite with thousands globally on Halloween—including those online and a "kindred contingent" back in Pittsburgh– who would be joining Tom Kenyon's internet-based meditation to transmute exploitive, predatory consciousness into Love and interconnection.

It was humorous to think that on the night representing horror, demons, devils, death and spooks, thousands would be meditating to shift human consciousness to remember its divinity. In actual fact, the ancient Celtic origins of Halloween—Samhain, as it is called by the Celts—celebrates this as the time of the year when "the veil that divides the realms of the seen and the unseen worlds is the thinnest," allowing for deepened connection and communication "between the worlds." We would certainly be appreciating that favorable condition of multi-dimensional support as we proceeded.

As we drove back to the farm guesthouse, we began mulling over various aspects of our adventure. Grandmother Dona related the ancient Cherokee story told to her, of the Serpent, Uktena.

Uktena was the legendary great poisonous serpent, whose heart was finally pierced, releasing its poison, so that it was able to transform and become a major planetary healing force at the

Serpent Mound. And Grandmother Dona felt that recalling this story now was important, since her heart had been miraculously released today of all its accumulated poisons, just like the Uktena.

"The Great Serpent is showing us how to release the traumas, hurt and poisons in our hearts, on behalf of a larger transformation that all are a part of," Grandmother Dona marveled.

We both became aware of the sense of interconnection we felt that our Serpent Mound explorations were having with author Lucia Rene's own adventure, described in her book, *Unplugging the Patriarchy*. In Lucia Rene's story, the long-hidden secret was revealed, that the serpent had bitten the hearts of the ancient Egyptian priestesses (and Lucia had been one of them in that incarnation), in the service of numbing them to the millennia of pain women would endure under Patriarchal rule, as women collaborated with men in a long journey of separation to explore the experience of the misuse of power. And, like in *The Three Seeds* story, the priestesses knew there was a real risk that the journey into separation and misuse of power could mean we might not make a successful return to unity.

Both in Lucia's story and now in the unfolding of all that was being revealed to us at the Great Serpent, we were being shown tremendous healing and movement toward wholeness, whispered earlier by the wind: "perfection."

"And we haven't even done the October 31st ceremony that we came here for," Grandmother Dona reminded me, laughing. Dayenu! We arrived home and wearily but happily retired to sleep.

Chapter 11 - Assisted by the Fairy Folk

. . . .

GRANDMOTHER DONA AND I FINALIZED OUR preparations to synchronize our ceremony with the global Tom Kenyon meditators at the designated 6 PM time at the Serpent Mound. As we tuned in through our inner work and prayers, I noticed an irresistible impulse to make a connection with the Nature Spirits prior to completing this 6 PM ceremony. Although I had never had a direct experience with Fairies, I took this prompting quite seriously.

I recalled that Grandmother Dona had both knowledge and experience about Nature Spirits. Now she explained to me that in ancient times, the Fairy Folk, or "Little People" had been collaborators with humans. But as humanity began to descend deeper into separation consciousness over millenia, these Nature Spirits had to shift into dimensional frequencies where they were less and less visible to humans so they could continue their work as Nature guardians, especially in guarding the ancient sacred sites.

As humanity's descent into separation deepened, and predatory attitudes of domination, greed, control and exploitation became pervasive, Nature Spirits could no longer risk collaboration with humans. They disappeared out of human experience and memory, and into the realm of myth. Then the term "myth" itself devolved, being redefined as meaning "untruth" rather than meaning "encoded wisdom."

Fortunately, we have some modern-day exceptions to this sad loss of connection and collaboration with Nature Spirits. These are the well-documented nature experiments and research at Findhorn, Scotland and at Perelandra in Virginia. I had read about both of these projects many years ago, and been very moved by the respectful co-creative collaboration of humans informed by the knowledge of the Nature Spirits. The spectacular results of their collaborations demonstrate how wise it is for us to reclaim this multi-dimensional collaboration at this precarious time on our planet.

Back when I did my 13-month vision quest process with Grandmother Spider, I learned that in addition to my Snake Medicine abilities regarding transformation and rebirth, I also have Fairy Medicine. This means that I carry a strong energetic and heart-based connection to Nature Spirits, and an ability to be receptive to their communications and wisdom. So I wanted to honor this opportunity to learn more now, through whatever synchronicities might open to us.

Grandmother Dona suggested that we pay a visit to another ancient mound site nearby the Serpent Mound, called Fort Hill, which was part of the ancient original mound-works system. In fact, she reminded me, the dolomite stone we visited yesterday was able to emit tonal sounds clearly to the Fort Hill location. And she knew that there had been recent reported Fairy activity there. Perhaps our songs and intentions yesterday from that dolomite stone had even emitted our frequencies to Fort Hill, sending an alert to the Little people in advance, regarding our current wish to connect with them. That all sounded wonderful to me.

We reviewed our *Sacred Path* guidance cards for the day, opening our sacred listening process. Grandmother Dona's card was Coral, representing nurturing. She felt this message was indicating a continued and deepened focus on her heart, as healed, whole, and restored. She marveled how this also fit in with Tom Kenyon's guided meditation plan for later today.

And the teaching of Coral also expressed the recognition of our "belonging to the Planetary Family," through the red blood that runs through the veins of every creature on the earth. That red flowing blood in our physical bodies correlates with the flowing waters of Mother Earth, which are considered to be her blood. So the coral symbolizes our nourishing connection to the waters/blood of The Mother of All Things, Mother Earth.

Her animal *Medicine Card* was Swan, expressing grace, and accessing the realm of miracles. We could sure use that energy of miracles to support this global intention of shifting humanity out of separation consciousness. And I knew it would require both grace and miracles if we were to experience any sense of contact with the Fairy Folk.

My *Sacred Path* guidance card was The Field of Plenty, representing ideas and needs being manifested. Not only was it an additional reassuring message about the intentions of the global meditation being successful, it reminded us that anything that is needed exists already within the Field of Plenty. We only need to come to Great Mystery with a grateful heart, giving thanks prior to receiving, and being willing to share.

My animal *Medicine Card* guidance was Lynx, who was both the Keeper and the Revealer of ancient esoteric secrets. That intrigued me, suggesting that something may be surfacing in connection with the lost knowledge of the Nature Spirits as we pursued our connection with the Fairy Folk.

I also pulled a card from the *Feathered Omen* deck, which was the Sea Gull, advising an attitude of adjusting behavior and communication. As I read this, internally I heard the word "communion" instead of the word "communication." I intuitively grasped that if we were graced with any connection with the Fairy Folk today, our communication would need to be adjusted to a deeply reverent and heart-based sense of "communion." This instantly reminded me of a powerful dream I had had years ago.

This dream had only audible words, with no visuals at all. In the dream state, I heard a conversation fragment, where my voice was asking the Source of Higher Guidance: *How shall we communicate then?* I was asking this question as if there was a major obstacle in communication to overcome. And I heard a Cosmic Voice offering the answer: *Through only Love.* This dream memory now felt like internal instruction to remind me what communion felt like, and how to access that state through Love. I made note of it.

We gave gratitude for our messages of synchronistic alerts, and set out on our way. We arrived at Fort Hill not long before their closing time, which seemed to be a consistent pattern to how our work unfolded.

Grandmother Dona led us up a hill with a narrow trail in the direction of the previous Fairy reporting. Shortly after entering the area, we paused and respectfully asked the Little People for permission to proceed further into their realm. Grandmother Dona spotted a fluttering leaf—one of the few leaves remaining—on a shrub nearby where we stood. She explained that this kind of leaf fluttering was their classic signal of acknowledgement and permission.

As we walked slowly, respectfully and alertly, we entered into a grove of many young sapling trees, stripped bare of their leaves from the recent fierce, cold winds. We paused there for a bit. I had an interior image of the Fairies hiding, stationed behind these young saplings, spying on us. For some reason, this image hit my funny bone, and I broke into uncontrolled laughter, almost to the point of tears. I had to take several deep breaths to reground myself, struggling to suppress giggles. Grandmother Dona waited patiently for me to settle, so we could proceed.

We walked further into this grove of bare saplings, and suddenly I held out my arm to stop Grandmother Dona and exclaimed, "Look!" as I pointed to a phenomenon just ahead of us.

There were hundreds of delicate, horizontal spider web filaments, draped across these bare tree branches on either side of the trail in front of us. They were glinting in the sunshine. I could see actual rainbows of light traveling along the webs; all the colors of the rainbow, moving along each web, from right to left. They were subtle to perceive, but absolutely breathtakingly beautiful. These horizontal webs were yards long, but amazingly, none of them sagged at all. The flowing rainbows illuminated all of the webs, revealing hundreds of little flowing strands of rainbow light. It was absolutely enchanting.

We both felt a deep recognition that the Fairy Folk were present. We again asked for permission to proceed, acknowledging that we would have to proceed through the array of webs, and we didn't want to destroy the delicate, luminous horizontal filaments. There was a dilemma, however. There seemed to be no way to proceed without destroying them. They were everywhere.

Nonetheless, we spotted the same signal to proceed: a nearby leaf, one of the few remaining attached to its limb, fluttered us onward. As we walked forward slowly and respectfully, I looked down at my black coat, which I expected to see plastered with these fine spider webs, but there was not a single web on my coat. *So we were not destroying this beautiful phenomenon after all. But why not? How was this possible?*

Before I could comment on this anomaly, Grandmother Dona spotted a log off the trail to our left. "There! That is a Fairy gathering place. See the little lichen structures that are shaped like huts, shelters and seating areas along the top of the log? And see the Turkey Tail Fungus? That is one of their favorite foods."

We walked to the log, admiring its natural miniature lichen village. We sat on a bare portion of the log, and offered the Little People gifts of nuts and tiny crackers that we had brought. Grandmother Dona spoke aloud, in blessing and invitation, making our request to have a shared conversation with the Nature Spirits. After a pause, she turned to me and said, "They are here listening, but are very guarded and cautious. Victoria, why don't you sing to them?"

That felt right. I was recalling the "communion" guidance, and a heart-song or two seemed just what was needed. I spoke my greetings to them. I recalled a song created by a SisterGoddess friend, Gail Ransom, back in Peaceburgh, about our four converging rivers. Our community had sung it to honor the Mayan Elders when they came to Pittsburgh and blessed our converging rivers' link with their 2012 prophecies of unity. It seemed perfect. I sang the chant to them several times:

"There is a river of peace, and a river of love, and a river of understanding. They long to become the River of One, to heal our Mother's family." ©

Grandmother Dona said, "Well, they liked that a lot, but are still feeling distrustful."

So I then proceeded to explain aloud to the Fairies why we were here: "We will be participating in a ceremony soon, at the tail of the Serpent Mound. It is our own contribution to amplify the effects of a global meditation that will be joined by thousands of people this Halloween, when the veils that separate the seen and unseen world are the thinnest. The intention is to shift humanity out of the predatory attitude of exploitation and to assist humanity to remember our divinity so we can co-create a world that works for all Life, not just humans. As part of this process, we have been singing the Spanish Renaissance song, "Riu, Riu Chiu." That song is recognized as a power song that protects the innocent from the predators."

I proceeded to sing that song aloud to the Fairy Folk, adding to its original verses in Spanish the names for calling in the power animals as additional guardians with God: Arana the Spider; Rana the Frog; and Serpiente the Serpent—representing the particular animal spirits of several of the ancient effigy mounds legendary to this area.

After singing the power animal version of "Riu, Riu Chiu," I added that it was our deep prayer and intention that humanity chooses to return to a higher consciousness of unity. I explained that this state of unity was the opportunity prophesized by the Mayan Calendar's Long Count. The Maya and other Indigenous peoples were tracking the 26,000-year-long rebirth process, now culminating in our lifetimes, of the 2012-era Shift-of-the-Ages. As part of this shift, Grandmother Dona and I intended that it once again becomes safe for the Little People to collaborate openly and visibly with humans. It was part of our New Earth vision that humanity would again remember and respect Nature Spirits and appreciate them.

I concluded by telling them about the plans for the Celebration of Unity in Pittsburgh, also aligned with this intention to shift out of predatory consciousness and into the power of Love, and honoring the ancient Indigenous wisdom teachings of unity. I spoke all this from a deep heart-centered place of passionate presence.

Grandmother Dona commented quietly, "They are listening with great care and interest."

I then told the Little People that I wanted to sing a song to them from my heart, that I would spontaneously create for them. I wanted to sing it from my essence to theirs, so that they could feel more deeply into my heart and intention. And I opened my mouth and began singing in an imaginary language of the heart.

As unabashed as a child, I simply allowed a melodic flow of syllables and tones to emerge. I sang, vividly imagining and feeling that my heart was able to remember their ancient Fairy language, so that my song would be understandable to them. I imagined and felt that they would be able to enter into heart-communion with me, understanding me and the purity of my motivation to connect with them.

The song felt loving and moving to me. When I finished, Grandmother Dona exclaimed, "What an enchanting, beautiful song! What language was that in?" Before I could explain, she cocked her head in a gesture of listening and exclaimed, "Oh! They were very touched by your song. They want to whisper a secret into your right ear."

I sat still and quiet, listening. I distinctly sensed that they now had a song for me. Then in my right ear I heard that the song was from Arana, Spider. I heard the first line, *"Come weave a web with me..."* and then I heard an instruction that the rest of the song would arrive soon. I was now my turn to be quite moved and I thanked them.

Grandmother Dona then asked the Little People if we could become visible to each other, or perhaps connect in some other more comfortable way—maybe simply by touching hands through the dimensional veil that hid us from each other, on this day of Halloween, when the veils between the seen and unseen are thinnest. In a gesture of trust and openness, she extended her hand out in invitation.

At that moment, an autumn leaf landed in her outstretched hand. We both marveled at this, since there were no trees arching over us, the trees nearest us were bare, and there was no breeze at that time. We smiled, acknowledging the connection, and gave them our thanks.

****

I must stop right here and tell you what began happening, right now, as I was reviewing this section of my writing. As I was sitting outside on the little deck of my home, re-reading these last lines that I just wrote, I was aware of a fleeting thought that perhaps a leaf landing on Grandmother Dona's hand may not seem like sufficiently convincing evidence of actual contact with the Fairies to some readers.

Then with my hands still poised on my keyboard, still entertaining that thought, I heard a commandingly loud rustling of leaves. The noise startled me, especially because the wind had been calm during all of this unseasonably warm March day, the entire time that I had been outside writing and editing. The rustling noise was coming from the only tree in the neighborhood that still had any dried autumn leaves left on it, three properties away. The whole tree was shaking.

As my attention riveted to this phenomenon of the loud rustling and the tree shaking, I began to discern a whirlwind circulating around the tree. It was a whirlwind making all that rustling noise in the brittle leaves. The whirlwind shook all the branches of this tree, now lifting a hundred or so leaves off its branches and swirling them into its wind-spiral.

As I watched in awe, the whirlwind brought the dancing cloud of leaves directly over to my deck, from three houses away. Most of the dried leaves were deposited right onto my deck in front of my writing table. This perfectly-timed whirlwind phenomenon was even more profound in its poignant contrast to the lack of wind all day.

I realized in amazement that it was at the exact moment of my doubting thought, that the Fairy Folk immediately sent me another, even more dramatic, synchronistic message of communion through the leaves. They seem to be quite determined that my report is believed. It seems clear that the Fairy Folk want to be taken seriously. It's like they were laughing and demonstrating that, *"Okay, if some humans won't want to believe one leaf, how about a hundred? Will a hundred leaves do?"* And they delivered the leaves onto my deck on cue.

So I am acknowledging the beloved Fairy Folks right now, and sending them gratitude and love, laughter and joy. Here is the New Earth revealing itself, and speaking engagingly to us all, right now.

****

Back to the story at Fort Hill...

Shortly after that poignant moment of the leaf contact, the alarm from the Fort Hill gift shop sounded, signaling their closing time. It was 5 PM. We jolted back into linear time. We realized that we still needed to make a stop at the artesian well on the way to the Serpent. We wanted to gather more of the sacred waters that connect the Serpent site with the converging four rivers in Pittsburgh, to use in our ceremony at the Serpent Mound at 6 PM.

We explained to our Fairy friends that we had to leave for the appointed ceremony, and we gave them our deep blessings and gratitude, bidding them farewell. Despite feeling a bit rushed, we left filled with a sense of grace and awe.

After stopping to fill our bottles with the sacred well water, we arrived at the tail of the Serpent with our sacreds. As Grandmother Dona spread out her blanket for the base of our altar, I suddenly called out, "Look!"

In the grass where we were setting up, and in the bare branches of the trees beyond the overlook at the Serpent's tail, there were hundreds of the same kinds of luminous, horizontal, rainbow-lit spider webs that we had seen at Fort Hill. Again, they were unbelievably long, extending yards and yards in length, without sagging, even in the variable intense winds that were beginning to reappear. They were everywhere. We had not seen anything like this before at the Serpent—or anywhere else—before seeing them today at Fort Hill. Now here they were again. These long luminous webs were not here at the Serpent Mound even yesterday.

"Grandmother Dona," I called. "The Fairies are here. They are here to join us in this ceremony! So this is what they meant when they whispered the first line of that song in my right ear: 'Come weave a web with me.' They are here to co-create this ceremony with us!" I felt elated.

I saw that Grandmother Dona's eyes were teary. We carefully scanned the area all around us. We saw that these rainbow web filaments were like a vast horizontal web wrapped around us—a web of Life—as far through the bare branches as we could see beyond the overlook, and through the grass all around us at ground level, as well. The Little People were participating in this momentous, transformational ceremony with us, and our designated spot had been made ready by them. I was moved beyond words.

The beginning line of the song whispered into my ear, had been their secret message; their way of tipping us off to this surprise for us. And it was also their way of letting us know that they were accepting our unspoken wish to collaborate. "Come weave a web with me," was the first line of their reciprocal invitation for a collaboration between our two worlds, of the seen and the unseen.

We had indeed made a communion-connection through the veil. And the rest of their song was still to come. *Dayenu*, I acknowledged silently. Remembering the animal guidance card from earlier, I also sent a brief thanks to Lynx, the Keeper/Revealer of ancient esoteric secrets, for facilitating this revelation from the Nature Spirits. And to Swan for grace and miracles.

It was now 6 PM! Time to begin with the planned guided visualizations. We each internally followed Tom Kenyon and his Hathor guides' meditative outline. I imagined the thousands of Lightworkers going through this process with us in over 100 countries—the aligning of our heart chakras with our pineal glands (the inner third eye area) and with our Higher Mind/Soul connection—to shift out of the life-destroying attitude of the love of power and into the life-generating attitude of the power of Love.

Inwardly, I began to see that same solid-looking pillar of Light that our cameras had framed during the recent sunset, but would not photograph. I could it see within, and feel that solid axis of Light transecting the sun, as it began penetrating down through the core of my body and continuing down into the Earth. As I experienced all this, it seemed that this *Heaven-Human-Earth alignment* was being established as the reconfigured "New Human Unit." It seemed that now humans could walk the Earth in this aware, interconnected, divine configuration as an embodied union of Heaven, Human, and Earth. It was a perfect visual for this unified divine human identity. I felt moved to be witness to this revelation: the shift into becoming "Homo Divinicus"—Divine Humans.

At the completion of the ceremony, I opened my eyes. I checked on Grandmother Dona, who was also reorienting herself. The sun was getting lower in the sky, and it was cold—around 40° Fahrenheit (4.5° Celsius). The winds had resumed as intense as yesterday—around 20 miles per hour. I looked up to see if the fragile web filaments had survived on the trees beyond the railing. They were still there, luminous, with their characteristic rainbow lights traveling along each one. Again I wondered how this was possible.

Just then something caught my attention and I refocused. "Look, Grandmother Dona!" I pointed to the central bare tree just on the other side of the railing at the overlook at the Serpent's tail, among the many trees decorated with the rainbow-glinting web filaments.

We stared, witnessing around 50 tiny winged creatures hovering together like a cloud to the left of the tree. They were bobbing up and down, in what appeared to be a coherent dance with half of them moving upwards, interspersing through the other half as they moved downwards. It looked like they were doing an interweaving dance, of weaving together Heaven above and Earth below, in perfect rhythmic choreography. The winged creatures were luminous, each one surrounded by a little field of light.

"What are they? Are they some kind of insect?" I asked, even though they didn't seem like any I had ever experienced.

Grandmother Dona scrunched her eyes and studied them from where we sat. "It's too cold for insects. The time of the year for bug hatchings is long over now."

We stood up and held out our hands, calling to them. We were amazed to witness the entire group of luminous winged creatures flying toward us.

They crossed over the railing as a unified group and approached us, half of the distance between us and them. As we began to walk closer toward them—still with our hands out—the entire group of them retreated back to their original position beside the tree on the other side of the railing. They resumed their Heaven and Earth interweaving movements with precision.

"I don't think this is bug behavior," I chuckled to Grandmother Dona.

"No, these are some kind of manifestation of the Fairies," she conceded in awe.

We each picked up the remaining gifts we had brought for the Little People, that in our rush to leave we had not had time to give them at Fort Hill. Grandmother Dona had a Peruvian mother-and-child doll, and I had my lavender flowers. We slowly walked toward the tree at the railing. As we got closer, I could see that each winged creature was about an inch high, and had a pair of wings on the top half of a slender body and another pair of wings on the bottom. Each had luminosity to it as it danced, gracefully moving up and down.

As we reached the railing at the overlook we each tossed our gifts over it, onto the cliff-ledge below, speaking aloud our blessings and gratitude. Grandmother Dona's doll landed just on the top edge of the precipice, and hung there, rather than tumbling all the way down the cliff.

Suddenly, the entire group of 50 or so winged dancers disappeared. They did not fly away. They all simply vanished simultaneously. In the very next moment both of us heard dozens of distinct, rhythmic footsteps tromping just below the cliff ridge where the doll had landed. It had been completely silent below, until the moment that the group of luminous dancers had disappeared. Now these tromping footsteps sounded audible all along the 100-foot span of the ridge below the overhang.

Grandmother Dona and I exchanged silent looks of awe, and grabbed each others' hands. We continued listening, verifying with each other all that we heard.

Yes, these were definite footsteps tromping rhythmically through the fallen autumn leaves below. No, they were definitely not the scampering sound of squirrels or other animals. And it sounded like the footsteps were from many beings—dozens of them. Some of the tromping seemed to be coming closer, making their way up the cliff ridge, to the higher area where the doll was resting.

In the next moment, a smaller group of the dancing winged ones reappeared in their original location to the left of the central tree. They simply reappeared, in an instant, as a group. The group looked about half of their original number, and they resumed their interweaving dance, alternating up and down among each other, choreographed in spectacular precision. The tromping footsteps continued below.

Grandmother Dona noticed the repeated calls of the Flicker and the Piliated Woodpecker, delivering their perfectly-timed medicine messages as we continued our Sacred Seeing. The Flicker's call affirmed "new rhythms of spiritual growth and catalysts for major change." The Piliated Woodpecker signaled a "new sensitivity to the heart as it awakens to new healing energies, in connection to the heartbeat of the Earth herself." How affirming, beautiful and perfect, we realized.

It was getting dark quickly. The footsteps below continued their tromping, but we still could not see their source. We only felt the deep knowing that they were from our allies, the Little People. Since we had no flashlights, we realized that we would have to be the ones to disrupt this connection and leave this celebration first.

We departed with an inspired offering of a childhood song we both knew, that we somehow felt was apt to sing for this moment:

"Everything runs in a circular motion/Life is like a little boat upon the sea/Everything is a part of everything anyway/You can have it all if you let yourself BE!/Why-o? Be-cause!/Why-o? Be-cause!"

I felt playful with the words. "Hmmm… be-cause: BE the *cause*. Create the New Earth from this divine BE-ing."

We giggled and sang, and immersed ourselves in the wisdom and perfection of this moment. It all felt so simple, so pure, so happy, and so true. We kept singing the ditty as a round, while we packed up our sacreds.

I bundled up my serpent stone, the Serpent Mound's gift to me from yesterday, grateful for its presence in this ceremony with us. We poured some of the sacred well water onto the ground, and saved the rest for me to take back to Pittsburgh, to pour into the four converging rivers. We acknowledged water's capacity to carry memory, like the magnet of a computer disc, within its molecules. We thanked the water for recording all of our prayers, feelings, intentions and experiences of today's ceremony. We bade farewell to our Nature Spirit friends.

As we drove back home reliving the magic of the day's experiences, we savored the first line of the promised song from the unseen realm of the Fairy Folk, "Come weave a web with me." We were eager to receive the rest of their song-gift.

When we got home we ate a simple dinner. Despite the late hour, we were determined to do another Peruvian Despacho ceremony of gratitude. Neither of us felt that we would be able to settle into sleep without it.

We gathered together materials for our give-away bundle, to burn as an offering of thanks to Pachamama—Earth Mother. We chose items symbolic of our awe and appreciation for the magical process we were experiencing, along with items of nature's beauty. Grandmother Dona brought forth the preserved round body of a pumpkin-orange orb spider that she had collected from a web under the eaves of her home and lovingly placed her in the bundle. We placed everything in the bundle with prayer and blessing.

We took our lovingly-wrapped bundle out to the bonfire that Grandmother Dona had lit in her patio hearth fireplace. We placed the bundle in the fire, turning our backs to it as it burned, in the traditional manner. As we turned, we were positioned to view the segment of the night sky that was displaying several constellations relevant to the Sacred Feminine.

We recognized how timely this act of witnessing was. We were now synchronistically positioned to pay attention to the star allies of the day's ceremonial work. We were being called to affirm and reclaim these Feminine star-connected energies of Creation, and to acknowledge their contribution to restore balance and reverence within human consciousness.

We were able to view Cassiopeia, Queen of Ethiopia; the Pleiades, the Seven Sisters; and Draconis, the Heavenly Dragon or Celestial Serpent—which was mirroring from the heavens our beloved Serpent Mound effigy below, with its serpentine Kundalini Life Force of Mother Earth. It was so perfect.

We spoke aloud, honoring the Sacred Feminine within us; within all women and men; within the Earth; within the Cosmos; within all of Creation. We recalled the message from Sacred Law, guarded by Crow who had appeared a few days prior to my journey here: "All things are born of women."

At that moment Grandmother Dona noticed that the smoke trail from the Despacho bundle was undulating upwards in a serpentine trail toward this Feminine section of the sky. At the same time, there was a cloud formation in this section of the sky which was undulating downward toward the Earth. The smoke trail and the cloud trail moved visibly toward each other as we watched in silent awe.

After another few moments, the two serpentine streams—the one from Earth and the one from the Heavens—intermingled visually and merged. We were blessed to witness this phenomenon as yet another profound message confirming the promised union of Heaven and Earth, like the interweaving dance of the winged ones earlier today.

We held each others' hands, witnessing in reverence, waiting for the prayer bundle to finish burning. Then, more magic happened. We heard a coyote howl from each of the four directions, north, south, east and west. The howling continued in a call-and-response until we were surrounded by the coyote chorus. Next we heard a sound that Grandmother Dona identified as the beak-clicking communication of owls from nearby trees. And then we heard the snorting sounds of deer nearby. The animals were participating as an active part of our sacred ceremony of gratitude and interconnection.

Grandmother Dona and I hugged each other in celebration of this magical moment of Oneness.

Grandmother Dona then looked up at the bare branches of the Elder Tree we were facing. My eyes followed. We were both struck with the odd patterns of flickering light cast there by the activity of the fire. The flickering light patterns gave us both the impression of something like a visual Morse-code message being sent off into the Heavens; to the Star Nations. Perhaps Spirit was making its own smoke signals from our gratitude bundle to the Star Nations. All that was happening felt expressed as a sense of unity; as the perfection of harmony.

We stood now with our arms around each others' waists. Tears were streaming softly down each of our faces. As we supported each other, we simultaneously felt held and supported in the even larger embrace of Mother Earth and all the vast beauty of Creation. The fire became quiet. The ceremony was complete. Our gratitude was boundless.

Back inside, sipping tea before going to bed, we marveled at the continuous flow of participation from all levels of Creation in today's ceremonial process. It was like Grandmother Dona and I were being shown how to live in a communion of oneness with all elements of Nature—with the insects, the animals, the birds, the cloud beings, the elements of earth-air-fire-water, the Star Nations, and even the unseen Nature Spirits. All levels of Creation were participating together with us in writing the story of the New Earth and our next Golden Age. They all had a stake in assisting this ascension process with humanity—this consciousness shift into unity and oneness—because we are not separate from one another.

It was like Gransmother Dona and I were among those forerunners who were being allowed to glimpse these revelations of the New Earth to bring back the news.

Ahhh... so *this* is what it is like to live in such sacred alignment with all of Life, that everything speaks the same language of

Creation—the language of Love, the language of communion—just as my dream had foretold.

This was the best Halloween ever! We had truly reached through the veils of separation. We were clearly, lovingly and consistently shown how profoundly this Shift of the Ages process was being assisted by *all* of Creation.

As my guidance card for the day had indicated, surely we were entering the Field of Plenty. Our highest visions and heartfelt yearnings for the New Earth were being manifested, as we gratefully observed with Sacred Seeing the many revelations of its appearance.

Now if we could only harness more awakened, conscious *human* participation.

We went happily to bed.

Chapter 12 - The Gift of the Fairy Song

. . . .

I AWOKE THE NEXT MORNING FROM a hilarious dream. I dreamed I was at a big conference with thousands of women and men in the audience. The women were distributing packages for the men only. The men were to open their packages right then at the conference, with the commitment to use the contents faithfully, to assist in integrating the knowledge being taught. The women were not in need of this assistance, so they were not receiving such packages. They were just watching as the men opened their gifts. So the men all opened their packages— and each man pulled out pink boxer shorts imprinted with a flying dragon located right over the crotch. The next scene showed a crowd of men in the hotel bathroom trying on their new pink dragon-imprinted boxers. They looked great.

I giggled as I got out of bed and rolled into the shower. So, the men were being given their own Dreamtime immersion into the Feminine and the Kundalini serpentine life-force. Fabulous!

As I stood in the streaming waters of the shower, the rest of words of the Fairy song suddenly began arriving, as promised. A beautiful melody arrived with the verses. I was astonished. I am not a songwriter, musician or singer, so I was relieved to be able to recall all the words as well as the melody. The Fairies' song was magnificent:

> "Come weave a web with me,
> A Rainbow web of Harmony
> Come weave a web with me.
> Come weave a web with me,
> Beauty for all to see,
> Come weave a web with me.
> Weaving, weaving, weaving a New Earth Dream,
> Weaving, weaving, weaving a New Earth Dream.
> Come weave a web with me,
> Fulfillment, joy and ecstasy!
> Come weave a web with me.
> Come weave a web with me,
> All Life expressing Unity!
> Come weave a web with me.
> Weaving, weaving, weaving a New Earth Dream,
> Weaving, weaving, weaving a New Earth Dream."

I repeated the words in amazement as I wrote them down. The song melody stayed with me in a mesmerizing way. I came out to the kitchen as Grandmother Dona finished drumming her prayers in grateful welcome to the morning sun. We made breakfast and I sang the Fairy song to her.

"What an enchanting melody... and the words are such a perfect message. The Fairies are so clear about co-creating this predicted Golden Age right along with us. Their dancing yesterday showed us the interweaving of this New Earth Dream that is uniting Heaven and Earth. We are so privileged to have participated in all this, and to have experienced all these revelations."

"So true," I responded. "With our Sacred Seeing."

"And Sacred Saying," she said.

We finished breakfast, savoring all the details. Grandmother Dona helped me document all the many amazing elements of our adventure in my journal.

As we took our dishes to the sink, we were about to move the large jug of sacred well water. Grandmother Dona pointed to the lid of the bottle. "Look, Victoria, a tiny baby crab spider is sitting right here on the top."

We both peered down at this little translucent crab spider with its oversized front arms. It turned a bit too, and positioned its body as if to return our scrutiny. Grandmother Dona noticed this, held up her hand in a gesture of friendship, and waved at the wee spider. "Good morning, little one!"

The tiny spider astonished us both. It lifted up one of its front arms holding it high in a return gesture of salutation!

We were so glad that we both witnessed this together. We may not have believed our own eyes if the other one had not been present to verify what had just happened. The magic of oneness was still present. I sang the Fairies' song to the wee spider. We sent it our loving blessings and gently moved the jug over a bit to clean up.

The communion of oneness continued. As I packed my car for the drive back to Pittsburgh, Grandmother Dona and I saw a magnificent cloud formation. It looked like a massive butterfly-woman with an elegant, huge wingspan. We were reminded of the tiny butterfly-woman visible in the light-beams of the heart crystal that we had both witnessed on our first morning together a month ago. Now this cloud image was like a macro-cosmic, enlarged version of that image. It seemed to be a magnified confirmation, a Heavenly acknowledgement, of our mission fulfilled. "As below, so above."

Before I left, I remembered that I wanted to loan Grandmother Dona a profound book I had recently completed. I dug through my belongings and succeeded in finding it for her. It was Peter

Kingsley's book, *A Story Waiting to Pierce You: Mongolia, Tibet, and the Destiny of the Western World*. It was a moving and heavily-researched story documenting how ancient shamanism had "seeded" all the Indigenous cultures at the dawn of humanity on the Earth.

On the book's cover was an arrow, representing the particular shaman's tool that was capable of piercing humanity's hearts and minds in a transformative manner. As I finished describing the book, and handed it to Grandmother Dona, we hugged. As we hugged, she glanced upward again at the sky and called out in astonishment.

"Victoria, look!" She watched me as I turned my face upward, and smiled as my mouth dropped open. The cloud language now visible was showing a new image. This new cloud formation was a huge long straight arrow shaft, with a clearly hooked point. We were quite astonished.

"Okay, I will definitely read this book," Grandmother Dona laughed. Obviously, the theme of acknowledging the modern significance of ancient shamanism was to be emphasized in our attention as we continued our adventure. I would definitely stay alert to this theme, especially since I had been shown my own Shaman-like experience at the Serpent well. We hugged one more time, and I headed home.

As I drove, I had plenty of time to wonder whether the revelations of this New Earth would somehow continue to express, as we each returned to our usual, mundane lives.

Chapter 13 - Unexpected Appointment with the Sacred White Buffalo

. . . .

MY FRIEND FRANK VALLEY HAD BEEN urging me to go with him for a day trip to experience the waters of the Youghiogheny River in the Ohiopyle area of Western Pennsylvania. He understood my deep spiritual connection with the converging four rivers in Pittsburgh, and knew that I would appreciate the opportunity to connect with more sacred waters. I had finally agreed to clear my plans and accompany him to that area. Today was the day.

Picking my *Sacred Path* card for the day in my now–established practice with Grandmother Dona of sacred listening, I was intrigued to see that I pulled Power Place. I recalled that the Power Place card had been my first card guidance for the initial visit to the Serpent Mound. Sitting with the card now, I found myself sensing the strong possibility that today's trip may offer surprises. So I instinctually went to gather up my sacreds for the trip. I was experiencing that familiar sense of high alert. I packed my yellow serpent-faced stone, the serpent-shaped staff that Grandmother Dona had given me, and a few other items, including my journal. I smiled, thinking, *this journal has become one of my most-used sacred objects!*

I paused and went back to include my Biogeometry BG-3 pendulum in my packing for the day. I always carried a regular pendulum and collapsible dowsing rods in my purse, so they would be handy for quick energy checks as I had been trained to use them. But this particular pendulum was really calling to me today, perhaps because Frank had studied the ancient Earth-energy-based science of Biogeometry, too. I didn't waste time analyzing the reasons, however. I just trusted the impulse.

As I waited for Frank to arrive, I recalled the Indigenous teachings of Power Place, about being nourished by Earth-connection to support our capacity to become "catalyzers" of transformation. The card also spoke about the ability to do ceremony that utilizes the body consciously as a living antennae to bridge Heaven and Earth. Each ceremony done at a Power Place establishes that unifying connection.

I had come to love the instructions in this card's teaching. I felt a sense of loss that such beautiful teachings about conscious co-creation through attunement with Nature have been nearly forgotten by most of humanity. I sent a prayer of thanksgiving to Jamie Sams for her book and for all the other Indigenous tribal people who had preserved such teachings across the centuries of their persecution.

After Frank picked me up and we were on our way, he asked me if I had ever met the Sacred White Buffalo, cared for by Nemacolin Woodlands Resort near our destination. I was aware that a White Buffalo had been born in Western Pennsylvania in 2006, but I had not had the privilege of an encounter with him. Frank advised me that, in that case, experiencing the presence of this sacred being needed to be a part of the day's plans. I immediately agreed, reassured by whole-body goose-bumps. An encounter with the Sacred Buffalo felt highly important. Nemacolin was a bit under two hour's drive, and close by the Youghiogheny River area where we were headed.

As we drove, we helped each other recall the significance of the birth of the Western Pennsylvanian Sacred White Buffalo and its female counterpart, the Sacred Black Buffalo. Each White Buffalo birth is subject to Indigenous tribal verification. Once it is determined not to be a hybrid or an albino genetic anomaly, the White Buffalo is recognized as a spirit-infused being born into its chosen location in order to bring to the local people a message of harmony, peace and unity.

The White Buffalo's sacred message calls the people of all nations to return to a spiritual path of unity. Its presence signals that now is the time to choose: to turn away from greed-based living and to join together in love, sharing, understanding and unity. The White Buffalo's presence brings urgently-needed attention to this crucial time of choice for all humanity as we stand at the crossroads, at the end of a 26,000 year cycle. Do we choose separation and greed or unity and peace? This choice determines our future.

I grabbed my cell phone and excitedly called Grandmother Dona. It seemed vital that she be informed of this new development, of our plan to visit the Sacred Buffalo. She answered from her Ohio home, and I filled her in.

She was delighted and told me, "My guidance card for today is the North Shield that tells the story about the Sacred White Buffalo." I was not surprised.

As Frank and I drove, I put my phone on speaker so he could hear Grandmother Dona too. She continued. "Interestingly, when I asked for guidance just a bit ago about what was needed for the day, I clearly got: "Victoria." I thought that was a bit different, and had to laugh! But right now it is starting to make sense. I am getting a strong feeling of knowing that important work is opening up with you and Frank there. You will be anchoring sacred energy somehow. I am getting a strong message that you also need to go to East Millsboro, nearby in the area of the White Buffalo. That feels vital."

She explained further, "I was told by an Indigenous Algonquin man here in the Serpent Mound area who has also been researching sacred sites, that there are Native American petroglyphs—ancient rock drawings—at the Francis Farm in East Millsboro, Pennsylvania. This man also was a researcher for NASA, by the way. He told me about his experience of the extraordinary power of that East Millsboro site. The petroglyphs on the farm are linked to the Indigenous myths of the "Underwater Panther," and there are some clues that the petroglyphs may be Mayan. That farm is private property now, so visitors aren't allowed. Since you won't be able to go to that property, we will have to see where guidance directs you after your meeting with the Buffalo."

I was appreciating that Grandmother Dona had spent so many years as an instructor and researcher at Kent State University, in their Multicultural Education Department, specializing in Native American Studies. What a perfect ally; intuitive plus informed by research.

She continued, "The Underwater Panther was an underwater being recognized by hundreds of Indigenous tribes across North America. It was described as having a combination of attributes from many animals, including the wildcat or lynx, and the serpent. And it had serpentine properties that were extraordinarily powerful and sometimes terrifying. From what I recall, this Underwater Panther was the underworld compliment to the Thunderbirds above-ground. Both of these were life-forces that had to be held in complimentary balance—probably representing yin and yang forces of the creative/ destructive feminine and the creative/destructive masculine."

"Anyway, I am getting that there is some kind of ceremonial work you are being directed to do there today, beginning with the

White Buffalo and ending somewhere in East Millsboro. More will be revealed with the White Buffalo. Oh, I want to be with you so much. I have met three other Sacred White Buffalo, but not this Pennsylvania one. This one has been verified by several tribes as authentically fulfilling the prophecies of unity. Well, I will at least be able to be with you by phone." She said goodbye, agreeing to check in later.

"Wow," Frank said before I could utter the same thing. I looked at him to further investigate his reaction. I knew Frank to be a person of tremendous spiritual depth, knowledge and training, who was devoted to planetary service. He was a true Kindred Spirit. I had trusted him with the details of my first trip to the Serpent Mound, which he had taken in stride, and in a reverent manner, As I scanned his face now, I was reassured by the fact that he was grinning.

"I am up for this adventure!" he said. "After hearing what happened at your trip to the Serpent Mound, who knows WHAT might open up."

"Well, then I had better fill you in on the details of the second Serpent Mound trip just last week on the Halloween weekend." I smiled. As we continued to drive, I told the wondrous story. Just as I concluded my tale, we arrived at the hilltop summit—the highest elevation in the area. It was 1:11 PM. This synchronicity was not lost on Frank, who commented immediately.

"Well, there is the spiritual punctuation to your story: 1:11 PM—a variation of the 11:11 numerology depicting the union of humanity and divinity, the symbol for "as above, so below," and appearing exactly as we reach the peak elevation at the highest perspective point of this area. Wow."

I smiled and realized what a perfect ally I had in Frank for whatever this adventure would reveal.

We stopped at the Youghiogheny River, making our visit there more brief than originally planned, to allow time to visit the Buffalo, and allow for the East Millsboro mystery. We went down to the riverbank and Frank collected some river water in a bottle. We did a simple water blessing ceremony at the river's edge, and immersed ourselves in the fresh air, beauty, and uplifting energies of the site. Then we journeyed on to meet the White Buffalo.

After a bit more driving, I phoned Grandmother Dona to let her know that we were pulling onto the long driveway leading up to the 33-acre meadow that Nemacolin Woodlands had contributed to the care of the Sacred White Buffalo, and his female counterpart, the Sacred Black Buffalo.

As Frank turned the car onto the narrow road that parallels the fencing surrounding the Buffalo's meadow, I could see the stable at the crest of the hill at the center the acreage. There was the White Buffalo, resting on the grass alongside the stable. As soon as my eyes landed on the magnificent creature, he arose to standing, and began to journey down the hill toward the road we were on.

"Grandmother Dona, Frank! I see the White Buffalo now. He is coming down the hill to the bottom, to where the fence is. I am going to get out of the car and walk the rest of the way down this driveway. I am so excited to meet him."

Before I could hang up, Grandmother Dona told me in an intense tone, "The White Buffalo is going to give you the song to connect to the frequencies of the Underwater Panther site there in East Millsboro." Frank and I exchanged wide-eyed looks without a comment.

I exited the car with half of the driveway distance left to walk. Frank followed a few feet behind me after parking the car. My eyes were glued to the Sacred White Buffalo. He was halfway down the hill approaching the double fencing, and the female Sacred Black Buffalo was now following not far behind him.

I suddenly realized that I would arrive at the fence at the same moment that the White Buffalo would. Goosebumps covered my body. *It is as if he is keeping an appointment with me, and he is exactly on time. Or maybe I am keeping an appointment with HIM,* I mused silently.

Sure enough, we arrived at the doubled fence at the border of the road at exactly the same moment. The White Buffalo came as close to the wire fence as was possible. So did I. We immediately connected eye-to-eye.

His fur was currently a yellowish color, having darkened from the original white. I had been told that the prophecies indicate that his fur will also turn red, brown and black—the colors of the races—to show the coming time of unity of all the races.

After turning to present his magnificent profile to me three times, as if for me to properly admire him (which I certainly did), the majestic Being returned to face me directly again, locking his midnight-black eyes into mine. I felt electrified with attention as I stared deeply into his eyes, and heard his heavy breath up close. We maintained a deep connection like this for about 20 minutes, with the White Buffalo occasionally breaking eye-contact to scratch, move a bit, or nibble a bit of dried hay, but always returning his gaze to mine, looking deeply into me.

I silently sent the Sacred White Buffalo my love and gratitude. I mentally communicated to him that I understood that now is the time of the Great Shift of the Ages, and so many of us are grateful that he and the Sacred Black Buffalo are here in fulfillment of the prophecies of unity. I let him know that many were collaborating to bring forth this predicted world of unity—the New Earth— that was to become a world ruled by love instead of domination; characterized by sharing, compassion, joy and peace. Silently I asked him if he had a song for me. I listened from my heart.

We continued to stare into each other, I was so aware of the intensity of his deep black eyes. His breath felt like substantive energetic matter. His powerful snorts seemed to punctuate with intention the silent essence of our communion. His horns were majestic. As I was taking all this in, I heard internally the word, Thunder.

At that moment, the White Buffalo moved over to allow his female partner, the Sacred Black Buffalo to come forward to encounter me. I did not know yet that her name was Thunder. She also positioned herself as closely as possible to the doubled fence. She also locked into my eyes intently. We gazed at each other for several minutes. Looking at her was like looking into midnight. Everything about her was pitch-black. She felt as gentle as the White Buffalo had felt intense. I sent her my gratitude and blessings. After a bit I internally heard the word, Lightning. Then she moved aside and the White Buffalo stepped back into view. I did not yet know that his non-Native name was Lightning. He resumed his gaze into my eyes and we continued communing for a few more minutes.

Suddenly everything shifted energetically and felt complete. Apparently the White Buffalo agreed, for at that same moment he turned away and began walking back up the hill, with the Black Buffalo following along. They continued on together over the hill until they disappeared from view. I gave a prayer of gratitude.

Frank stepped over to me and we quietly tossed into the meadow our gifts to them, with honoring and love. Frank left three tumbled gemstones, representing Grandmother Dona, me, and himself. I made my offering of frankincense and myrrh.

Still basking silently in the sense of communion with the Buffalo, we turned around to view the sky opposite the field. The heavy grey clouds that had thickly covered the sky—and even had delivered snow flurries earlier—gave way, allowing the sun to break through over the mountainous landscape. The peak of the nearby mountain strongly resembled the hump of the Buffalo.

As we watched, the clouds streamed into an intense display. A deeply-darkened stretch of horizontal clouds gathered above a layer of brilliantly-lit horizontal clouds wedged below it. The sun was situated at the exact threshold between the two layers of clouds. Half of the sun's disk was visible in the dense dark cloud layer above; the other half of the sun's disk was visible in the light-filled cloud layer below. An intense laser-like shaft of light shone downwards from the sun disk to the Earth.

Frank and I marveled together, curious that the sun's light was projecting downward only, as a solid beam, with none of the familiar radiating streaks of sunlight we were used to seeing.

Again I was reminded of this same axis mundi, or world-axis image that Grandmother Dona and I had witnessed in our cameras at the Serpent Mound, as well as during the Halloween ceremony meditations. However, the columns of Light each of those times had traveled in both directions; up to the Heavens and down to the Earth. This one was emitting only the downward shaft of the solid white laser beam from the sun to the Earth. It looked as though a Heavenly dose of Light was giving Earth its medicine.

Frank and I memorized this amazing sky display. The powerful cloud-language was speaking to our hearts. We finally had to break our attention to remind ourselves that there was more to attend to. Even though we were not sure what. At least we sort of knew where. Even if we didn't know exactly how to get there yet. I broke into a grin, surrendering to the mystery of it all.

We returned to the car, aware of the late hour. If we were to find the East Millsboro site and have time to do whatever it was that we were supposed to do before sundown, we would have to get going.

What WAS it, about all these ceremonies occurring just in the nick of time at sundown? I wondered.

Frank and I called Grandmother Dona as soon as we got back to the car. I described what had happened with the Sacred Buffalo. I reported that no song had been part of the experience, but I had heard the words Thunder and Lightning.

"Well," Grandmother Dona said, "no song has arrived yet, but those words you heard are the non-Native local names for the two Buffalo. The White Buffalo is called 'Lightning' and the Black Buffalo is called 'Thunder.' Frank verified this, saying he had read the display signs while I was communing with the Buffalo; these names were explained on the placards.

Oh my Goddess, I thought, *it was as if these sacred animals were each introducing their partner to me! They were so completely attuned to each other, like yin and yang; like profoundly-aligned sacred partners, honoring each other.*

I was still feeling deeply inwardly-focused, as Frank and Grandmother Dona tried to figure out directions to get to East Millsboro from Nemacolin. Frank had a sketchy, fairly unhelpful map. Grandmother Dona was on her computer trying to get directions for him and convey them by phone.

Frank handed his map to me so that I could navigate as he drove. He was so determined to get us to our mystery location in East Millsboro, which we knew could not be at the private property of the Francis Farm where the petroglyphs were. I admired his spirit.

I looked at the map he gave me. I didn't have the heart to remind Frank that I am directionally impaired. I have no sense of direction, and can get disoriented and lost even in familiar areas. But I accepted my navigator's assignment. Today was an out-of-the-ordinary day. So instead of protesting, I took out my Biogeometry pendulum and held it over the map to rely on its instruction.

Good-naturedly, Frank decided that my pendulum method was as good as any of our other flailing-about efforts for directions, since we did not even have a definite landing point. And at least he had gotten a sense of general directions from Grandmother Dona and his sketchy map. As I held the pendulum over the map, pointing to various routes, it swung widely in a clockwise direction and verified the next leg of our journey. I gave Frank that information.

At that moment, a song began arriving.

I heard the distinct words and grabbed my journal, writing as fast as I could. The song was arriving along with a melody. It began:

> "White Thunder, Black Lightning
> Flowing underground.
> What was rent apart,
> now restored within sacred sound."

Frank's voice penetrated my deep inner listening. "Hey, Victoria, will you check to see whether we should take this next turnoff?"

I dutifully held my pendulum over the sketchy map, after locating the route number in question. The pendulum circled clockwise, indicating yes. I made this report, and returned to my song-catching.

The same haunting melody was returning with the next lines:

> "A time of separation
> Holding in protection
> Earth's final gestation,
> Birthing Holy Ground."

Seeing that I was writing intently, Frank interrupted this time with an apology, "Hey, sorry, but what should we be doing next? We are close to East Millsboro in the vicinity of the farm. But where should we go? I am not familiar at all with this area."

I held the pendulum over my map again, moving it from road to road. It liked East Millsboro Road, swinging clockwise happily. As Frank made the turn onto that road, he reported, "Wow. I am suddenly feeling a shift of energy. I feel really relaxed, and feel a deep sense of peace."

As he spoke these words, my energy also shifted dramatically, and I was now becoming tearful. This was a familiar signal from my inner truth barometer. I shared this with Frank, and also explained that the song Grandmother Dona had predicted being downloaded to me from the Sacred White Buffalo was still in process of arriving. Frank nodded respectfully and gave me space as best as he could, driving a bit more slowly.

As I tuned back in, sure enough, the melody resumed once again, with more words:

> "The song within arising,
> Light and Dark uniting,"

As I recorded these words, I noticed that a small dark spider, the exact matching color of my reddish brown coat, had jumped onto me. I recognized her as a sacred ally, representing the weaver of the web of the New Earth dream, from the fairy song, and I blessed her presence as the final lines of the song arrived:

> "Humanity, Divinity,
> Forever re-bound."

As the dictation of the lyrics and melody concluded, I was filled with the understanding that once we were directed to the mysterious location, I was to sing this song. Then I would need to sing a spontaneous flow-of-heart-soundings, or tonings, as I tapped the Earth with my staff.

This all felt quite holy; sacred. I accepted it in trust. I realized that the cloud formation we had just witnessed was demonstrating and confirming the song's message of "Light and Dark uniting: Humanity, Divinity forever re-bound."

My body's truth barometer of goose bumps and tears was going haywire, even though I didn't understand why the Sacred Buffalos' colors were reversed in the song, as White Thunder, and Black Lightning. But I trusted that it all served a still-hidden purpose. Maybe it had to do with righting a reversal, represented by the phrase "flowing underground." Maybe it would become clear as we did the ceremony. I realized that the ceremony was important, and I did not need to consciously grasp its elements and purpose, other than the song's punchline: "Humanity, Divinity/Forever re-bound." Inwardly I replayed the song, felt its power, and settled into trust.

Frank had slowed down, approaching a Y in the road. "Which way do we turn here?"

Again I checked the map with my pendulum. "Turn left." We turned onto Upper River Road. I told Frank that the complete song from the Sacred White Buffalo had arrived, and it was magnificent. I hummed the compelling melody aloud, committing it to memory, as I continued holding the pendulum over the map. The pendulum's rotation had intensified and it was circling nearly horizontally at great speed.

The road was running parallel to a railroad track. We continued along. Now we were driving through a run-down trailer park. Then the paved road ended, and a narrow gravel path appeared, going right into the woods.

Frank stopped the car. He saw that the pendulum was still circling furiously. If it hadn't been strongly anchored to the cord, it would have flown off. We assessed the situation.

The gravel path into the woods was barely wide enough for our car. "We will have to drive out in reverse," Frank observed. "There isn't room to turn around. I can certainly do that. Should we proceed?"

"The pendulum is indicating absolutely yes," I answered. "I gave the pendulum instructions to stop at whatever location we need to be for our ceremony. We will drive into these woods until the pendulum stops."

With great trust, Frank drove forward slowly onto the narrow path. He proceeded into the woods as I looked down watching the pendulum. At one point I glanced up, and farther ahead I saw a large branch lying partway onto the path. It was shaped like an undulating snake. I looked down saying nothing. The pendulum was flying like a helicopter blade.

"Victoria, there is a branch ahead that looks just like a huge serpent in the road."

"Yes, I saw that," I responded, without looking up. Frank continued moving forward slowly. It somehow felt comforting that a serpentine presence was showing up.

Suddenly the pendulum stopped. It just dropped, limp and wobbly, like the electrical force propelling it had been unplugged. I called out, "STOP HERE!"

Frank stopped, trying to pull over off to the side as much as possible on this narrow gravel path. We got out of the car to look around. As we walked around behind the car, I saw that the serpentine branch was exactly at the rear left wheel of the car. Frank noticed this as well.

The serpent-shaped branch was pointing across the gravel path to a rather large blackish stone on the right side of the car. We walked over to it.

This black stone was about 10 inches across, and the left side was shaped like a large arrow point. The opposite side looked straight and blunt, like it had broken off from a larger formation. It was very heavy and hard, but had striated layers with irregular fractures that had created raised patterns visible on the top part of the rock. It had millions of tiny pin-point sized sparkles in it, glinting with light.

I was getting the image that I was to place my smaller, yellowish serpent stone, from the Serpent Mound, atop this dark stone, and that Frank was to pour the waters from the Youghiogheny River over them both, uniting them with the water element, as I sang the song from the Buffalo. Then I would finish with the toning and tapping the staff into the Earth to ground all the energies.

I explained this to Frank as I pulled my serpent stone from my backpack and got my serpent staff. Frank stopped examining the blackish stone and redirected his focus to retrieve his bottle of river water. We noticed that the sun was quite low in the sky now, and we were aware that we would have no light to see the narrow path as we backed the car out of the woods in reverse, if the timing of this took us beyond sunset.

I knelt down to place the yellowish serpent stone on the black stone. As I did so, I was completely astonished by what I saw. "Frank, look!" I pointed to the black stone. "Right where I am about to place the serpent stone, can you see here, on the black stone, there is a raised outline of a serpent head in profile that nearly exactly matches the shape and size of the profile of my serpent-faced stone from the Serpent Mound? Look how exactly their snouts line up together on each other." I positioned the lighter-colored stone with its snake profile aligned atop the darker snake profile. It looked like perfectly-fitting puzzle pieces.

Frank shook his head in wonder. "It looks like this black stone has a serpent template that was created to match the shape of the light yellow stone. Wow."

"Well, I guess we found the right spot for this ceremony—for whatever purpose it is meant to fulfill." I recalled the powerful words to the White Buffalo song.

"The words and melody downloaded to me from the Sacred White Buffalo reveal clues to the purpose of this ceremony. Listen to this song, while you pour the river water over these two serpent stones—light and dark stones—as I sing it."

I took a few moments to open sacred space and honor the seven directions—South, West, North, East, Above, Below and Within. I sent out prayers to honor and align with the Creator, Great Mystery, the Divine Ones, the Ancestors, the Fairy Folk, the animals, the elements, and All Our Relations. I nodded to Frank, who began pouring the water in a reverent manner as I sang:

"White Thunder, Black Lightning, flowing underground.
What was rent apart,
now restored, within sacred sound.
A time of separation, holding in protection,
Earth's final gestation,
Birthing Holy Ground.
The song within arising, Light and Dark uniting:
Humanity, Divinity
Forever re-bound."

After singing this holy song, I allowed my heart to direct my voice in toning a wordless melody, the way I had done with the Fairies. I felt into the highest vision of the arriving New Earth of unity. And I rhythmically tapped my serpent staff into the Earth as a physical anchor to the process, intending that the Highest Purpose of the Light be served in this mysterious ceremonial process. I toned until it felt complete. I gave thanks and opened my eyes, aware of how natural and effortless it had all felt. The whole ceremony had only taken a few minutes. There was still sunlight.

I quickly called Grandmother Dona. She answered immediately. I described all that happened. She spoke strongly but in sobs of tears, "You DID it! What you did was more important than you'll ever know. I have been drumming outside on my property ever since we hung up. I have been holding the energies for this great healing. I saw an incredible cloud formation with dark clouds layered overtop of light-filled clouds. And the sun was sitting right in the middle of them where they joined. It was breathtaking! Five deer came while I was drumming and they stayed close the entire time. Deer represent compassion, overcoming obstacles with love. It has all been so perfect."

Now I was tearful too, but Frank was motioning that we had to get out of the woods while we could still see. I didn't even have time to tell Grandmother Dona that she witnessed hundreds of miles away the same cloud language that we had seen here, and that the song gifted to me from the Sacred White Buffalo had described "Light and Dark uniting."

I prayed: *May it be so, that Humanity and Divinity are forever re-bound. May we become the awakened eyes and mouthpieces for God, for Creation, to bring forth the next Golden Age of a New Earth.*

Then I chuckled. *This ceremony was certainly putting some kind of puzzle piece into place to facilitate that,* I realized. *Those stones were literal puzzle pieces, meant to be reunited.*

I jumped into the car that Frank had packed with my sacreds— which now included this serpent-faced large black stone—and slowly we backed out of the darkening woods.

When we finally re-emerged from the woods, it was nearly nightfall. We drove home in awe, reliving the day's amazing adventure. We shared a hearty laugh about my navigating with the Biogeometry pendulum. "I am so glad I listened to my guidance to go back and bring it," I giggled.

After a bit of silence Frank mused, "Just imagine... your ancient serpent-faced stone traveling from the ancient sacred site of the Great Serpent Mound, Ohio, to arrive at East Millsboro, Pennsylvania, on a remote wooded pathway... to be reunited with its ceremonial stone counterpart, as directed by a pointing serpentine branch... the light and dark serpentine rock-templates to be locked into place, united by water and a song from a prophetic animal of unity—the Sacred White Buffalo, with his counterpart, the Sacred Black Buffalo! Wow. Who could even make up such stuff.

I laughed, but I couldn't even utter a reply. I had been thinking along the same lines. And I was humbled by being gifted with these song downloads; first from the Fairy Folk and now this from the Sacred White Buffalo—especially since I am not a singer, musician or songwriter. *Why me?* I wondered.

We marveled at the message in the song from the Sacred White Buffalo. I pondered over the information reflected in the words of the sacred song that was very correlated with other spiritual information I had been hearing. Specifically, I was intrigued with the words that indicated the time of "separation" was "holding in *protection*" Earth's "final gestation, birthing Holy Ground." Our heads were swimming.

I recalled that I had received a guided message in meditation, in 2006, from Gaia, Mother Earth. She was asking Light-workers, as her midwives, to help bring forth the New Earth in the following manner:

> *… sing with me our songs of the New Earth…*
> *being birthed in radiance and grace.*
> *You are my birth attendants.*
> *Sing to me the sounds of transformation with*
> *your mantras, chants, and tonings.*
> *Sing to me the sacred songs that open my birthing in joy.*

Now I understood that this was not just a metaphorical message. Four years later, here I am being given specific, profound songs to sing, to anchor in the New Earth energy and assist its birth. And I am being directed with guidance for how to use the songs and sacred sounds in ceremony with Kindred Spirit friends. It was so good to experience that I was not alone in this Divine Assignment, and that so many other Lightworkers were receiving similar guidance.

I was gratefully aware of several spiritual sources which addressed the state of separation-consciousness on Earth. Most of them indicated that humanity's journey into separation had been an agreed-upon plan long ago. One source had even indicated that Earth had to be held in a state of quarantine to protect it from the rest of the Universe, until humanity's consciousness, planetary events, and astronomical alignments all converged to make the Great Shift into unity a workable process. And several sources were also indicating that sacred sound, tonings and songs were a necessary part of the activation needed for the Great Shift of the Ages.

I stirred from my musings grappling with a question, that I directed to Frank.

"I have to say, Frank, I was a bit puzzled that we were led to an area in the woods, rather than by a river. I really felt that we were supposed to be by a river doing this ceremony. And weren't we on a road called Upper River Road?"

Frank mused a bit, then responded, "Tomorrow I will check an online map to see where exactly we were. I really couldn't get my bearings. Maybe the river was once in the area, but has since shifted its course."

Frank pulled up to my Pittsburgh home and parked. "Thank you, Victoria, for such sacred listening and deep trust. And for a totally amazing adventure."

"I must thank you too, Frank, for exactly that. We made it GOOD, Honey!" We hugged goodnight.

The next morning I got a call from Frank.

He instructed me, "Go to your computer and enter 'East Millsboro Road, East Millsboro, PA.' on your map search. Then zoom in closer on the aerial map. You will see that we were about 600 feet from the eastern shore of the Monongahela River, which was obscured to us by the woods." As Frank waited, I did so, and could see how close we really had been to those waters.

"Now, Victoria, if you zoom out and view our site from the vantage point of East Millsboro, the town, you will see something stunning. Remember what we were saying last night about all the synchronicities? That ancient serpent-faced stone traveling from the ancient sacred site of the Great Serpent Mound, Ohio, to arrive at East Millsboro, Pennsylvania, on a remote wooded pathway, to be reunited with its ceremonial stone counterpart as directed by a pointing serpentine branch, their serpentine templates to be locked into place, and all that?"

"Yes…"

"Okay, now add another impossible miracle. Take a look at the aerial view of the meandering shape of the Monongahela River where we were at East Millsboro. See the river's curving "M" shape? Then take another look at the veining on the top of your yellow Serpent Mound stone."

I already saw that the river's shape where we had been directed to do the ceremony yesterday was a visual match for the veining in the yellow serpent stone. I gasped.

"That stone from the Serpent Mound is a MAP to this site in East Millsboro!"

"Exactly," Frank replied.

I said the only thing I could utter, "Ecstatic!"

****

Almost a year and a half later, as I am recreating this story from my journals, I still puzzle over understanding the full purpose and the spiritually-intended impact of this East Millsboro ceremony. I understand that it was connected to the reuniting of humanity and divinity, in the service of birthing the New Earth. The words from the White Buffalo's song revealed that much. But was there anything else I still needed to understand?

So, as I am taking a moment to ponder my questions, I notice feeling drawn to retrieve another book that Grandmother Dona gave me, Barbara Marciniak's *Earth: Pleiadian Keys to the Living Library*. I open the book with a prayer for guidance, and spontaneously land on pages 57-59. The words there reveal something riveting, illuminating. I read and re-read every vital word, as my understanding opens up. I articulate key phrases aloud, savoring their instruction:

"When you visit ancient sacred sites... you *experience electromagnetic formulas for higher consciousness....* Most [ancient] civilizations have *stored data in stone...* with stones being the bones of the Earth.

[The consciousness of the] *Earth reads you* as you live and breathe on her, and She *knows the stage of your development and your ability to accept responsibility.* Sacred sites, therefore, become activated by individuals who can use their own *keys of consciousness to unlock the sites,* remembering and releasing the knowledge stored and experienced in them...

When you enter sacred sites and intentionally imagine... the sites become activated. *Imagination is the most powerful force* available to humankind.... To recognize *that you are a spiritual being is a key to the corridor of the future you seek....*

As visitors at sacred sites, you are *opening the time locks with keys of consciousness and triggering energy combinations* that have been holding memories of events until you demonstrated that you were ready to receive them. When you infuse yourselves with energy and *surrender and work with intention in sacred sites, you literally send bolts of great change around the globe.*"

I repeated these passages until I finally integrated the big picture they portrayed. All I can say to all of this is: *Thank You, Great Mystery.*

Chapter 14 - Another 7:32

• •

THE PHONE RANG. IT WAS GRANDMOTHER Dona. She wanted to share her updates.

"I was awakened by a sound this morning, like a drilling noise. I woke up and saw the clock. It was 7:32! Again! This is the fourth time for that numerological message. But I cannot get anywhere with why that time keeps appearing. First it showed up with you, two times, and then twice now it has shown up with me. What IS that? And when I actually woke up, there was no sound of drilling, either. I think that sound was a dreamtime way to wake me up in time to notice the 7:32 thing again. So why no clues for what it is trying to tell us?"

I had no answers either.

"All I could recall upon awakening was a dream fragment," Grandmother Dona continued, "where I was being challenged and frustrated by people I know in real life. And in the dream, I kept being reminded that I am now anchored into my new way of Being— living from my Indigenous Soul that sees only beauty. So I need to stop dragging it through the garbage of lower-vibration perceptions and feelings. And then I heard your voice in the dream, reminding me, 'be that Love Presence—that energetic vortex—generating the radiance of Love, and elevating everything around it.'"

"I realized that everyone who is waking up on planet Earth, during this time of the Great Shift, could have this Love Presence way of being. What a profound sense of purpose everyone could have: to generate love, to see the highest and best, to embody that way of beauty and connection that the Indigenous Soul knows."

I was moved by her dream, and replied, "What a powerful message. And it was punctuated by this 7:32 phenomenon. I am not sure what the 7:32 part means yet either, but it seems that it appeared this time to emphasize your dream's message. I get that we must take this dream's message to heart, and apply it."

"Agreed," Grandmother Dona replied. "AND, I pulled the Power Place card this morning. My guidance is strong that I am to come to see you next weekend, and we are to go to the Sacred White Buffalo together. I need to have an encounter with Lightning myself. Interestingly, next weekend will be the time of his fourth birthday. We will see if there is any guidance about further ceremony when the time arrives. Will that work for you? And can Frank come too?"

"I'll have to check with Frank, but it works for me. And of course you can stay with me."

We began making plans. Grandmother Dona would drive to Pittsburgh, arriving the day after Lightning's fourth birthday. Frank agreed to be available to escort us to the White Buffalo the next day. Our mutual friend and collaborative transformer, Kathy Evans-Palmisano would accompany us as well. We would all follow the Trail of Guidance collaboratively, from that point on. These soul-friends were excellent sacred listeners in their own rights. I trusted that we would make it GOOD, Honey.

Chapter 15 - Stone Heaven

· ·

WHILE WAITING FOR GRANDMOTHER DONA'S ARRIVAL later in the day, I agreed to have breakfast with another local transformational ally and Shamanic healer, Kimberly June. She had been waiting for an opportunity to hear about my experiences at the Serpent Mound, and I wanted to show her my smaller serpent stone, with its profile that looked like a miniature of the serpent face in the cliff ledge at the head of the effigy mound.

As we ate, I told her the stories from the two Serpent Mound visits, and from the recent visits to the Sacred Buffalo and the East Millsboro sites. Afterward, I handed Kimberly the yellow serpent-faced stone with the map to the Monongahela River on its top facet. She examined it, and then looked at me, explaining that she felt drawn to meditate with it. I gave her my permission, then I sat quietly as she did so.

As Kimberly tuned in, almost immediately she began having a vivid visual experience. With her eyes closed and the stone in her hands, she described it aloud as it occurred. I had brought my journal, so I recorded her experience:

"I see my Shamanic Self in warrior garb. I am appearing as a male, in deerskin leggings and a headband only—no headdress. I am holding your serpent stone over my head, doing a ceremony. There is a fire and the tribe is gathered around. It is dark. I am chanting and shouting loudly, to the sun, even though it is dark. I keep hearing, "There is something inside this rock.""

"I keep shouting and chanting. I am calling all the tribes. We are all to perform the same ceremony together—all across the world, and at the same time. The shamans are doing it, everywhere, all together.""

"What we are doing is opening a transformative vortex, as a group. I see the smoke from the fire, coiling upwards like a serpent, as our unified chants rise. I am turning into an eagle. I rise up as Eagle Woman, rising with the ascending coils of the serpentine smoke." She went quiet.

Then Kimberly opened her eyes, drew closer toward me, and continued. "Wow. This vision is now reminding me of the dreams and meditations that I have been having this past week. In those, I keep seeing the same visual, where I turn into the Shaman, Eagle Woman, and I FEEL wings and flight. I feel my talons grabbing something off a Cliffside, and I continue to fly. I look down and see that my talons are carrying a grand serpent. As Eagle Woman, I am taking the serpent high into the Heavens."

"Since the eagle flies the highest of all birds, most Indigenous peoples understand eagle to be the intermediary between the Earth and the Heavens. These visuals show me that the Kundalini serpent force of the Earth is being elevated into the Heavenly realms. It shows the unification of the Earth with the Heavens."

I nodded. "Yep, you are having an inner revelation that is another confirmation—a visual intuitive one—of all that I am being shown on my end." I was smiling. So were my goosebumps.

I giggled to Kimberly, "Too bad stuff like this can't be on the nightly news. People in general sure could benefit from a peek into all the subtle shifts and transformations occurring just below the radar, as an antidote to all the doom-and-gloom. And I know that if these experiences are happening for a group of Pittsburgh spiritual workers, they are happening all over the planet. Here are you and I, Kimberly: two Lightworkers, disguised as mild-mannered Social Workers. Frank is a Lightworker disguised as a mild-mannered Healthy Home Consultant. Now I am off to meet another Lightworker, disguised as a 70-something, mild-mannered retired University instructor."

Kimberly laughed her agreement, nodding, and we hugged, saying our goodbyes. I still had some free time to luxuriate in savoring our conversation, before Grandmother Dona arrived later in the afternoon.

Inspired by Kimberly's experience, I decided that I would go to my personal Pittsburgh power place, to my Sacred Tree in the local cemetery, and see what happened if I, too, meditated with my serpent stone. I chided myself for not trying this before. Then I realized why I had not done so as instinctually as Kimberly had. I still carried the old belief that I am not a "visual" person. Well, I would certainly set the intention today that information from the stone could come to me through any of my ways of knowing—not only visual.

I arrived and settled in at my Sacred Tree. I felt reassured by the comfort and sense of belonging that I had from my 25-year history of connecting with my beloved Power Tree, in gratitude, ceremony, prayer and journaling. I relaxed into the familiar sense of its welcome, and opened to my love for it.

I was enchanted to notice the neighboring tree. The upturned tips on each of its bare branches were lit up, each tip sparkling with sunlight, like little jewels. I had never witnessed such a phenomenon before.

I opened a sacred space with prayer in my usual way, and opened my heart in deep attention. Much to my surprise, a clear impression of a scene—a visual scene—began running like a movie.

In this meditative state, I see myself dancing on a hilltop in the dark just before the sunrise. The setting full moon is my only illumination. I am alone. I am holding a serpentine branch in each of my upraised hands, dancing a slow rhythmic movement. I understand that I am functioning as a Shaman-Priestess of the Serpent Mound. I am connecting with the Kundalini life-force of the Earth through my movement.

As the full moon begins to set and the rising sun simultaneously appears in the opposite sky, I continue my dancing. I dance, positioned between the moon and the sun, anchoring the balanced feminine and masculine energies they represent.

Through my dance, I am now going to each of the directions, South, West, North and East. At each direction, I first dance in a counter-clockwise spiral, to un-bind the frequencies of the old paradigm of separation consciousness, and then dance in a clockwise spiral to re-bind humanity into the new paradigm of unity consciousness.

I am enacting a ceremonial un-binding from ego and re-binding into divine essence; as divine humans; as conscious co-creators with Spirit. I do this same spiraling dance sequence of un-binding and re-binding, in the remaining directions of Above, Below, and Within, to include all seven sacred directions.

As I complete the dance by drumming and circling around the directional points of this re-binding, a brilliant dawn floods the sky. Simultaneously, thousands of people flood the hilltop from all directions, encircling me. The words of a chant become louder and louder, and all are chanting it with heart-full intention:

Heartbeat of Creation: Heaven, Earth and Human!
Unify! We can thrive! Now in Right Relation!

At that moment I heard the sharp call of a Blue Jay penetrating my movie-like revelation. I opened my eyes. There was the Blue Jay on the tree with the sparkling jewel-tipped buds. I recalled that the Blue Jay is often called The Announcer. And its medicine teaching is about the right use of power.

I could still feel the drumbeat of our collective chant from the vision. I sent out silent gratitude. And a prayer: *May this be so: humanity's shift from ego to divine essence. May we reclaim a sacred world.* I felt full; moved; inspired; complete.

As I left my personal power place to drive home, I grappled a bit with my habitual inner conditioning of invalidation. That cynical degrading inner voice was trying to convince me with the thought, *You just made all that up. It doesn't mean anything. Kimberly likes to make stuff up, too. So what?*

Immediately I recalled one of my favorite quotes from one of my favorite humans, Albert Einstein. He said, "Imagination is more important than knowledge. Knowledge is limited. Imagination encircles the world." I have a poster at home of Einstein and that quote. *Hmmm, I choose to listen to Einstein over you any day*, I shot back mentally to my inner critic.

To put that invalidating inner critic in its place, I now said to it aloud, with some intensity, "Yeah, and remember, Einstein also said, 'No problem can be solved from the same level of consciousness that created it.' That is why the wise ancients have called this historic timeframe of the 2012-era 'THE SHIFT of the Ages.' GET IT? We must shift our consciousness into unity as the way out of the global messes we have created. Band-aids won't work anymore."

As I sat at a traffic light in this animated conversation with myselves, I glanced out my window. The passenger of the car stopped at the light beside me was watching my lively hand gestures with great interest. We waved at each other as the light changed, and we moved on. I giggled with embarrassment and relief, that that was not someone I knew.

That was when I saw that I had just missed a call from Grandmother Dona. I called her back.

"I am almost to Pittsburgh," Grandmother Dona reported. "I just had to call and tell you of these two license plates that I kept driving behind for a time—they seem like synchronicities. We will have to stay alert to discern their meanings. The first one was "STONHVN." I am reading that as "Stone Heaven." The second license plate was "SUMATRA." Isn't that unusual? I am not clear what all that portends, but the cars with those license plates kept repeatedly signaling to change lanes right in front of me, insisting on capturing my attention."

"Okay, we will keep that in mind and see if it connects any dots," I replied.

Grandmother Dona arrived an hour after that call. Once I got her settled and refreshed, we set up an altar to create proper sacred space for the evening's plans. I had arranged for my small group of "Skull Keepers" to come and meet Grandmother Dona, and to meditate and hold ceremony with the "Peaceburgh Community Skull" as we called it, that I had received from Mayan Grandmother Flordemayo, of the 13 Indigenous Grandmothers, in her most recent visit to Pittsburgh a few months before.

During that visit, some of us had arranged for Grandmother Flordemayo to teach our community about the ancient crystal skulls from her Mayan lineage. She taught us that, to the Maya, the skull represents the human cranium's capacity for divine wisdom and knowledge. The original ancient crystal skulls were encoded with the frequencies of unity and unconditional love that are needed to assist the Great Shift of the Ages.

As a Mayan Priestess and lineage carrier of the skulls, Grandmother Flordemayo is a Keeper of one of these ancient "Grandmother Skulls." She explained to me that she had ceremonially facilitated the duplication of these frequencies of wisdom from the Grandmother Skull into this jadeite skull, which was now ready and available for being part of a community that would honor it and use it for transformation.

I knew immediately that this jadeite skull needed to be part of the growing Peaceburgh community of unity. So I made arrangements with Grandmother Flordemayo and a promise for it to be properly cared for and used in a sacred manner. Thus, a circle of aware and committed "Peaceburgh Community Skull Keepers" was born. And tonight, most of them would meet Grandmother Dona.

As the other Skull Keepers arrived, I introduced Grandmother Dona to Tenanche Rose Golden, Miguel Sague, Kathy Evans-Palmisano, and Frank Valley. We settled into a circle that included a table set with the altar that Grandmother Dona and I had created.

We all gathered to attune to the altar of stones and sacred symbols, expressing our group commitment to follow the Trail of Guidance toward Unity. Along with the jadeite stone Community Skull from Grandmother Flordemayo, the altar's various stones were from Grandmother Dona's and my journeys connected with the evolving Serpent Mound adventure.

In addition to my yellow serpent-faced stone, which was sitting nestled on top of the larger black East Millsboro stone with its matching snake-template shape, were stones from Grandmother Dona's latest journeys to earthwork mound sites nearby the Serpent Mound effigy. These sites included Fort Hill and Tarlton Cross Mound.

Grandmother Dona described one of these stones as "the Tree of Life" stone, since the markings on this stone resembled that universal sacred image found in all religions and spiritual traditions. Another stone that she found on a dry earthmound site looked like a piece of white tubular-laced coral the size of a baseball. This stone was particularly intriguing. How could coral be found embedded in the Earth's surface at this earthwork site in Ohio?

Another stone Grandmother Dona brought was heart-shaped and looked like a streak of lightning was painted across it. She advised us that many such heart-shaped stones are found in the creek beds surrounding these earthwork mounds of Ohio.

My beautifully-preserved baby rattlesnake from my Altar of Surrender had a prime spot on the altar along with the snakeskin gifted to me by the Spirit of the Serpent at the Serpent Mound. I had also placed on the altar the Mayan glyph given to me by Grandmother Flordemayo. Its image showed the spirit of the Feminine receiving the serpent-shaped staff of power from the Masculine, at this timeframe in history. A black metal sculpture of a Goddess arising from the mud of the Earth was central on the altar. Standing tall, as a backdrop to the entire altar, was an African sculpture from Mali of The Ancestral Couple appearing to oversee everything.

Grandmother Dona's magical-looking butterfly-shaped stone from the Fort Hill site was given a special spot on the altar, as well. Grandmother Dona passed it around for everyone to hold. She explained, "The heavy weight of the small two-and-a-half-inch butterfly stone suggests that it derived from celestial debris of a comet or asteroid. This makes sense, because the Serpent Mound area has been verified as a site of crypto-explosion, indicating the entire area was impacted by a comet or other such cosmic debris thousands of years ago." Of course, we all noticed that the butterfly shape—symbolizing transformation—was relevant for this great Shift of the Ages.

Our group admired the visually-powerful assembly of stones surrounding the Goddess sculpture, the jadeite stone Community Skull, the baby serpent, and the Mayan glyph. Then Grandmother Dona retold the story of the synchronistic license plates, "STONHVN" and "SUMATRA," on her drive to Pittsburgh.

Miguel laughed heartily when he heard her report, and declared, "Well, just look at the altar we are sitting in front of here; all those sacred stones. THIS is Stone Heaven! We have established Stone Heaven right here at Victoria's home." That made perfect sense. We all joined Miguel in laughing about our cosmic joke.

"Well, what about the 'SUMATRA' license plate?" Grandmother Dona asked. Miguel mused a bit, and then answered, "Remember what is right outside beside Victoria's front door? She has an Indonesian Rice Goddess of fertility and abundance there, to grace all visitors upon entering. Sumatra is a part of Indonesia. Again, it appears that the Sumatra location that the license plate was indicating, is right here, at this sacred site of Victoria's home."

"Perfect," the Skull Keepers concurred unanimously, chuckling.

We next focused our attention on the magnificent unity drum that Grandmother Dona had brought along. It had been given into her keeping from Indigenous Lakota friends after they used it at a sacred Sundance Ceremony at the Rosebud Reservation in South Dakota. She recounted the meaning of its symbolism.

The frame for the drum was crafted from the sacred Cottonwood tree pole used in the actual Sundance ceremony. The drum stand was crafted from the Tulip Poplar, representing the Tree of Life. The drumhead, made from buffalo hide, was painted with concentric circles of red, white, yellow and black. These sacred colors represented the colors of the human races, calling all of humanity to come together in Unity. The colors also represented the four truths of unity, balance, love and peace.

Grandmother Dona had used this unity drum with Grandmother Flordemayo at the Serpent Mound on the Summer Solstice, just prior to Grandmother Flordemayo introducing the two of us.

Now Grandmother Dona instructed the circle of Skull Keepers: "We want to infuse the drumbeats of our ceremony today with the frequencies of the New Earth of Unity. So we must *feel* the Universal Heartbeat rhythm as we drum with the beaters, sending out that intention of Unity from our own united hearts. The heartbeat of Mother Earth is the new rhythm of this Great Shift into the New Earth of Unity. Let us co-create it together now."

Then she added, "And I am wearing my ceremonial buckskin dress, honoring my family's Mohawk lineage, through my Great-Great-Grandmother's blood. This sacred prayer fan of Crow feathers is all that I own from her." She placed the prayer fan and her beautifully beaded ceremonial prayer staff in the altar area.

After smudging each other and the drum with sage, four of us took the beaters and began drumming the unity drum. Grandmother Dona guided us more deeply into the meaning of our drumming: "The heartbeat rhythm of Mother Earth is the same rhythm that fetuses hear as they grow in their mothers' wombs, and it is the same rhythm detectable within the Earth and throughout the Universe. *The heartbeat is the rhythm of all of Creation.*"

I felt a rush of goosebumps followed by affirming waves of energy. I was happily recalling the chant from my revelation earlier today when I had tuned into my serpent stone. *Heartbeat of Creation: Heaven, Earth and Human! Unify! We can thrive! Now in Right Relation!*

After a few minutes of drumming the soothing, harmonizing rhythm, I became aware that Grandmother Dona had gotten up, retrieved her Crow feather prayer fan, and was dancing with the heartbeat rhythm. I saw tears streaming from her eyes. We drummed until the energy wanted to wind down and settle. Then we sat together in silence for several minutes, inwardly following our own meditative promptings.

Finally the energy shifted again as one-by-one we began stirring and opening our eyes. Each of us shared our inner experiences, meditations and intuitions.

Tenanche shared her visual experience of the presence of the Sacred White Buffalo, which conveyed a sense of affirmation and blessing on our gathering and our intention of Unity. Frank shared that the Stone Heaven altar seemed to come to life, especially the Mayan glyph, and seemed to be conveying to us how to live in a sacred manner. Kathy felt vibrations from the Stone Heaven Altar encompassing us, like a transformative vortex of energy. She saw the jadeite Community Skull gathering information from the other stones, then saw that it sent a column of bright light upwards to the Heavens and downwards into the earth, in the axis-mundi configuration.

Miguel experienced a visual replay of a peak memory, of canoeing in a tiny canoe along the Allegheny River for two weeks, to arrive at an Indigenous Indian reservation. He heard his own Taino ancestors' voices chant a song that is sung in community when they do an inner shamanic journey together: "I have a canoe/I travel in beauty/in my canoe." He understood that this visual scene was an affirming message of humanity learning to journey together in community, within a sacred consciousness of oneness. We were the forerunners for humanity of that journey returning to unity.

I shared my internal imagery of seeing rainbow-colored spiraling twists of DNA, followed by the sense that these rainbow-colored web filaments of my own cellular DNA were emanating outwards from my whole body, connecting to the stars in the various constellations in the Heavens. It seemed to be a message that humanity's DNA is activating into a Universal divine connectedness.

Then Grandmother Dona spoke. Her voice shook, and her eyes were luminous. "I felt my Great- Great- Mohawk Grandmother come thorough the heartbeat rhythm into my own heart. She came through to honor me and thank me, and she really wanted to dance. So I had to get up and dance. I could not sit. I felt her dancing through me. I was moving to her Spirit. She was once again experiencing the sacred Heartbeat Dance of Life—only this time, it was through me. She was so happy. I felt the Crow feather prayer fan come alive with energy and memories. It was a miracle!"

Grandmother Dona continued, "I recalled the song:

'I saw tomorrow look at me
Through little children's eyes
How carefully we would plan,
If only we were wise.'

"Then I looked at this miracle of stones collected on our Stone Heaven Altar, with the Ancestor statue standing guard over everything. I was stunned to realize that the spirit of the ancients moved these rocks to where they needed to be for us to find them— for us to touch these ancestor stones from our side of the veil of Life that separates the world of the seen from the unseen.

"Holding any of these stones is like holding the hands of my Great- Great- Grandmother, and the ancestors before her, who touched them long ago in sacredness at the Earthwork Mounds. Now the cellular memory of the past and the future is in them and in us simultaneously. We are connected with the ancestors through these stones, in sacredness and wisdom. This experience we are having collectively today is an alchemy of stone wisdom, here in the Stone Heaven of Peaceburgh's Sumatra, in Victoria's living room!"

We were all listening in rapt attention at Grandmother Dona's revelation, in various stages of tears and gasps. Each of us felt the resonance of the Truth in her experience, in our own experiences, and in the alchemy of the ancestral stones.

We grounded the experience, and the wisdom, with more sacred drumming. We realized that this memory of our ancestral connection through the Earth's bones—these stones—was necessary for the New Earth of Unity. Unity included All Our Relations, even the Ancestors. We recognized that it is upon their bones and their wisdom that we travel our path into a future of wholeness, peace and unity.

We ended the amazing, revelatory and transformative ceremony. Reluctantly we departed from our sacred circle, hugging our good-byes, and returning to our individual lives as mild-mannered ordinary people with extra-ordinary awareness, who trusted in a soon-to-be established New Earth of Unity. We had already had shared a preview of Heaven on Earth today, in the "Stone Heaven, Sumatra of Peaceburgh."

As Grandmother Dona and I prepared for bed, we savored our amazement of the messages and miracles of our Stone Heaven altar. And we hadn't even gotten to our main plan of Grandmother Dona meeting the Sacred White Buffalo. Dayenu! This would have been enough. But there would be even more tomorrow.

Chapter 16 - Grandmother Dona's Appointment with the Sacred White Buffalo

· ·

THE MORNING BEGAN WITH OUR USUAL process of tuning in to guidance. Our guidance cards for the day were the *Sacred Path* card, Whirling Rainbow: Unity, Wholeness Achieved, and the animal *Medicine Card*, Butterfly: Transformation. These messages certainly captured our feelings after the Stone Heaven ceremony yesterday. And the cards were a completely apt portrayal of our intention for bringing forth the highest collaborative expression possible of Heaven on Earth, in our New Earth of Unity. It was a perfect synchronistic affirmation to send us off to meet the Sacred Buffalo today.

The image on the Whirling Rainbow card also struck me as an uncannily similar visual replica of the spiral dances I saw myself doing during my serpent stone meditation yesterday, tracing the un-binding of humanity from ego-based separation, and the re-binding of humanity into divine essence. My goosebumps alerted me to the card's synchronicity on all levels, but in this moment I was aware of its specific message as a cosmic pat of reassurance to me, further quieting my inner skeptic's response to yesterday's meditation. Even if I *had* made up all that stuff yesterday, it was all nonetheless contributing transformational energy in service to this great intention. I smiled sweetly to that inner critic: *So there!*

Grandmother Dona wanted to pull a Ted Andrews *Feathered Omen* card for good measure. She picked Dove, the popular image for peace, also representing New Cycles of Opportunity. Grandmother Dona twinkled, "Ah ha! I felt that there was one more message that needed to emerge from Source. This too is perfect."

Our sacred escort and driver, Frank, arrived. He hugged us both then turned to Grandmother Dona to report, "I awoke this morning to a beautiful dream that the White Buffalo wants to honor you, Grandmother Dona—for WHO YOU ARE." She squeezed Frank's hands, thanking him.

Then Kathy arrived and after another round of hugs, we departed to honor the fourth birthday of Lightning, known as "Kenahkihinen" in the Lenape Indigenous language, meaning "Watch Over Us."

On the 90-minute drive, we were thrilled to witness the sky language. We saw double sun-dogs—the double rainbows in the clouds encircling the sun. They were omens, a real-time image in Nature mirroring and confirming the message earlier of the *Sacred Path* card, the Whirling Rainbow of unity and wholeness. We also witnessed several cloud formations of serpent-shaped undulating clouds ascending. It felt like the Universe was in direct communication with us. We were in awe.

"Dayenu! And we aren't even there yet!" Grandmother Dona exclaimed. Seeing Kathy and Frank's puzzled looks, she explained the meaning of our private joke, and we all grinned.

We arrived at the meadow with its central hill protected by double fencing that was the home of the Sacred White and Black Buffaloes. Lightning and his female partner, Thunder were both already down near the edge of the double fencing. We parked the car to make the walk in a mindful manner, up the gravel road to greet them, all our eyes glued on the sacred animals.

As we came closer to them, Grandmother Dona's legs buckled and she suddenly fell toward the ground. Fortunately, Kathy and I, who were on either side of her, quickly caught her, preventing her from collapsing. Frank caught up with us and assisted.

"I can't feel my legs!" Grandmother Dona exclaimed. "My whole body is vibrating, as if it is singing, with a big vibratory energy." Kathy and I held her closely on either side, stabilizing her. Despite the disruption to her ambulation, Grandmother Dona's eyes remained glued on Lightning and Thunder, and her face looked ecstatic. Clearly, she was not in the least concerned with this challenge.

With all of our assistance she was able to resume walking, but with great difficulty. We finally made it to the edge of the fence. After quietly watching Lightning and Thunder graze, Grandmother Dona finally stabilized her stance, holding the fence for support.

At that point, the White Buffalo moved into a position facing Grandmother Dona from his side of the double-fencing, and we could see their eyes lock into a mutual gaze. Grandmother Dona's face was luminous. She spoke softly from time to time, directly to Lightning, and he was responding each time by nodding his enormous head, three times. It appeared that they were in a deep, mutually acknowledging conversation. Then Lightning moved aside, to make room for his female partner, the Sacred Black Buffalo, Thunder, to have her turn in the conversation, just as he had with me during my visit last week.

Thunder moved into the position facing Grandmother Dona. The process of this intimate, mutually-flowing communion and acknowledgement repeated for several more moments, between human and animal. Then the two sacred buffaloes reconnected with each other, moving alongside of each other as if on cue, and walked along the fence's edge together.

The four of us watched in amazement at what we were being shown. The movements of these two sacred animals were slow and deliberate, and appeared matched—synchronized—as if by cosmic choreography. They looked like white and black mirrors of each other, doing a dance of unity between opposites.

When the head of one of the buffalo bent downwards, the other's head would follow downwards at the same angle—only it was impossible to discern which one had initiated the movement. If one of them took a step with the right front leg, it was instantly matched by the other, as their subsequent steps likewise flowed in matched choreographic perfection. It was impossible to tell whose movement was being followed by whom. Professional dancers could not have done a better job of this synchronized, mirrored movement. My initial impression of them as yin and yang sacred partners was amplified.

We were in awe at what we witnessed—this deeply unified interconnected movement between the sacred male and sacred female prophetic buffaloes, whose miraculous virgin births were global summons into unity.

It was as if they were demonstrating that what seems impossible is indeed possible: the union of opposites; of the Light and the Dark; of human ego with divine essence; of the races; of the genders... even unity with animals as sacred way-showers. Yes, Unity at all levels IS possible.

We were privileged to be here as four witnesses to this revelation. We were so moved and in awe of the ways that *all levels of Creation* kept revealing themselves as aware and participating in co-creating unity, again and again on our adventures. And here, once more, was this poignant demonstration, with Lightning and Thunder. And prior to them, with the Cloud People through their sky language on our drive here. What was needed in this picture of aware conscious co-creation was for more of humanity to wake up, tune in and commit to this higher path of embodying unity.

I kept wondering, *If the animals can do this, why is it so hard for humans? What is stopping us?* As far as I could tell, it was simply a matter of awareness and choice. Now the question is, do we humans, as stewards of the future, choose this unity or not?

The Indigenous prophecies of the past 500 years consistently portray the imperative of each individual's choice in this timeframe of history, at the ending of the Great Cycle—the 26,000-year completion of the Precession of the Equinoxes, and the simultaneous ending of the Mayan Calendar Long Count of our 5,125-year "Fifth Sun" age. All the Indigenous wise ones remind us that there are two paths: the path of separation with fear, greed, domination, exploitation; or the higher path of unity with love, respect, peace, sharing. Only by choosing the higher path of unity is it possible to collaborate to create Heaven on Earth—a world that serves the greater good of all.

I sent out a heart-full prayer: *People! Please: Choose! Choice is an inward and continuing conscious act of commitment and co-creation. Please, choose unity. It is time! We are all in this together!*

The reverent witnessing and inward musing of the four of us was interrupted by another vehicle arriving on the gravel road, with other visitors also wanting a private experience with the sacred animals. We wanted to respect their turn. We made room for them after conveying our gratitude and blessings to Lightning and Thunder. As we were leaving, we observed the posted placards along the fencing that portrayed the story of the White Buffalo in Indigenous culture.

The placards conveyed that, according to Native American sacred stories, the Sacred White Buffalo chooses to be born where its message is needed most. By no coincidence the land of Kenahkihinen's (Lightning's) birthplace here in Western Pennsylvania adjoins the land of the historic battlefield where the French and Indian War began in 1754—"the war that made America."

The historical impact of this war birthed a new nation but initiated the death of a people who were the original inhabitants, an estimated 20 million Indigenous individuals, of what was once called "Turtle Island." The resultant genocide that followed left less than 250,000 and began an era of forced assimilation and cultural decimation for many generations to follow. There is more Native blood spilled in Pennsylvania than in any other state in our Nation. How fitting then that this sacred animal would be born here.

On our drive home, we asked Grandmother Dona about the phenomenon of her legs giving way. She said, "As I saw the Sacred Buffalo, I began to recall the story of White Buffalo Calf Woman, and to feel her presence."

I felt the energy in the car intensify. Kathy, Frank and I exchanged looks. "Please tell us more!" Kathy urged.

Grandmother Dona took a moment to gather her thoughts, and then spoke:

"In the ancient Lakota Sioux sacred teachings, White Buffalo Calf Woman was the embodiment of Great Spirit that came to the people to remind them of their connection to Source—like Jesus, Mohammad, Krishna, Kwan Yin, and other Holy Ones. She brought to them the teachings of sacred ceremony, and gave them the sacred pipe, so that they would always have a shared practice for integrating spirit and ego; a practice for experiencing their unity with All Our Relations—all of Life.

"And White Buffalo Calf Woman foresaw all the anguish that humanity's journey into separation would generate, especially for the Red Race, and their near-extinction. But she promised to return—as all religions' Holy Ones have—to assist in the return to unity, when all the races finally come together in harmony. When my legs gave out I was overwhelmed with a big energy. I felt the certainty that that time is NOW, and that sacred unity is what we are creating together. We are creating that unity with the assistance of All Our Relations, and most magnificently today, with the assistance of the Sacred White and Black Buffalo. The prophecies say that the Sacred Buffalo are here for all people—not just for the Indigenous ones—for ALL people."

She finished with tears, and a great sigh. Our conversation felt complete, as we each mused in silent wonder and awe at the seamless demonstration of the story that we were privileged to witness today.

Chapter 17 - A Ceremony With the Steelers

• •

THE NEXT DAY, FRANK, GRANDMOTHER DONA and I had agreed to gather in ceremony near The Point: the State Park where the fountain, fed by the fourth underground river, marks the place of the converging three/four rivers in downtown Pittsburgh. Kathy was assisting us by holding sacred space for the intention and ceremony from her remote location, since she was not able to join us in person. We had all received similar guidance about this collaboration.

As we joined together in sacred listening, we received confirmation to do a ceremony at The Point to anchor in the highest vision for Pittsburgh's future as a center for spirituality and healing, and then for Pittsburgh to serve as a catalyst for other cities to rise up to their highest paths as well.

We were inspired to continue the process of envisioning our City's highest path that had been initially foreseen in meditation by local spiritual workers, Nance Stewart and Frank Keller in 2006. My report of their visions in my article on the Mayan Calendar and the Shift of the Ages had been the catalyst for Mayan Elders Don Alejandro and Grandmother Flordemayo's visit, and their confirmation of Pittsburgh's three rivers link to the Mayan 2012 prophetic teachings of unity.

Don Alejandro was a 13th generation Mayan High Priest, Mayan Calendar Day Keeper, and Grand Elder of the Mayan Council of Elders of Guatemala. Grandmother Flordemayo was the Nicaraguan Mayan Grandmother of the International Council of 13 Indigenous Grandmothers. Together, these cultural dignitaries were conferring on our city quite an unusual cross-cultural acknowledgement of spiritual interconnection. I wondered whether any other such historic linking had occurred in modern times, connecting a modern city and an ancient prophetic culture.

I was quite moved by Don Alejandro's generosity during that visit. He had taken care to copy and bring with him from Guatemala a piece of paper, written in his Quiche Mayan dialect, of the "Statement of Revelations and Prophecies." That statement was the information that summarized the ancient Mayan 2012 prophetic teachings linking our three rivers with their prophecies of the promised return to unity. We worked with his wife and translator, Elizabeth, to translate that paper before his return home.

After sharing his "Statement of Revelations and Prophecies"— and thereby confirming the Pittsburgh three rivers/ Mayan 2012 connection foreseen by Stewart and Keller and referenced in my article—next he offered an extraordinary traditional Mayan T'zite Oracle ceremony to foresee the City's future. That oracle reading also ended up confirming what Stewart and Keller had foreseen about Pittsburgh's highest future path.

From that point on, my head was perpetually swimming with this unclassifiable knowledge. This was stuff movies were made of: stranger than fiction. And it was really happening, right here. And I was becoming the designated guardian and spokesperson for all this unusual interconnecting information.

A modern city's link to Mayan 2012 prophecies; Pittsburgh's rivers as a Universal Portal mapping the Milky Way. What was I to do with all that?

Over time, an inspired core of 30 or so unity-dedicated "transformational leaders," as I called them, had emerged who valued and understood the information. I was so grateful that I had actually honored them at an event I organized called "The Peaceburgh Transformational Leaders Tribute." I recalled the saying that "misery loves company." What I deeply realized along the way is that "unity loves company," too. So I identified my company of Kindred Spirits, honored them, and now we travel this journey into unity together. They have chosen to remain connected as an ongoing community of unity, re-named as Transformational Alliance Peaceburgh.

Now, with some of these Kindreds, we would co-create a ceremony for a fulfilled future New Earth, starting with Pittsburgh— "Peaceburgh"—and catalyzing other cities to rise up with ours.

Together we reviewed the highlights of the transcript of Don Alejandro's 2007 T'zite Oracle forecast for the future of this catalytic City of Pittsburgh; a city that did not yet widely know about our Mayan prophetic link. Nor did most of its residents know about our identity as a Universal Portal—an ancient earth-star landscape— correlated to the rivers of stars in the Milky Way's Heavenly Portal, which was a cosmic zone central to the galactic alignment of the 2012-era Shift of the Ages. The T'zite Oracle highlights read:

"Choice, there are two paths: the city is still walking the path down into a dark ravine, to a low place, but there are those still trying to find the better, healthier path.

The challenge: How can Pittsburgh emerge together in a safe way from this dark, low ravine? How can this be done, with so many in Pittsburgh who are asleep?

In Pittsburgh and in the world, there are entanglements of greed and confusion that do not lead to the greater good, but the times are changing, and Pittsburgh is being **born now into destiny** to assist this change, this transformation....

In time, Pittsburgh's work on that higher path will be like the force of a tornado. This tornado swirls like a woman's skirts and hair, and when she swirls, her movement brings others into the higher force. Pittsburgh is the spirit of that movement....

Not far into the future, more and more people will join together to deal with the big problems. A big community of women and men, a big community involved...

Pittsburgh is moving onto the higher path, and step by step we will see the beneficial effect. Do not fear, but keep working together using intelligence and awareness, not force....

Here in Pittsburgh, we will link with other cities in similar struggle who will also rise up, and join us, seeing our higher path."

The four of us had especially tuned in to this final statement for our highest vision of today's ceremonial work. Focusing on our three (four) rivers portal we would first uplift Pittsburgh, then link with other cities in similar struggle who will also "rise up and join us, seeing our higher path."

Not a bad plan. It was a dirty job, but somebody had to do it! We were all in good spirits in anticipation of our collaborative Divine Assignment.

Before leaving to meet Frank, Grandmother Dona and I spent a few moments meditating and tuning into sacred listening at our Stone Heaven altar. Again, I received clear guidance, similar to what I had received prior to our initial Serpent Mound ceremony. *Your intention: it is done. Now simply trace that highest vision from the Future back to the Present, as Sacred Seer and Sacred Sayer.*

I also got guidance to sing the songs I had been given, to energetically activate that vision. I shared this with Grandmother Dona, who nodded, "Of course, all that makes sense. And I am getting a strong feeling-message of joy. It is a lovely confirmation."

I went to get the *Sacred Path Cards* book and the *Medicine Cards* book to access further synchronistic guidance, and to continue the committed practice we were now accustomed to doing prior to our ceremonial work. I pulled my guidance cards. They were, Thunder Beings: Usable Energy and Raven: Ceremonial Magic. *Perfection*, I thought.

I brought the books to Grandmother Dona. As I offered them to her, I was surprised to notice a third book that I had inadvertently picked up with the other two. It was a book that Grandmother Dona had loaned to me, but I had not yet read. The book was Barbara Marciniak's *Earth: Pleiadian Keys to the Living Library*.

I gave Grandmother Dona the other two books, and looked back down at Marciniak's book, still in my hands. I intuitively realized that this was no mistake. It was a synchronistic prompt indicating that there was a message imbedded somewhere in the book, necessary for our purposes, which would shed deeper understanding on the process—like a bonus synchronistic boost. My job was to locate the relevant information quickly as it was nearly time to leave.

I excused myself, retreating to my bedroom to give each of us private time for our inner work before we left. I said a mental prayer, *"Thank you for this bonus information about to be revealed and help me to locate the message quickly and accurately."* Without further thought, I simply dropped into my heart, felt my gratitude, and opened the book randomly (to page 181). The words that my eyes landed upon were anything but random. They left me breathless. They read:

"Time is a construct. On Earth, you have been under the assumption that the present springs from the past. We suggest that the present springs from the future as well. *The assignment you are on involves changing your past, as you spring from the future, in order to create a different present."*

WOW. I got that message big time. I mean, *really!* It felt like an unseen divine coach had leapt out of the pages to affirm and instruct us.

What potent verification, affirming how we were being shown to do all our ceremonies, underscoring my earlier guidance of tracing the future back to the present. This synchronistic message also confirmed ceremony as a potent event that can actually shape-shift reality. I gave a prayer of thanks.

Then I couldn't resist reading more of that chapter, even though we really had to leave now to meet Frank.

This chapter, called "Riding the Corridors of Time," continued on to describe time corridors throughout the Universe that are connected to the "webs... fibers... rays of light... lines of time that carry you into another now... the web of light that is the vital grid-connecting existence, which is everywhere alive... web lines transporting intelligence... great light corridors...."

Wooosh!

My skin was prickling and the hair all over my body was trying to stand straight up. These phrases reminded me of the unexplainable, impossibly-long, horizontal, luminous, spider-web-like filaments of light that Grandmother Dona and I had witnessed. We had both seen them, strewn all along the grass and interconnecting the bare trees, at both Fort Hill and at the Serpent Mound at our Halloween ceremony. It had truly felt like we were wrapped within and fully surrounded by these endless web filaments of light. They were all around us, everywhere. And we had witnessed rainbows of light streaming from right to left, traveling along the impossibly-long horizontal web filaments.

I was getting goose bumps on my goose bumps. *Why was I being led to this information at this moment? Were those magical endless web filaments somehow connected to this mind-bending material?*

I heard Grandmother Dona calling me. It was time to leave.

I just couldn't resist a bit more tantalizing information. Now I was excited to read about the Maya from that same chapter:

"The purpose of the Maya was to come onto the planet to establish a paradigm for the future… through collective consciousness. The Maya were an experiment to affect the future and seed this planet… for a future that is now. The Maya were Keepers of Time… they knew that one day their time would come and they would leave the planet… to transport to another dimension… where they still exist and flourish… and they knew that one day, their knowledge, their keys, would be uncovered and discovered by the Family of Light—by you. We suggest that there are some people who have discovered these keys already."

I could feel my eyes popping as my mouth dropped open.

Grandmother Dona's summons was more insistent now. I grinned apologetically as I emerged from my bedroom, promising to fill her in on the synchronistic discoveries from her book that had jumped out and into the process of the day's ceremony. We got into Beauty, and sped to the Point engaged in excited conversation. I tucked the book into our backpack of sacreds for our ceremony, so that I might have more peeks into its irresistible information along the way.

When we found Frank at the overlook above the Golden Triangle at The Point—where we had an aerial view of the rivers converging—we realized two things: 1. Thousands of spirited Pittsburghers were gathering for a Steelers game downtown, making access to The Point extremely challenging, and 2. it was starting to rain. We stood under our umbrellas, looking down at the congested Point area, reconsidering our plan.

These circumstances appeared to be obstacles to our plan—crowds complicating our access to the Point, and rain making the conditions cold and miserable—when Frank spoke.

"From some of my spiritual studies, I have learned that whenever there is a collective consciousness of many people focused in a spirit of unity and joy—the way our Pittsburghers feel when they come together for a Steelers game—that creates useable energy for any synchronized ceremony that shares that same intent; like ours today does!"

I laughed and said, "Okay, that makes sense on its own AND I pulled the guidance card for today of Thunder Beings: Useable Energy."

Grandmother Dona piped in, "Yes, and looking at the storm clouds gathering momentum with this rain, we may also be gifted with Nature's expression of useable energy, in the form of lightning and thunder. That useable energy source is also expressed in the teaching of Victoria's Thunder Beings card; the renewal of Creation through the union of Mother Earth and Father Sky during a storm."

Frank was grinning and could not resist adding, "Well then, that form of Lightning and Thunder must be summoning the Sacred White and Black Buffaloes, calling them to us by name. I guess they wanted their energy to be a part of this ceremony today."

We all laughed, agreeing.

Now I, too, was bursting with the need to add my next insight: "Just before we left I was guided to the book *Earth: Pleiadian Keys to the Living Library*. In the amazing chapter that I landed in, there was some incredible information about this same mass consciousness thing that you mentioned, Frank. It was explaining about webworks in the corridors of time that need a mass consciousness event on the planet to link into in order to anchor a new timeline onto the planet to assist a higher consciousness here. How about those Steelers, for providing our mass consciousness event?"

"How many viewers typically watch these televised NFL football games?" Grandmother Dona asked.

Frank and I exchanged glances. "Millions?"

"Easily."

Suddenly we all burst out laughing! We were all quite impressed and delighted with our astute catching of the abundantly-available guidance.

"I don't think we have over-looked anything!" Frank concluded.

"Well, I will just add the reminder here that my guidance was clear and simple: '*Your intention: it is done. Now simply trace that highest vision from the Future back to the Present.*' So we really don't have much to do but to recap and celebrate."

Suddenly the rain intensified.

"OK! Plan B: go to Grandmother Dona's sacred chariot!" I directed. "We will do the ceremony as we sit inside her vehicle overlooking the converging rivers' Universal Portal that mirrors the Milky Way's Heavenly Portal of star-rivers."

We all scrambled into the shelter of her vehicle. Once we settled inside, it really did feel more like a cozy celebration than a cosmic ceremony linking into the corridors of time. Nonetheless, I called on the animal medicine of Raven, which was the animal *Medicine Card* for the day.

"More perfection! I recall that Raven not only represents ceremonial magic, but brings a change in consciousness—one that 'may involve walking inside the Great Mystery on another path at the edge of time.' Maybe Raven is our escort through these mysterious corridors of time for today's work." We all chuckled.

"Listen!" Grandmother Dona interrupted.

We all directed our attention to the sound of amplified cheers arising from the Steeler game at the stadium below our overlook. The Steelers must have scored a touchdown. We joined in the cheers, knowing that we were linking them to an even more joyous and unifying event.

Amidst the rain, and punctuated periodically by cheers from the Steelers fans, the three of us traced the highest vision that we could imagine, from the Future back to the Present—of Peaceburgh, of the Celebration of Unity, and the emerging New Earth consciousness for our planet—emerging and being amplified city by city, all around the world.

We took turns speaking it into being, in our most heartfelt, vivid descriptions and declarations. We recalled our fourth, underground hidden ceremonial space-holder, Kathy, who was like the fourth underground river, adding to our visions with sacred feminine energy. We felt complete with our work. Then I sang the magnificent songs from the White Buffalo, and the joyous song from the Fairy Folk that I had been given to energetically activate the vision, as I had been guided.

We looked at each other with contented grins, sharing vibrant silence.

Then Frank pulled out a thermos of hot tea, and poured the tea into rounded glass tea cups each imprinted with a map of the Earth. We shared a warming toast to the New Earth. Then he pulled out a bowl holding 19 small acorns, all nestled in concentric circles, with their pointed caps upward. In an endearing show-and-tell style, he explained the potency and stability of the number 19 that radiates energy of wholeness. He uses this energetic potency of wholeness in his environmental healing work and wanted to add its numerology to the final touches of our collaborative work of New Earth consciousness today.

We collectively grounded the frequencies of wholeness into the intention and vision of our ceremony, and then ended with prayers of gratitude and loving appreciation.

We said our farewells and headed back to our homes.

After I returned home with Grandmother Dona, she repacked her chariot and got ready for her drive back to Ohio.

"We sure know how to make it GOOD, don't we?" she smiled, hating to go home.

We took a last moment together at the Stone Heaven altar. I received guidance that it needed to stay up for a total of eight days. I simply accepted this. "Yep, we sure do." I sent her off with hugs.

Alone again, after such a rich day of kindred-spirited co-creative fulfillment, I settled at my dining table with a cup of tea to record the events, miracles and insights. After a bit, my writing was interrupted by a phone call. It came up on my caller ID as Frank. I answered.

Instead of Frank's voice, I was surprised by the sound of loud music blasting out of the phone. It kept playing on and on. I was puzzled... *what was going on?* Finally after a couple of minutes, the music ended and Frank's voice came through. He spoke with an excited tone.

"Victoria, I had to call while this song was playing, so you could be part of the magic. Did you catch those lyrics? I was listening to this CD as I was driving home. Victoria, you will love this. This particular song track began playing at exactly 7:32 PM. And it is TRACK 19. There is your 7:32 thing again! And remember what I was saying about the number 19 generating the stable energy of wholeness? This is track 19 that came on at 7:32. And get this... the song is called, 'Joy to the Universe!.' Yep, to the UNIVERSE! We made it GOOD, Honey!"

"Ecstatic," I uttered, "Ecstatic."

Chapter 18 - Second Song from the Sacred White Buffalo

· ·

SIX DAYS HAD PASSED SINCE THAT extraordinary collaborative ceremony at The Point. The Stone Heaven Altar was still assembled upon the glass end table in my living room. I followed my inner instructions to keep the altar energized and activated for eight days, then to gather the available Peaceburgh Skull Keepers again for a ceremony to dismantle it.

Each time I walked through my living room, I felt the Altar's magnificent energy, and a feeling of profound promise... *but of what?*

I wanted to tune more deeply into this feeling. It was as if the Altar was an assembly of support; a vortex of multiple forces palpably expressing collective support from the unseen world; from the Ancestors; from that stabilizing energy of wholeness that Frank had addressed; from an Intelligence of Divine Love.

After days of feeling this irresistible call, I was finally able to give my complete attention to tune in to the presence of these energies at this Stone Heaven Altar. It was 10:30 PM.

I pulled my bentwood rocker, right up to the edge of the Altar. I gathered into my intention to receive whatever was most important, with clarity. I sat quietly, breathing into my heart, visually inspecting and savoring with awe each magnificent item on the altar, with vivid attentiveness.

I became present to an irresistible yearning to clarify for myself what was most important for me to know about the next steps of my Soul Work; about the highest purpose that I came here to serve. Feeling deeper into the intensity of this inner yearning, I followed the impulse to close my eyes and breathe into the yearning, allowing it to BE.

In my mind's eye, I immediately saw and felt the close-up face of the Sacred White Buffalo Kenahkihinen with his magnificent midnight-black eyes locking into mine. I responded to the potency of that connection with tears; my Tears of Truth.

Next, I began to hear words arriving; it was like a song in its rhythm and cadence, but without a melody. I opened my eyes in surprise. The words were continuing to arrive. I grabbed my journal and began taking transcription. The words were slowing down a bit, for me to recall and to catch up. As soon as I caught the first batch, more began arriving. I noticed a complex rhyming pattern and a rhythm that was engaging. The arrival of words, organized into five distinct groupings, or verses, felt complete. Everything became quiet again.

I was moved as I re-read all the words that I captured. I now began reading the song-message aloud to myself:

Second Song from the Sacred White Buffalo

"Indigenous Soul: Original Whole
Seeing with Sacred Eyes
Life's interconnection, speaking as Blessing
Divinity realized.

In a Sacred way, creative as play
Offering our self-expressions
As gifts freely given, joyously living
Abundance the lesson.

A new way to listen: Oneness the mission
Listening to Creation:
Animals, stones, trees, rivers and bones
Honoring All Our Relations.

Releasing the lies of shallow eyes,
Beholding each other's beauty.
Freed from the chatter, speaking what matters:
Heart, Soul, Community.

No more separation, now co-creation.
Relating essence-to-essence.
Original Blessing: joy, peace and sharing.
A New Earth expressing Love's presence."

I allowed myself to weep quietly in deep awe and reverent appreciation. *A second song from the Sacred White Buffalo? What a stunning description of what it is like to live from a restored, whole, Indigenous Soul; remembering how to live in Right-Relation with all of Creation, with All Our Relations.*

These words felt like a vivid description of life as it is meant to be lived in the New Earth of Unity; the New Earth prophesied by the world's Indigenous peoples, by the various world religions, and envisioned by the planetary visionaries and Lightworkers. I felt completely committed to be in service to this revelation of the New Earth and its description of our original, whole Indigenous Soul.

I offered a prayer of thanks.

I re-read the words again. They were so perfect. It described the Golden Age, of Heaven on Earth, in a song.

So why were these songs coming to me? I am not a musician, not a songwriter, and not even a good singer.

Hmmm, I noticed wryly. That unfortunate habit of discounting myself had not been eradicated from my brain-neurons yet. *I wondered if this old habit would still be with me as I entered more deeply into the consciousness of this New Earth of Unity. At least I had learned peaceful co-existence with it, through neutral witnessing.*

I refocused, determined to shift out of my head and return my attention to my heart. I suddenly recalled my Sacred Path guidance card for the day: Whirling Rainbow: Unity/Wholeness Achieved. *Wow, that is for sure,* I mused. Unity/Wholeness was the perfect description of the picture painted by this song's words.

And I remembered the animal *Medicine Card* guidance for the day was Turkey, alerting me that "you are being given a gift." I smiled. Whoa, what a gift. I felt my favorite mantra beginning to recite itself inwardly: *thank you/I love you/thank you/I love you/thank you/I love you,* over and over, joyously.

Even as I fell asleep that night, that mantra would not stop.

Chapter 19 - Another Song Download...
This Time In Rap Format

· ·

FOR SEVERAL DAYS, I HAD PONDERED a request from one of the Younger Tribe folks in our growing Peaceburgh community of unity, Kellee Maize. She and I had grown closer through an ongoing women's group we were part of, and she was also the youngest of my honorees in the Peaceburgh Transformational Leaders Tribute that I hosted. I had become a combination mentor, second-mother and soul-friend to Kellee. I was always amazed by her.

Kellee was a Hip Hop rap artist, songmaker, performer, entrepreneur and musical activist. Her heart, passionate determination and creativity were inspiring and unceasing. Her vision was to transform the world through music and she was good at it. She held a strong vision of the New Earth of Unity in her big heart.

Her request stopped me in my tracks when she told me a few days earlier, "Victoria, I keep getting the sense that I am supposed to help get your Fairy Song and White Buffalo songs out to a larger audience by doing rap versions of them. What do you think?"

Uh-huh. A rap version of the songs sent in from the Fairy folk and the Sacred White Buffalo?

Now *THAT* was a different idea; one that stretched my concept of what was possible, to be honest. How in the world would that work?

I looked into the steady and earnest eyes of this musical activist visionary, as I simultaneously felt into this possibility within myself. I noticed a *Yes* trying to open up from a tight bud into a flourishing flower. I also felt ambivalence pushing back.

I finally responded, "Wow, Kellee, what an offer. I will take it into my guidance and let you know." I was committed that my answer to her heart-inspired request would not derive from my ego-based personality.

So this inquiry had been simmering in the back of my mind for a few days already. I had lifted the lid and peeked into that pot before I went to sleep last night. *Yep, still cooking. Time to sleep, though.*

When I awoke the next morning, I was compelled to linger between the worlds a bit longer, in the luxury of the vivid remnants of a beautiful dream. I had savored the dream in great detail, then taken the time to record it in my journal before starting my day.

I dreamed I was at a rocky ocean beach. I was standing at a pile of unusual stones that were accumulating on top of a rocky ledge within reach of the gentle wash of ocean waves, as they rhythmically came ashore and returned out to sea.

Right at this junction of earth and water, at this rocky altar-like ledge, I stood witnessing a continuing miracle. With each wave, deposits of carved stone Zuni fetishes were being delivered onto the rocky altar ledge, by the hundreds—all crafted from rose quartz; the heart-stone; the pink stone of love.

These small stone fetishes were in the shapes of the traditional animals honored by the Zuni and other tribes: miniature bears, wolves, eagles, snakes, turtles, owls, frogs, crows, otters and others;

all made from the pink heart-stone of Mother Earth. As I continued witnessing this phenomenon, I realized that the accumulating fetishes also included little pink suns and stars and moons and planets.

With each ocean wave, more and more of these delightful treasures were deposited on top of the rocky altar-ledge as a direct manifestation of love from the Heart of Mother Earth. Her continuing love-gift was arriving in ongoing waves like the sacred ash that is generated and accumulates around the photos of the enlightened Indian saint, Sai Baba. More and more gifts of these pink heart-stone animals and stars and planets just kept washing ashore.

It was breathtakingly beautiful. I felt overjoyed to witness this continuous outpouring of creation from this ocean of love manifested for our joy, arriving directly from the Mother's Heart.

I still had my journal with me after recording this dream, as I went to take my shower. I smiled as I reminded myself of the guidance cards I had pulled for the day: Stone People: Records, Knowing Revealed, and Spider: weaving the Web of Life that interconnects us all. That dream of love-stones was already confirming the relevance of today's messages.

I was still immersed in the wonder and reverent feelings of the dream as I stepped into the shower. I felt the familiar deep gratitude for the water spraying over me, rejuvenating me, and spoke a blessing for the water. Then I recalled Kellee's request, and spoke a prayer aloud as I washed my hair, "Divine Mother, what do you want me to do about Kellee's offer to collaborate on rap versions of the Fairy Song and the White Buffalo songs?"

I can't say that I was expecting an immediate answer to my prayer. But I sure didn't expect what happened next!

Right there, in the shower, a *RAP version* of the Fairy song message and White Buffalo messages started arriving. Yes, and in the recognizable Hip Hop rhythm. It was as clear and distinct as if I were wearing headphones.

"Wow, Beloved Mother, thanks! Uh, can you wait for me to catch all this in writing? Can you slow this down a minute?"

I rinsed the shampoo from my hair and jumped out of the shower to grab my journal. Funny, how I had brought my journal into the bathroom. That was not something I usually do. Trying not to drip all over it, I took dictation as the rappy verses arrived:

"We are multi-dimensional Beings
It's through our hearts that we are seeing

The animals—they will speak to us
Nature Spirits will be real to us
The magic of the Earth—She will dream through us
Our hearts so open love will stream through us

We are multi-dimensional Beings
It's through our hearts that we are seeing

The songs of the Angels—they will sing through us
The Rivers' flow of Oneness—they will bring to us
Power stones—they will reveal to us
Ancestors' Wisdom—it will heal through us

We are multi-dimensional Beings
It's through our hearts that we are seeing."

I couldn't believe what was happening. But I was able to hear every word clearly and catch it as it arrived, and scribe it into my cherished journal. My sacred journals were bearing witness to some incredible stuff. And the song was really catchy.

But it wasn't finished. Oh my Goddess! Now the original Fairy song wanted to be woven into this spoken-word rap version, and to become a part of it. It was all happening with such precise clarity. These original rap verses were being repeated, and yes, in-between each rap verse was being inserted a sung verse from the Fairy song: *Come weave a web with me/a rainbow web of harmony....*

I smiled as I remembered again the messages from the guidance cards for today: the Stone People card and the Spider card. I re-interpreted their messages now: *knowings revealed, about the interwoven web connecting all of life... that is what this rap version of the songs emphasizes.*

I rehearsed the new song. The spoken rap song interwoven with the sung Fairy song sounded impressive to my ears. I couldn't wait to share it with Kellee.

I finished drying my hair and getting dressed. After I rewrote everything more legibly, with no water dripping onto the pages, I called Kellee.

"Hi, Kellee. I just received a surprising answer to your request to assist with a rap version of the Fairy and White Buffalo songs." I filled her in on the details then delivered a bashful rendering of the rap song.

"I am loving this!" she responded. "Come over to my recording studio and let's record it. It needs to be part of the Celebration of Unity ceremonial performance. Let's perform it together."

Perform it together? Now that was really stretching my sense of the possible!

I guess in the New Earth of Unity, even the impossible is possible.

Our collaborative performance of *We Are Multi-Dimensional Beings* became part of the Celebration of Unity honoring the Indigenous as Keepers of Wisdom for how to live into this New Earth of Unity. The rap song mirrored the compelling Indigenous wisdom teachings offered by three Pittsburgh Indigenous Elders in this community ceremony of life, and it helped us all in reclaiming our restored, Whole, Indigenous Souls. It was warmly received.

And Kellee was also inspired to render the second song from the White Buffalo in a spoken word CD track with spellbinding sound effects on another of her albums (KelleeMaize.com/Music).

Chapter 20 - A Third Serpent Stone

· ·

I FELT COMPELLED TO WALK IN my personal Power Place to pay a visit to my Sacred Tree. No matter what, doing this always grounded me. And recent world events were challenging my sense of stability.

I was so saddened by the recent news of March 11—that the media called Japan's "twin disasters"—of their massive 9.0 earthquake and then the tsunami, resulting in the nuclear reactor meltdowns. The impact of that unresolved disaster made staying grounded a necessity. And the very ground which grounds us was shifted on that day: the earthquake shifted Japan 13 feet closer to the U.S. and shifted the Earth's axis by 6.5 inches. I knew that such impacts could trigger further instability, both geological and human. Whew! Talk about the Indigenous prophecies of Earth Changes.

Yet, it was also very present in my attention that a couple of days *prior* to Japan's twin disasters, I had received a forwarded email originated by Szuson Wong, PhD, that was titled "THE GREATEST REVOLUTION IN HUMAN HISTORY BEGINS March 11, 2011: Uranus in Aries, The Revolution of Consciousness."

Wong sent an alert that, as the planet Uranus (known as The Great Awakener) enters the constellation of Aries on March 11,

2011, "the greatest revolution in human history begins, that will become known as the Revolution of Consciousness." She elaborated that, "Unlike revolutions of old, this revolution will be centered in the hearts and minds of the men, women, and children that inhabit planet Earth."

And it had not escaped my attention that two days before March 11, a massive X-class, earth-directed solar flare had erupted, seen as a catalyst for the March 11 earth-shifting events.

The resulting disasters had certainly served to jolt mass consciousness into a sense of heightened interconnectedness and compassion, as well as activating people to support each other and share resources. The earthquake-tsunami was responded to world-wide, with a massive wave of humanity's heart-opening—all mega-doses of unity.

It had riveted my attention that this worldwide disaster prodding humanity into unity consciousness was perfectly aligned with such an impressive array of celestial events. The well-documented divine parade of celestial, solar, stellar, astrological and planetary events was a dramatic demonstration of "as above, so below."

Reverberating from this context I needed to walk; to become grounded in beauty, in gratitude, holding space for the highest vision of an awakened humanity. And I arrived at my Power Place. As I crossed the threshold of the entry gates into the cemetery, I felt the familiar shift of energy in my body—like I was changing the channel on a radio from a raucous, blasting, harshly fragmenting channel into a quiet, peaceful, and attentively-aware channel.

I continued walking toward my tree, drinking in the beauty of this place. I realized that of all the places on Earth, this was my sweet spot, that I had adopted to love, to explore, to develop a relationship with over these twenty-some years. And I had become intimate with this place. I had become part of it. I felt how I belonged to it. And in return, my spot on Earth was teaching me reverent engagement, subtle attention, and deep listening. My heart softened. My entire body softened. I felt bathed in goodness. I was seeing, smelling, feeling and hearing Earth's Medicine. My drained energy shifted and became vibrant, sweet, enlivened.

I found myself wishing that everyone on this planet could have a relationship with a special place like this that would nourish and ground them, slow them down, train them in deep seeing and deep listening, and fill them with the beauty and awe of Nature. What would it be like if every human felt a sense of belonging to a place that would soothe and heal, open and reveal, in the magical way that Nature does?

Ever since I had received the song-downloads from the Nature Spirits and the White Buffalo—and the recently-arrived rap version integrating their messages—I felt inspired to sing these songs whenever I came to my Power Place. I sensed that each time I sang these songs, they were being anchored more and more deeply into the noosphere—the planetary grid of the collective consciousness. And so I began to sing each of these songs now—to the Earth, sky, trees, plants, insects, birds and animals here—affirming to All My Relations that the New Earth consciousness was indeed arriving. Regardless of the surface appearances of the news headlines, I knew that we were shifting steadily from the love of power to the power of love... even in the midst of tsunamis and nuclear meltdowns, or, more accurately, *assisted* by tsunamis and nuclear meltdowns.

Still singing, I rounded the bend in the road leading toward the pond. Looking down, I noticed a significant-sized stone right in my path, right in the middle of the road. I interrupted my song to bend down and inspect it. To my amazement, it had a distinct, serpentine-shaped face on one end. It had a snout profile that reminded me of my two other serpent stones: the yellowish one, from the Serpent Mound, and the blackish one from East Millsboro, Pennsylvania.

This stone was a mid-sized stone, compared with the other two. It had a similar ridge creating the serpent's eye in its profile, and a similar eye formation. Its coloration was a combination of the other two stones, a mix of yellowish and darker colors. The bottom of this stone had the same tiny sparkles through it, like the East Millsboro stone. I picked it up and gazed at it with amazement. Carrying it with me, I resumed singing the verse from the second White Buffalo song:

> "A new way to listen: Oneness the mission
> Listening to Creation:
> Animals, stones, trees, rivers and bones
> Honoring All Our Relations."

Suddenly my attention was again interrupted, this time by the appearance of several deer emerging from the pond area. They began to cross the cemetery road in front of me. I counted 12 of them. They gazed at me, not at all alarmed by my presence in the road.

As I bowed to them, and sent them love and gratitude silently from my heart, the lead deer crossing the road stopped to look intently at me. It turned to take a few steps closer, then stopped again and continued to gaze at me. As he did this, all the other deer following behind also slowed, and assembled to gaze at me as well. They were about 20 feet from where I stood.

I was incredibly moved by the phenomenon of all these deer choosing to stop and connect with me, with trust, without a trace of alarm. I softly repeated singing my song from the White Buffalo, this time offering my song to the deer.

All 12 of those deer, facing me in the stillness of attention, accepted my song to them. They remained focused on me, motionless, as I finished my song-gift:

"Original Blessing: joy, peace and sharing

A New Earth expressing Love's presence."

I bowed again to the herd of deer, and held up my hand in a gesture of blessing and love. We gazed at each other for several more moments. Then in a whispered tone, I explained to the deer that the song I was singing was a message from the Sacred White Buffalo describing the New Earth culture, as humanity remembers how to live from our original Whole, Indigenous Soul. All 12 deer continued in their attentive stance, remaining motionless. It was as if we were taking a stand together, animal and human, on behalf of this highest future path. Our communion of silent grace filled my heart.

Then one of the deer stirred and began grazing on a nearby shrub, and several others joined the picnic. They all began moving on in a relaxed manner. Our spontaneous shared ceremony was obviously complete.

With a final blessing, I turned and headed to my sacred Power Tree. As I arrived, I greeted it and connected with it. I touched my hand to its trunk, and waited until I could feel my heartbeat-pulse in synch with the pulse of my Tree. Once I felt connected, I told my Tree all that had happened, and placed the third serpent stone at the roots.

I sat on the ledge of the nearby Celtic Cross monument, and allowed my gaze to focus on the large pyramid monument opposite from where I sat. I was still filled with a sense of deep reverence and awe, wrapped in gratitude.

I was now remembering the wisdom offered to me by the Chinese poet-in-exile, Huang Xiang, while he had lived in Pittsburgh. I had interviewed him about his understanding and experience of the converging four rivers. He loved the four rivers and had written poetry about them. He asked me to share the interview conversation we had about "Rivers Alive in Us" with as many people as possible.

In that conversation, Huang Xiang explained that, "Our bodies are here, but they are also sitting somewhere else. That somewhere else might be called the One Life, or the divine intelligence or the greater flow of universal consciousness. Having our flow of consciousness move unimpeded—like a river—is a fundamental aspect for entering an experience of Oneness."

Huang Xiang further described that we must begin by looking at the world with different eyes—beyond our two physical literal-seeing eyes. We must "look at the world from the heart, aligned with the 'third eye,' (the area of the forehead just above and between the physical eyes) which connects us to spirit and imagination. When we do this, we discover that our bodies open to a sense of unity with the Earth and the Heavens, which become like an open book that we ordinarily can't see."

I realized then that the words from the White Buffalo's second song that I had just sung to the deer, taught the same thing as Huang Xiang had expressed: looking with different eyes meant seeing with Sacred Eyes.

Huang Xiang had emphasized that by looking with different eyes this way, we access a non-linear language—a language of imagination, unity and *communion*. We begin to see ourselves as part of the vast book of life, and to have a deeper experience of participation in this larger story.

Indigenous peoples of all cultures have preserved this language of unity and communion. Most of the rest of us have forgotten how to speak it.

As Huang Xiang described it, "the animals, they become our language. The birds of the sky are the punctuation to the words of the animals. We can comprehend how to read the book of creation through our bodies. It is like we are all writing a shared story together, living the same language through heart and spirit, entering the essence behind forms, and sensing the presence of the One Life that expresses as all life."

My experience with the deer today had been a vivid demonstration of this language of unity and communion. It was a teaching from Nature herself. Through entering the One Life, we can consciously participate in the story that we are writing together with the *"animals, stones, trees, rivers and bones/Honoring All Our Relations."*

Living that way would really make it GOOD, Honey!

I smiled, immersed in a sense of deep contentment, enveloped within a deep trust that humanity would indeed shift collectively into this expanded way of perceiving and being.

I realized that Huang Xiang's words and the message from the White Buffalo were expressing in poetic form the truth that quantum physics has recently verified: *"we are living in a 'participatory universe.'"* And as quantum science has demonstrated, our very acts of observing are continuously affecting the outcome of the experiment—the experiment we call Life.

I knew that by becoming intentional Sacred Seers and Sacred Sayers, humanity could create a better experiment of Life—a better story than the story of separation, fear and greed that we have been unconsciously creating for too long.

Either way, we were creating this story together, collectively. We had better make it GOOD, Honey, and soon.

Well, I acknowledged, the greatest revolution in human history had begun in earnest, with the arrival of Uranus in Aries, as The Great Awakener. I was definitely determined to stay tuned to THAT channel, not to the doom channel.

Renewed and re-grounded, I headed home with my third serpent stone. I couldn't wait to introduce it to the other two.

Chapter 21 - To the Serpent Mound with the Three Serpent Stones

. . . .

MY DEAR SOUL FRIEND AND SISTERGODDESS, Kathy agreed to join me on my next trip to the Serpent Mound. Not only did she want to experience the ancient sacred site, but I had received some very significant guidance that Kathy wanted to support. Another ceremony was being called for.

I reviewed the Divine Dot Connecting. Sitting with my three serpent stones in deep listening and meditation, I was prompted to stack the three stones one on top of another. As I did so, I was stunned to see how they all fit together. They were perfectly aligned by the shape of their serpentine snouts, as if they had each been stamped from the same template. The large, medium and small stones sat nested together in a trio of serpent profiles. I smiled, imagining that they were happy at this human-facilitated reunion, bringing them together from three sacred sites.

I am sitting in the presence of a restored geologic puzzle, I marveled. It had been impressive enough already, that two serpent stones had found their re-connection. But now, *three? Dayenu!*

Three, I mused. *That theme of three appears so consistently.*

I gazed contentedly at the three serpent stones' re-united configuration. Suddenly I received a deep and quietly profound sense of knowing: each serpent stone represented the Kundalini Life Force at the three levels of existence—the Human, the Earth, and the Heavens—reconnecting in a grand trinity of reunion.

How amazing was it, really, that each matching serpent stone, from three different locations, had found its way to me, for me to reunite them with each other? I knew from deep within my Soul, that a ceremony wanted to happen, and what the ceremony wanted to express. And I responded to all this with a mixture of awe and calm acceptance.

Kathy was excited to be assisting me. It was a beautiful day as we set out. The *Sacred Path* card for the day was Counting Coup: Victory, and the animal *Medicine Card* was Antelope: Knowledgeable Action. The Antelope is an ancient and traditional symbol of shamanic medicine and knowledge. Its message signified acting with a higher purpose with the Bow of Authority on behalf of self, family, clan, nation and Mother Earth. Antelope's presence urged, "Do it now. Don't wait any longer. The time is *now*, the power is *you*." I was completely moved by the affirming support of these messages aligned with the purpose of our ceremony. *A Victory for the New Earth is on the way*, I mused.

So Kathy and I were on our way to the Serpent Mound, the three serpent stones packed in a backpack with the Community Skull from Grandmother Flordemayo, along with some other symbolic ceremonial items. Grandmother Dona was unable to join us, but held sacred space for our work.

On the drive, about halfway to the Serpent, Kathy and I were inspired by the magnificence of the Cloud Language decorating the blue sky. The shapes of the clouds were breathtaking. Many of them looked like celestial paintings, with swirling brushstrokes. One cloud formation in particular amazed us. It was a perfect cloud painting of a hummingbird. The hummingbird's wings were fully opened, and each wing displayed distinct feathers. Its head was turned in profile, with a perfectly-positioned blue eye, and its long elegant beak was flawless. Its body was clearly shaped and its tail was fully extended with distinct feathers fanning downward. It was hard to comprehend how such a distinct, complex, beautiful image could have been produced by cloud vapor. I was able to catch a photo of it through the car windshield.

We translated this hummingbird Cloud Language as a good omen. In the Indigenous tradition reported by Jamie Sams and David Carson, the hummingbird represents joy. Its medicine is the ability to solve the riddle of the contradiction of duality.

"We could sure use big doses of THAT medicine on this planet," Kathy laughed.

"Well, that shift out of the divisive duality of separation, and into the awareness of our interconnection and Oneness is what the Shift of the Ages is about. Barbara Marx Hubbard, an amazing eighty-something futurist, describes it as the shift from ego to essence. I really love that. And the conclusion of this historic 26,000-year cycle that the Mayans have been tracking is ushering humanity into a timeframe where these shifts are amplified and accelerated." I acknowledged.

Inwardly, I began hearing the tune of the first song from the Sacred White Buffalo arising in my memory, with the distinct line *"Humanity, Divinity/Forever re-bound."* I sang this aloud to Kathy. She nodded with a deep sigh, her body softening in response to that promise.

I took a look at my photo of the heavenly hummingbird, examining it with the camera's close-up function. I gasped. "Kathy! There is something in this photo that I didn't see when I took the shot. There is a long, perfectly rectangular cloud that actually looks like a banner with distinct cloud letters—a whole string of them. The letters are a vaporous white and they look like they were stamped with precision into the cloud banner. The letters are incredibly uniform and they are all in capital case. They appear to be spelling something, but they are upside-down. The cloud banner of letters is right above the hummingbird."

Kathy speculated, "Can you make out the characters? I wonder if we caught a reflection of the vehicle ID number from the dashboard?"

We were coming up to a rest stop, and I would have the benefit of another pair of eyes to make some sense of the phenomenon.

After we pulled over, Kathy inspected the front and back vehicle windows. "Well, all I found was a serial number on the rearview window, but it has several lines of numbers, not any letters, and they are in black. The characters in your photo are white and cloud-like, clearly formed but a bit transparent, and they look like mostly letters, capitalized. I see the upside-down word, "MOON," if you read it flipped. I don't think you could have gotten a reflection of a passing road sign, because we would have been moving too fast for it to be this distinct, and there are just too many characters in this cloud-banner for a road sign anyway." Her possibilities for a reasonable explanation were running out.

I took a turn scrutinizing the photo. If I read the cloud-imprinted characters flipped upside down, I could discern fairly clearly the letters spelling "CHRISTO." Then the letters became a bit blurry. They almost suggested "CHRISTOPHER," but when I examined the image with more discernment, what I saw was "CHRISTO1 HHHMOON."

I took out my pendulum, and checked its response to the possible combinations: a clear and emphatic "no" for any of the "CHRISTOPHER" combinations; an emphatic "yes" for "CHRISTO 1 HHH MOON."

Kathy and I stared at each other, speechless. Our brains were cranking, trying to crack the code of the cloud banner of letters, pointed to by the hummingbird of joy whose medicine was to solve the riddle of the contradiction of duality.

I finally broke the silence. "What I am getting is that "CHRISTO 1" means that the Christ-consciousness in the past arrived in the form of singular deities, like Jesus, Buddha, Krishna, White Buffalo Calf Woman, Quetzalcoatl, and Kuan Yin. But in our era, *all of Humanity* represented by the H repeated three times for emphasis—collective Humanity—will express the Christ-consciousness. And we will access that higher consciousness through the Sacred Feminine, as represented by the moon. The intuitive Heart of the Divine Feminine will be our access to this expanded divine consciousness of compassion and Oneness." I glanced down at my previously resting pendulum. It was now spontaneously rotating in a vigorous clockwise yes direction. I felt relieved to have that confirmation.

Kathy was nodding thoughtfully, "That interpretation makes perfect sense to me. And it feels so hopeful, so full of promise. Whew! What a way to receive such a message. How is that even possible?"

We looked at the photo one more time. "Look," Kathy noticed. "There are two intensely bright objects below the cloud banner, just off to the right, above the hummingbird's right wing. I wonder if they could be extra-terrestrial spacecraft? They look solid and intensely bright."

I shook my head, chuckling. "Let's get back on the road to the Serpent Mound. Solving that Cloud Language sign is plenty of mystery for me. I am not up for another puzzle just yet."

Kathy laughed in understanding, and we resumed our drive. We arrived at the Serpent Mound by late afternoon. Stopping at the gift shop, we found out that Ross Hamilton was on site, along with some archeological researchers. "Dayenu already!" I muttered in gratitude. How perfect. Ever since my encounter with Ross at our inaugural visit to the Serpent, I wanted to reconnect with him again to learn more about his work that I resonated with so strongly. And I recalled that he was working on a new book about the Ohio Valley star mounds including the Serpent effigy, recovering the Indigenous wisdom about an ancient science of nature, whereby the separation between Heaven and Earth can be dissolved.

The Serpent was bustling with researchers and visitors, but we didn't spot Ross right away. We set the intention that we would cross his path easily, and we let go of any sense of effort. After taking Kathy on the allowed path surrounding the snake effigy, and giving her space to feel into the energies present at the site, we decided to climb the lookout tower. Kathy was tuning in, absorbing impressions and assessing energies in a mindful reverent manner.

I had described to Kathy the phenomenon of the unbelievably long, horizontal web filaments that showed up during Grandmother Dona's and my encounter with the Nature Spirits last Halloween. When we arrived at the top platform of the lookout tower, I noticed another odd phenomenon.

"Look, Kathy! Can you see that small fine strand of vertical web, moving through the air approaching us?"

I watched Kathy as she focused into the air in front of us, adjusting her gaze. "I see it. How unusual! The web looks like it is slowly heading straight for us."

That was exactly what was happening. The fine, nearly invisible web-strand was slowly and steadily approaching, in a stable, vertical position. I held up my right hand, in a gesture of blessing, honoring it. Amazingly, the web-strand navigated its way exactly to my upheld hand. It landed on my hand, anchoring itself perfectly positioned to connect my two fingers. The top part of its vertical strand attached to my upraised index finger, and the bottom part of the strand attached to my thumb.

"Wow! Let me try to get a photo of that." Kathy said with a tone of awe. I stood motionless, the web filament still connecting the index finger and thumb of my upheld hand. She snapped a couple of pictures on her cell phone and took a look. Disappointed, she reported, "The web filament is just too fine. It isn't visible in the photo."

"Well, at least I have you as a credible witness," I laughed. I gave blessings and thanks to the web filament, to Grandmother Spider and the vast Web of Life, and to whatever Nature Spirits had directed this web so precisely to us with its profound message of interconnection. Then I released it back into the air, and we watched it drift away.

Kathy shook her head as we arrived on the ground again. "That was so awesome… what a deep sense of connection with the Nature Beings here. This place is so magical."

Shortly after that we crossed paths with Ross Hamilton and his partner, Leslie. I approached them, introducing myself and reminding Ross of our encounter last Fall with Grandmother Dona. I told him that if there was any way that I could support his work and his compelling vision, I wanted to do so. Ross generously invited Kathy and me to sit under the picnic shelter and chat with him.

Kathy and I listened with keen interest as he described how his work was unfolding. He elaborated further about his vision of restoring the ancient knowledge of the Indigenous wisdom-keepers. His plan was to apply their original ancient science of nature to foster harmony between the Earth and sky energies for stabilizing weather patterns, and generating vital, usable energy. This work would also restore humanity's sense of a more meaningful union with the stars and the cosmos.

My deep attention to Ross's sharing was interrupted by the activity going on just behind him, in the field beyond the picnic shelter where we were sitting. I noticed the appearance of many fine, long, horizontal web filaments glinting in the air behind him.

They were incredibly long, like the ones that Grandmother Dona and I had seen a year ago. They kept appearing, only visible at all by virtue of the light they captured.

I refocused my attention to Ross's information-sharing, then again became distracted. The web activity mesmerized me. The air was so thick now with these long horizontal web filaments, that I could not resist watching. *Where were the multitudes of spiders that were producing such prodigious amounts of web? Or were they being generated by something else? Perhaps by the Nature Spirits and elementals?* I wondered. The entire time, I had not witnessed any bugs or spiders hovering around the area.

I finally had to apologize to Ross for my distracted attention. I explained what was occurring behind him. We all took a few moments to watch together in wonder.

The entire field was being blanketed in layers of these fine long web filaments. Yet no hint of insects was discernable. The grass glinted with the impossibly long filaments. They were everywhere throughout the large field. The field was shimmering in its gossamer cover, as the light danced along the webs.

It had all happened so quickly. None of this had been present when Kathy and I had walked through the same field just prior to encountering Ross. We marveled at this magical and mysterious phenomenon. I took a few photos, and was finally able to return my attention to resume this hoped-for opportunity to learn more about Ross's work and plans. I did my best to listen and not divert my eyes.

After a bit more inspiring discussion with Ross, I realized that it was getting late. I also realized that Kathy and I had not yet done our intended ceremony with the three serpent stones. We exchanged contact information with Ross and said our farewells.

As Kathy and I went to find a good spot at the Serpent for our ceremony, I chuckled, musing to myself, "Yep. Absolutely consistent.

Each ceremony I had been guided to do wasn't able to occur at each location until almost sundown. What *was* that? Just a weird series of coincidences?" I knew the answer was no.

But I wasn't sure of the significance of the sunset timing. Did it relate to the theme of the closing of cycles? Perhaps synchronicity was anchoring each of these New Earth ceremonies at day's end as a reminder of the grand 26,000-year ending of the Mayan Calendar, and the closing of the Fifth Sun Long Count in the same timeframe.

We arrived at the head of the Serpent and set up our sacreds at the overlook. We were quite aware that the surveyors were fairly close behind us, still doing their research. But this location was definitely calling to us.

I turned to Kathy, grinning, "I am sure being trained how to do potent ceremony in the most brief, abbreviated manner, with this get-it-done-just-before-sunset process that keeps recurring. Fortunately, I also keep being shown that it is already complete from the intentions and preparations, so that just a minimal process of tracing the future back to the present is enough. And here we go again!" I inspected the sun moving lower toward the horizon.

"I am at your service," Kathy bowed playfully. She then began assembling the altar with me, with intuitive confidence.

After we opened sacred space and honored the seven sacred directions, South, West, North, East, Above, Below, and Within, I described the symbolism of our ceremonial altar-stones:

I introduced the Heaven Serpent-Stone. "The biggest, blackish-grey stone on the bottom, from the East Millsboro site, has the outline of the serpent-snout, just off-center there. This stone represents the Heavens' Kundalini, that cosmic serpentine Life Force, moving throughout the Universe. See the zillions of tiny sparkles all through that Heaven's Kundalini stone? They are like the stars and multiverses in the Cosmos.

I introduced the Human Serpent-Stone. "This stone in the middle, resting upon that biggest serpent stone, snout-to-snout, is the serpent stone from my own personal sacred site. It has a blend of the yellowish and blackish colors from those two other stones. This middle stone represents the Divine Human's Kundalini; the serpentine Life Force awakened within humanity. And it is functioning as a bridge between the Heavens' Kundalini and the Earth's Kundalini, blending the energies of both.

I introduced the Earth Serpent-Stone. "And resting on top of that interconnecting human-bridge middle stone, is the smaller yellowish Serpent Mound stone. It represents the Earth's Kundalini, or serpentine Life Force. See this M-shaped veining on its top surface? That turned out to be a map matching the M-shaped segment of the Monongahela River right where Frank and I were directed to go, in East Millsboro, the site near the Sacred White Buffalo. That map on the Serpent Mound stone confirms its link to the blackish-grey stone, showing that they were meant to be re-connected."

Kathy nodded, adding, "And the exactly-matching profiles of the serpent-faces of all three stones verify that all of these three stones were meant to be re-connected for our ceremony today."

"Yep." I gave my SisterGoddess a big hug. I was grateful that Kathy quickly grasped these things with minimal explanation. She was clearly also a Sacred Seer and Sacred Sayer.

I silently sent out a quick prayer, that multitudes more of humanity would also find ways to step up to the plate of living from conscious intention, co-creating the highest good for a New Earth, instead of unconsciously living from cynicism, reaction, blame and victimhood. I was envisioning a Planetary Army of Sacred Seers and Sacred Sayers. That image made my military brat younger-self smile. I recalled that my Army-Colonel father had described himself as a Soldier of Peace. *The New Earth Army is arriving*, I grinned.

I refocused to co-creating our altar, as Kathy and I placed the other symbolic objects on and around these three foundational serpent stones. Then we took a few moments to speak our intention aloud, in an act of Sacred Saying:

"These three serpent stones have been mysteriously and miraculously brought back together in unity—representing the Heavens, the Human, and the Earth. Their reunion symbolizes the interconnected flow of serpentine Life Force being reunited and aligned throughout Creation. It is our intention that likewise, humanity too, will realign into cosmic unity. Humanity, too, will embody a unified and unimpeded flow of Life Force; serving once again as the conscious Bridge, connecting Heaven and Earth."

I felt an inner prompt to sing the first song from the Sacred White Buffalo:

"White Thunder, Black Lightning, flowing underground.
What was rent apart, now restored, within sacred sound.
A time of separation, holding in protection,
Earth's final gestation,
Birthing Holy Ground.

The song within arising, Light and Dark uniting,
Humanity, Divinity
Forever re-bound."

As I finished singing the song, I was moved by the realization that I had received this song from the White Buffalo within a few hours of the timeframe of our current ceremony exactly one year ago. And its words were a ceremonial description of what we had enacted, both then and in a more complete way, now.

I shared this realization with Kathy. Her eyes widened, then quickly became wet. We hugged and danced a little jig.

"Whew!" I marveled. "Today's ceremony apparently is phase two of last year's East Millsboro ceremony. That ceremony had acknowledged the two stones, the Earth and Heavenly stones, with their respective Kundalini energies re-aligned. Today's ceremony energetically included the Human element in that alignment, completing the trinity. Now we are fully acknowledging a reunion of Heaven, Human and Earth, with all their Life-Force energies aligned.

Kathy spoke her prayers of blessing and gratitude. We wrapped up the ceremony with gift-offerings to Earth, to Spirit, and to the Kundalini Life Force. I paused to allow an impression I was receiving to arrive more clearly. It was a felt-sense of the Kundalini Life Force as the loving, creative expression of the Divine Mother— freely flowing and sovereign throughout all of Creation. Joyous.

The sun was starting to set. The researchers had finished and left. And we were complete, too.

We walked the length of the Serpent back to Kathy's vehicle in mindful silence and in deep gratitude. That cloud hummingbird of joy whose medicine was to solve the riddle of the contradiction of duality had certainly added its magic to our ceremony of unity.

Chapter 22 - Cosmic Serpent, DNA, and Sacred Knowledge

. . . .

A FEW MONTHS AFTER OUR THREE-SERPENT stones ceremony, I received a phone call from Kathy. "Victoria, you have to take a look at the book Regina Rivers gave me. You know how deeply she is learning about Shamanism and shamanistic ways of knowledge and healing. Well, this book is profound, and it is calling your name. It is titled, *The Cosmic Serpent: DNA and the Origins of Knowledge*. It is written by Jeremy Narby, an anthropologist, who makes a fascinating scientific study of the interconnection between consciousness, shamanism, molecular biology, and the serpent. What Narby discovered about the serpent seems to validate on many levels the ceremony we did at the Serpent Mound in November. Pretty cool, huh? Did you know that the serpent is central to all Indigenous shamanism worldwide?"

As I listened to Kathy, my skin was sending me those confirming goose bumps. I was also feeling a burst of energy flowing through me signaling for me to pay attention to this. However, my attention was already riveted. "Go on, tell me more," I urged her.

Kathy continued to tantalize me, "Narby documents that the visions reported in numerous cross-cultural shamanic traditional ceremonies consistently describe the serpent in ways that closely resemble DNA and chromosome activity in molecular biology!

"Really? This guy is an anthropologist?" I asked.

"Right. And he has concluded that the shamans of the world experienced direct revelations of scientific knowledge that they described poetically. Narby says that their revelations were induced bio-chemically through their sacred plant medicine practices, like drinking the ayahuasca," Kathy elaborated.

"Hmmm... from accounts I have read about ayahuasca, I can believe that. New scientific research is calling the key chemical element of ayahuasca 'the God molecule.' And that God-molecule is present in our brain's pineal gland too, that spiritual workers associate with the mystical third eye."

"Oooo... awesome. Well, listen to this one," Kathy continued. "Narby thinks that shamans could also understand what science calls the 'cellular language' of bio-photon emissions—which is the light that living cells generate. Did you know that living things really do generate light?"

"I did hear something about that," I strained to recall.

"Shamans always refer to spirits as beings of pure light. And they communicate with spirits through this light. Narby thinks shamans are actually perceiving cellular bio-photon emissions, and amplifying these communications of light-encoded information with their ritual use of quartz crystals! Quantum science has already determined that light transmits information, and quartz crystals are used in radio transmissions."

"Whoa, what was that bio-emissions and quartz connection again?" I was not quite following this part.

Kathy thought a moment then replied, "Okay, here it is. Narby is basically saying that the hallucinogenic sacred plants and the quartz crystals are the equivalent of scientific tools used by the Indigenous shamans to tune into the knowledge of—TA-DAAA!—*the cosmic serpent of DNA within all life.* That is how they accurately accessed information about the serpentine DNA at the molecular level, in their shamanic revelations. Tuning in to the DNA as the bringer of life and knowledge gave shamans their cosmic serpent."

"OH! I got it now! Wow!"

I was loving this! It made so much sense. Of course. We carry the serpent in our human bodies as the intertwining double-helix of DNA strands. Our bodies have this serpent knowledge encoded within us. And that same image of intertwining serpents has been adopted by the medical profession in their Caduceus symbol of the healer.

"Wait until you read this for yourself. Multitudes of Indigenous creation stories worldwide consistently depict the origins of life and knowledge as arising from a snake-like vital principal of cosmic origin; a cosmic serpent. I am talking about cultures across millennia including Aztec, Mayan, Egyptian, African, Chinese, Peruvian/Amazonian, Australian Aboriginal, Hindu, Siberian... and I seem to recall Narby mentioning Sumer, Persia, the Pacific, Crete, Greece, Scandinavia and Celtic as well."

"Awesome, Kathy," I responded. "This reminds me of Grandmother Flordemayo's explanation that the Serpent taught the Maya about movement in time, mathematics, space and velocity. She said that the snake represented all that knowledge. Actually, Grandmother Flordemayo said, "the Serpent *is* knowledge." Whew! This is fabulously validating. It is sad that so much patriarchal religion has demonized the snake, making the serpent the demonic force of Satan, when this very principal is the life-force within our human DNA and in the DNA of all creatures."

Kathy chuckled, "I thought you would resonate with this material."

"Resonate? I am ecstatic! You know how passionate I am about linking ancient spiritual wisdom and modern scientific understanding. More and more I am seeing that these are simply two languages describing the same reality: a right-brain, poetic language and a left-brain concrete language. And it sounds like Narby qualifies as a Kindred Spirit. He does a beautiful job of cross-translating these two languages by demonstrating correspondences between science and shamanism; between molecules and mythology. Go Narby! Yep! Sign me up! How soon can I get the book from you?"

"It is on its way, SisterGoddess."

I hung up the phone, grateful for my Tribe of Kindred Spirits in and beyond Pittsburgh, who shared my passions and perspectives, as well as an integrative spiritual path. These unusual topics and stories we discussed were not the expected sound-bites, chit-chats, gossip, and television-episode reporting of typical workplace conversations that I had experienced. I recalled how, for so many years, some of my best allies and friends were the inaccessible authors of pioneering books on human consciousness and spirituality. Now I finally had an accessible multi-faceted Tribe of co-journeyers as well as my remote author-mentors.

When Narby's *The Cosmic Serpent* book was finally in my hands, I dove into it. I was fascinated to learn that Narby's systematic process of tracking correlations between science and shamanism also proved to be a catalyst for his increasing ability to see with Sacred Eyes. As Narby revisited shamanic texts and art, he opened deeply to grasp Indigenous shamanic mythologies, recognizing them as poetic descriptions of universal knowledge. And at the same time, he understood them in the corresponding terms of scientific constructs.

I couldn't help but grin triumphantly, as I read from Narby's chapter titled "Myths and Molecules." There Narby tracked correspondences that connected shamanic myths around the world with scientific information about DNA molecules, each depicting snakes as "life-creating" and "knowledge-imparting":

"DNA is the informational molecule of life, and its very existence consists in being *both single and double*, like the mythical serpents."

"DNA is a *master of transformation*, just like the mythical serpents. In 4 billion years, it has multiplied itself into an incalculable number of species, while remaining exactly the same."

"Scientists often compare the form and movements of this long molecule [DNA] to those of a snake. Molecular biologist Christopher Wills writes: 'The two chains of DNA resemble two snakes coiled around each other in some elaborate courtship ritual.'"

"To sum up, DNA is a snake-shaped master of transformation that lives in water and is both extremely long and small, single and double. Just like the cosmic serpent."

If the microscopic DNA in the human body was uncoiled, Narby notes that it would extend 125 *billion* miles! How far from Earth into space would that cosmic serpent be connecting us? If the Shamans were perceiving that aspect of DNA, it would most certainly have to be described as a cosmic serpent.

Narby's exhaustive investigations revealed to him that Shamans had discovered firsthand the hidden unity of nature precisely because they could actually access the reality of molecular biology through their own science of sacred plant medicine and quartz crystals. And their ancient firsthand knowledge of the unity of nature was confirmed by modern molecular biology.

I was in serpentine heaven!

I refocused on Narby's journey of discovery, as he detailed numerous connections between DNA and the cosmic serpent, the axis of the world, and the language of the spirits of nature. I was impressed that a rigorously-trained anthropologist would have read Mercea Eliade's information, "that shamans almost everywhere speak a secret language, 'the language of all nature,' which allows them to communicate with the spirits."

Reading about this secret language of all nature immediately reminded me of my recent experience at my Power Place communing with the herd of deer. I again recalled the teachings of my Chinese poet friend, Huang Xiang. I bet he was describing Shamanic teachings from his own Indigenous heritage, when he taught me that it is possible to "read the book of creation *through our bodies,*" and that by looking with different eyes, connecting to the heart and third eye area of the forehead, we can enter a *non-linear language of unity and communion.*

WOW.

And at that moment phrases from the second song from my beloved Sacred White Buffalo also came distinctly to mind: *"Indigenous Soul/Original Whole/Seeing with Sacred Eyes"*... and especially this phrase: *"A new way to listen/Oneness the mission/Listening to Creation/Animals, stones, trees, rivers and bones/Honoring All Our Relations."*

WOW. WOW. WOW.

I allowed a rush of gratitude-filled energy to wash over me. I felt full, and Tears of Truth began to flow—so much Divine Dot Connection.

I took a deep breath for re-grounding. Once more, I returned to the richness of Narby's material. I read a bit further. Then I actually had to stand up and cheer when I read Narby's next epiphany:

"What else could the Ancient Egyptians have meant when they talked of a double serpent, provider of attributes and key of life, if not what the scientists call 'DNA'? Why are these metaphors so consistently and so frequently used unless they mean what they say?"

I gave Narby an encore of cheers when he noted that dragons were often interchangeable with serpents in these Indigenous creation stories and myths, and when he finally surrendered to this conclusion: "There, I thought, is the source of knowledge: DNA, living in water and emitting photons, like an aquatic dragon spitting fire."

"Wooo Hooo! Go Narby!" I hooted out loud. I was so grateful that Narby's book had also documented his own transformation. "Jeremy Narby," I declared, "you have definitely graduated to being a Sacred Seer and a Sacred Sayer!"

And I knew that, if this shift to integrative understanding of oneness was occurring within anthropological science, it would soon happen in other institutions of knowledge. Anthropology would be a potent catalyst and a cultural bridge to integrate ancient spiritual wisdom and modern science.

I settled into a deep feeling of assurance of humanity's promised return to this ancient New Earth way of living and being; living from our Original Whole Indigenous Soul.

Chapter 23 - More Divine Dot Connections

· ·

FOR SEVERAL DAYS, *THE COSMIC SERPENT* material held my attention. It catalyzed my awareness of the many arenas of consciousness-shifting on the planet that were propelling humanity toward our longed-for unity. My thoughts were flooded with the proliferating evidence of global transformation, flowing together like the converging rivers of Pittsburgh, that kept affirming humanity's promised return to oneness. The Hopi prophecy phrase arose in my thoughts: "There is a river flowing now, very fast...trust that this river has its destination."

Any single transformational breakthrough in any single arena—quantum science, biology, anthropology, medicine, economics, religion, spirituality, art, music, journalism, media—could have the impact of the proverbial butterfly whose wings fluttering on one continent starting a tsunami on the other side of the planet. And there were hundreds of thousands, millions, of these transformational shifts occurring faster than could be counted.

In fact, one of my favorite You Tube videos is Paul Hawken's *Blessed Unrest*, where he documents this very phenomenon, that he describes as "the biggest movement in the world that no one saw coming." He shows that simply viewing a running list of the names of transformational organizations—millions of them—would require continuous days and nights of viewing. And the global list is growing exponentially.

Narby launched me on this train of excited thought by giving me a glimpse of this consciousness shift within the field of anthropology, and his own shift, into seeing with Sacred Eyes of oneness. And now, just to stop my head from spinning, I had to sit down and review highlights of the other transformations occurring in various fields of human endeavor. They still mostly occurred below the radar of the nightly news reports. How sad is that? Most television viewers I knew were in a constant state of alarm or despair. But I knew better.

I began checking off mental highlights in every area I could think of. Let's see… the emerging science of human consciousness: Lynn McTaggart made information about quantum physics, applied to human consciousness, easily accessible through her bestselling books, *The Field: The Quest for the Secret Force of the Universe*; *The Intention Experiment: Using Your Thoughts to Change Your Life and the World*, *The Bond: Connecting Through the Space Between Us*. HeartMath Institute was also conducting global research on the capacity of unified human intention to increase social harmony and peace, with their Global Coherence Project. Quantum physics experts, such as William Tiller, PhD, of Stanford University, were working on a model for expanding traditional science to include human consciousness and human intention as capable of significantly affecting physical reality, with his plan called Psychoenergetic Science. I just love him for that.

Bruce Lipton revolutionized biology with his *Biology of Belief* research, demonstrating that human cellular DNA is influenced by an individual's thoughts and beliefs. Because he had integrated quantum physics and human consciousness into cellular biology,

Lipton had been acknowledged internationally as bridging science and spirit.

Similarly, Candace Pert, a neuroscientist and pharmacologist was acknowledged for bridging science and heart with her research, *Molecules of Emotion.* She demonstrated how body, mind and spirit cannot be separated, and how "feeling good and feeling God are one and the same." Wooo Hooo! I really liked that one.

The field of medicine was being transformed by integrating Eastern concepts of energy-based mind-body medicine, Reiki, yoga and meditation practices, in ways that were exploding. A noteworthy area was the tapping healing modalities, such as the Emotional Freedom Technique (EFT) that uses the knowledge of acupuncture meridians for tapping on the body as an acupressure for the emotions. EFT is an accessible, effective and simple tool to heal emotional trauma and other illnesses and disorders. Wholistic, homeopathic, naturopathic and quantum physics-based healing applications were showing up at an incredible rate.

In the field of economics, revolutionizers included Charles Eisenstein's work on *Sacred Economics* and Lynn Twist's *The Soul of Money*—both focusing on shifting consciousness out of greed and into sharing, generosity and contribution. The micro-lending movement alleviated poverty in developing countries by empowering women through small business loans, with the incredible ripple effect that these women were then able to uplift their entire communities. The movie and subsequent social movement, *Thrive,* exposed the economic hidden tyranny of a global elite controlling the world currency. The international Transition Town movement introduced local currencies, cooperatives and community gardens to build resilience in response to global economic instability, as oil-based economies flounder. The Occupy movement stimulated awareness, conversations and experimental processes in participatory democracy, and challenged corporate-controlled economics. The

Global Commons Trust movement mobilized a plan to protect the shared natural resources necessary to sustain life, such as water, air, and food. Internet-based crowd-funders such as Kickstarter and Indiegogo provided an easily-accessed platform for anyone's vision or project to be financed by social network-based sharing.

The domain of new planetary culture was originally inspired by visionary author Jean Houston and her international work of social artistry, including her consulting to the United Nations, and to national and international leaders. Her work and vision opened the pathway for other cultural evolutionaries such as the online *Evolver Network*, spearheaded by consciousness authors Daniel Pinchbeck and Jonathan Tallat Phillips. *Evolver* sought to bridge economics, the arts and spirituality. They used international networking to create an emerging planetary culture based on ecological values and creative collaboration. Phenomenon such as the Burning Man Festival also provided creative experiments in establishing more interconnected, authentically-expressed cultures. Festivals such as these bridged the domains of the new planetary culture and the arts.

Art, music and the performing arts were increasingly being used to accelerate social change. I didn't have to leave home to experience examples of these social change artists. Pittsburgh boasted several of these transformers: Sheila Collins' InterPlay troupe employing improvisational story and movement for noble purposes; Pittsburgh's Playback Theatre enlisting live audience participation; Kevin May's spoken word philosophic Flow-etry; Kellee Maize's conscious rap; Vanessa German's magical spoken word social commentary. The *Playing for Change* music CD and their worldwide musical collaborations exemplified the global reach of such art for social change intentions. Then there was Alex Grey's sacred art. His mystical paintings of the human anatomy depicted humans as luminous, energetically-flowing, divine, interconnected beings. And he created a Chapel of Sacred Mirrors to display this series of paintings in a space that looks and feels holy. Jose Argeulles was taking the concept of art to a whole new level—envisioning Earth herself as a collaborative work of art. Described in his book, *Manifesto for the Noosphere,* he described how conscious humans will mindfully enact and co-create our highest vision of life on Earth, as our collective work of art—our "collective cosmological dream, regularly and ritually rehearsed and enacted." Now that's MY kind of art!

Religion experienced several cracks in their institutional walls. The exposure of Catholic priests sexually abusing children resulted in a public outrage. Ireland's answer to the Vatican's inadequate response was to close Ireland's embassy at the Vatican. On another front the Vatican wobbled: In the face of ongoing petitions from various Indigenous groups, including the International Council of 13 Indigenous Grandmothers, The Vatican quietly removed from their books the 1493 Papal Bull. For 500 years, that inhumane document had authorized the removal of rights and lands from Indigenous "pagan" peoples and justified Christian domination, genocide, and exploitation of Natives. However, the Vatican was still resisting a public apology, and the pressure continues. Then there was the issue of the Vatican dealing with the Nuns. Substantial transformational presence and influence from the Nuns arose within the Catholic Church, through the Leadership Conference of Women Religious, but the Vatican cracked down on them. Through all this, the voice of the Sacred Feminine emerged gloriously, anyway, through catalytic mouthpieces such as Sister Joan Chittister, and through unprecedented presentations depicting the Feminine Face of God at the Parliament of World Religions Conference. In these less-rigid contexts, the progressive spiritual leaders properly welcomed and acknowledged the Divine Feminine and the Indigenous spiritual traditions. In the Jewish sector, Judaism evidenced a more integrative spirituality, with its Jewish Renewal Movement, which even incorporated connections to Shamanism.

Spirituality—as distinct from institutional religion—boomed with historic discoveries of esoteric wisdom such as the Gnostic Gospels and the Dead Sea Scrolls, revelations about Mary Magdalene's stature as Christ's beloved and his primary apostle, and lost histories of the Goddess cultures that preceded patriarchal religions for hundreds of thousands of years. Spiritual visionaries populated the internet, airwaves, and book industry, from the Dalai Lama to Eckhart Tolle; Deepak Chopra to Oprah and Tich Nhat Hanh; to the visionary Mamas Barbara Marx Hubbard, Jean Houston, and Marianne Williamson; to the visionary Grandmamas—The International Council of 13 Indigenous Grandmothers. Viral DVD movies such as *I AM, Tuning In: Spirit Channelers In America,* and *For the Next 7 Generations* invited open exploration of spirit. Spiritual Cinema Network financed the creation and offering of spiritually-focused movies via DVD. The proliferating offerings of such visionary spiritual teachers, videos, books, trainings and music was gathered and delivered at the online site, *inspire.TV.* Spiritual adepts channeled the Ascended Masters, the Archangels, and Divine Mother. Meditation was now a household word, and a common practice. Prayer was moving out of churches and into hearts.

Journalism and media were transforming too—being reclaimed by the masses to expose cover-ups of political, cultural and religious oppression and untruths—ranging from using Twitter and Facebook in the Arab Spring revolutions and the Occupy Movement, to the women's citizen journalism of *World Pulse Magazine,* that trained grassroots women leaders to become voices of change, to *Kosmos Magazine's* mission of giving voice to Global Citizens Creating the New Civilization.

Education was slowly making transformational inroads. Kindergarten through 12th grade education had alternative home schooling and wholistic-education-based private schooling movements, such as the Waldorf and Montessori Schools. These schools were based on wholistic educational philosophies that emphasized fostering reverence for life, passion for learning, and supporting the student's capacity for an identity based on connections to the natural world, spiritual values, community and life purpose. Too bad that agenda wasn't included in the public schools, which were still held hostage to political mandates focused on teaching to the achievement-tests' contents so that outcomes look good on paper. Graduate level education had some new prototypes: Wisdom University was dedicated to "providing full-spectrum transformational learning;" SEED Graduate Institute specifically incorporated Indigenous wisdom, ecology and quantum physics; the California Institute of Integral Studies included a School of Consciousness and Transformation.

Even the field of law was undergoing a shift into the heart, with movements toward restorative justice, mediation, and collaborative divorce.

Then there was politics. I had to admit, I couldn't come up with any examples of transformational unity-consciousness shifts that were revolutionizing politics, other than the appearance of global grassroots protestors. Hmmm. Maybe that indicated that our political/governance structures were simply too embedded in the old paradigm to be transformed? From what I could tell, politics was too deeply mired in polarized ego, with extreme agendas to look good (read: *be right*) by making the other side look bad (read: *be wrong*), and it was sinking to hate-mongering and negative fear-based tactics to achieve control and domination. Not much room there for a shift. Politics was effectively serving as a model for all that does *not* work in the New Earth of unity, which I admit is a role necessary to provide contrast.

Well... 13 domains transformed out of 14 wasn't bad. But politics and governance was a mighty big arena that held an awful lot of folks hostage with some pretty bad ju-ju.

I sat back, reviewing these promising transformational highlights, and felt reassured. Not just reassured, but inspired. Not just inspired, but excited, even proud of being an awakening divine human.

Divine human... Narby's DNA and the cosmic serpent... there, I was spinning off again. Next my whirlwind thoughts were dot-connecting to Gregg Braden's book, *The God Code*, where Braden documented that divinity is encoded into our DNA.

I had followed Gregg Braden's writings for years. He had become one of my spiritual mentors through his writings. Part visionary, part scientist and part scholar, his Divine Dot Connecting abilities were vast, bridging ancient wisdom and modern science. I shared this area of passion.

In his *God Code* book Braden used the ancient practice of gematria, the numerology assigned to sacred alphabets such as Hebrew, to determine a way to translate the numerology of our human DNA chemistry into a decoded message—derived from the atomic mass numbers of human DNA bases of Adenine, Cytosine, Guanine, and Thymine. He discovered a surprising translation: our cells carry the message, "God/Eternal within the body." That is the message that is decoded when the numerical chemistry of our DNA is translated by gematria into the letters of ancient Hebrew.

We are divine humans. We all carry serpent medicine of the cosmic serpent in our DNA. *And it is divine.*

Maybe now, with all this breakthrough information, the extreme, fundamental religions would stop demonizing the serpent—bringer of life and knowledge. And I could finally relax completely and talk openly about the serpent being my within power animal.

What would it be like today if we had never forgotten that we are divine humans? What will it be like when we all finally remember?

I remembered now, when my older son Adam was six, and requested to see photos of how a baby was made. Thinking resourcefully, I showed him Lennart Nilsson's breathtaking book *A Child Is Born* with its fetoscope photography of conception, the progress of fetal development, and photos of the baby emerging from the mother at childbirth. I will never forget his response.

After sitting reflectively for a few moments, he turned to look into my eyes and said with a tone of wonder, "I guess we all started out as miracles, huh, Mom? Even the criminals, right? But I guess they forgot that they were miracles."

True. Too many of us have forgotten that we were miracles, criminal or not.

And I recall the incident of my younger son Jake's response to me, when I apologized to him for being impatient with him at bedtime. He was three years old. He looked at me thoughtfully, with soulful eyes, lovingly took my hand, and said, "Mama, I forgive you always." Remembering that still takes my breath away!

Clearly and thankfully, young children have not forgotten yet who they really are: divine miracles full of love and compassion. Key word: YET. How do we reclaim a sacred world so that this core essence-self does not get buried, broken, or forgotten?

First step: climb out of material literalism and remember our divinity, and our interconnection with all Life.

Chapter 24 - Learning to Speak
the Cosmic Language

. . . .

FOR TWO DAYS, ON JUNE 5TH and 6th, 2012, humanity's eyes were unified in a collective act of witness, to the rare 105-year cycle of the Transit of Venus across the Sun.

I personally felt especially tuned in, riveted to this event. I had many astrological connections with Venus in my natal astrological chart. And I was astonished to learn that my birthdate, translated into the Mayan Calendar, corresponds with their day-glyph "Lamat" which means star, specifically the morning/evening star of Venus, whose transit is central to the Mayan creation story of the Popol Vuh. That really lit me up. My Mayan birthdate is "Lamat: Star, Venus!"

My energy field was buzzing. I sensed that my personal response to this Cosmic event was important; something to be mindful of, and to offer in service to the collective consciousness, to the noosphere. It was as if my eyes were to serve in an act of Sacred Seeing, to function as a proper filter through which to process this rare event on behalf of humanity, adding my symbolic understanding and my Sacred Saying. And I was up for this Divine Assignment.

Some confirming guidance flashed in. I recalled Gregg Braden discussing in his *Divine Matrix* book that we have the power to transform our lives by gaining a better understanding of our relationship to the "Matrix of All That Is"—to the Cosmos—*by learning how to listen to its messages, and learning how to communicate in its own language.*

I was excited about this homework. As a Sacred Seer and Sacred Sayer, I definitely wanted to refine my ability to communicate with the Cosmos in its own language.

As I studied the Language of the Cosmos occurring with the Venus Transit, the first thing I noticed was that the Transit would last two days. Two represented duality, the predominant experience of this material world. It did not necessarily mean polarized divisiveness, but it too often did. One of these challenging polarities was the lack of integration between the feminine and the masculine, between the logical left-brain and the relational right-brain. And so it was significant that on these two days, humanity would witness in the Heavens a Cosmic Union—a conjunction of the feminine and the masculine—embodied in the event of the feminine planet Venus transiting across the masculine Sun. This image of Cosmic Union above would support the transmutation below, of ego-based, divisive duality into partnership... Sacred Partnership. Duality in its transformed state is Sacred Partnership.

I understood that this phenomenon of "as above, so below" was an important aspect of the Cosmos speaking to humanity in its own language, the Language of Unity. Humanity was being invited to participate as a global witness to this feminine-masculine union in the heavens. And as this occurred in the heavens above, we would be assisted with integration of the masculine and feminine below, on Earth; consciously or not. I preferred consciously.

The next thing I tuned into was that Venus is the planet named after the ancient Roman Goddess of Love, and represents in the

Heavens that archetypal energy of the sacred feminine and the heart of love. The symbolism used by the ancients to represent Venus included the rose, the pentagram and the heart—all symbols that still express love and the divine feminine.

And amazingly, these symbols are the exact geometric patterns which science recently verified that Venus traces in her orbits! Venus actually traces a pattern of a five-petal rose as she orbits the Earth, each petal appearing as a heart-shape; and Venus traces a pattern of a pentagram, or five-pointed star, as she orbits around the Sun. *How did the ancients know?* Once again, science catches up to ancient knowledge.

I translated this Cosmic Language, portraying its meaning through my Sacred Seeing and Sacred Saying as a clear intention, and spoke it aloud in Earthly dialect:

"As this Venus Transit occurs, Earth and all her inhabitants are being bathed in this cosmic sacred geometry of Venus, the Love-bestowing Divine Feminine. And her Love-gifts are being amplified and supported by the solar energies of the Life-bestowing Divine Masculine, the Sun. The Sun is magnifying and propelling Venus's Love patterns towards Earth. The Feminine and Masculine heavenly forces of Creation are generating their beloved energies together, in divine union. The Feminine and the Masculine are unified. And humanity receives these upgraded-energies on Earth, integrating them. Earth is transmuting into the Home of Love."

There. That is strong, beautiful. That is a vision I am committed to stand for, I thought with satisfaction.

I continued to prepare for the first day of the Venus Transit Cosmic Union by pulling my guidance cards. My *Sacred Path* card for the process was Rite of Passage, depicting a ceremony that celebrates a person's change of status into the next milestone of Life. What a perfect a description of the intended impact of the Transit: humanity's global Rite of Passage. Into the heart of Love.

And my animal *Medicine Card* for the first day of the Transit was... TA-DAAA! None other than the Snake—that attentive Cosmic Serpent and my within animal guide. Of course the Serpent would be with me, facilitating humanity's global Rite of Passage and administering its profound medicine of transformation. What a synchronistic validation of all that was indeed in process.

The first day of Venus's Transit began. All across our beloved planet, in coherent, rapt attention, connected with technological eyes—of the internet, television, Facebook, online videos, telescopes, smart-phone downloads, emails, texts and tweets—and in live gatherings sharing the wonders of the event, humanity's eyes were glued to Venus. She began her rare 105-year cyclical transit across the Sun. This was the twin transit she began eight years ago in 2004. And humanity will have to wait another 105 years to bear witness to this twin transit process again, in the year 2117.

I arrived with friends at a our local community of unity event at the Mesa Creative Arts Center, joining a circle of Kindred Spirits organized by the Center's owners Brad and Kate Silberberg and led by Taino Elder and Mayan Calendar expert, Miguel Sague.

It was perfect that my dear friend and collaborator Miguel was the key presenter of the afternoon. With his animated storytelling he enacted the ancient Mayan creation story, the Popol Vuh, demonstrating the way that Venus's orbit has her appear both as the morning star and the evening star—the twin star. He told how Venus also represents the twin heroes descending into the underworld to defeat the Lords of Negativity at this moment in our historical cycle, at the closing of this Mayan Long Count. This timely Venus Transit of 2012 represents a long-fought victory over those Lords of Negativity, who have been holding all beings in a life-denying trance as they ruled with their domination, arrogance and greed for over five millennia.

We all listened, engrossed. What a fitting description from this most ancient story of our current moment in history, as the people collectively confront the arrogant greed of the 1%. *How did the ancient Maya see so perfectly into our future?* I wondered.

Miguel turned the group over to me. I passed out printed images of Venus's rose orbits, her pentagram orbits, and telescope photos of her small but mighty black dot moving across the flaring plasma rays of the vast orange and red Sun.

And I spoke of the power of the Sacred Feminine, as the power of Love, returning to defeat the Lords of Negativity.

I reminded those gathered that Venus is all about relationships and the feminine consciousness of the heart. The Mayan Long Count had tracked the 5,125 or so years of separation consciousness under the domination of Patriarchy, which severed the head from the heart, over-valued the linear, logical left-brain and under-valued the interconnective, intuitive right-brain. During this long timeframe, all levels of relationship had gone out of balance: relationship with self (the inner heart and self-love); relationship between the genders; relationship with Earth; even relationship with Spirit. All were negatively impacted due to a damaged relationship to the heart, to the inner and outer feminine, leaving the realm of relationships a big mess.

We have some major clean-up to do. This Fifth Sun—the Final Long Count era—of separation consciousness is now ending. The Patriarchal experiment of the love of power is now transitioning to the Power of Love. And with the Venus Transit, we are infused with Cosmic-level macro-assistance. It is our job to integrate it.

Now is the time: the opening to take our transformation as high and as deep as we can possibly imagine. We are entering the Great Transition, aka the Great Cosmic Clean-up. We are being supported above and below. And we need to make it GOOD, Honey! It is time to become Cosmic translators, speaking the Cosmic Language of Unity and Love.

It is amazing to be alive to experience the end of the Long Count of 5,125 years of Patriarchy, synchronized with the ending of the vast 26,000-year cycle of the Precession of the Equinoxes. Witnessing Venus and receiving her Love frequencies is part of this collective Rite of Passage into the arriving New Earth of Unity and the transition period into an emerging Golden Age, when at last the love of power is replaced by the Power of Love!

The second day of the Venus Transit arrived. Live-streaming computer images kept me transfixed with her cosmic transmissions and I wove them into my day's activities. Her energies were so palpably present with me. I noticed feeling buoyant, uplifted, and light-heartedly happy.

I received an email with a link to international photos of the Transit. The images were stunning views of Venus crossing the Sun, seen through the Sacred Eyes of my brothers and sisters all over the world. I couldn't resist printing several photos and creating a magnificent Grand Altar of Venus on my living room floor, adding to them the rose and pentagram images of her Earth and Sun orbits.

I gazed at these Venus images, and noticed a subtle inner swirling feeling like I was re-patterning my brain and my cellular structure. I wouldn't be at all surprised if that were really happening. Not to mention my heart. I just felt *so happy* viewing them.

My dear friend Tenanche came to join me in admiring the Grand Altar of Venus. She is the creator of Rosaflora Flower Essences, and I playfully referred to her as the Rose Queen. It delighted me that her middle and last names, Rose Golden, embodied that regal stature. It was her research that provided my introduction to the phenomenon of Venus's rose transit pattern, and also to the Hubble telescope photo of the new "Rose Galaxy" recently created by two galaxies colliding to unify into one—forming a celestial Rose. The image of that Rose Galaxy was also on the Venus Altar. It was so perfect for the Rose Queen to join me in honoring Venus.

In conducting research for her rose flower essences, Tenanche also discovered the microscopic rose-pattern visible within the cells of human connective tissue. We marveled at the evidence that humanity was infused with the Rose energies of Love both inwardly and outwardly. "As above, so below; as within, so without." Macrocosmically and micro-scopically, Love was appearing as the glue of the Universe; of Life. Tenanche and I were ecstatic about that secret emerging to become substantiated by left-brained science, in the service of LOVE made visible.

We couldn't stop gazing into the imagery of it all. And Tenanche also pointed out that the pentagram star-shaped pattern of Venus's Sun transits is mirrored in the pentagram form of the human body. She stood up to demonstrate the vertical head-and-trunk line with the four out-reaching radiating limbs of arms and legs: the pattern of a human star. We smiled, understanding the Cosmic Language reminding us that humans are divine-human star-beings.

That observation triggered the memory of a magnificent chant created by another cosmically-aligned friend of mine, Gail Ransom. It went:

> "We are, we are we are *Stardust*
> We are, we are we are *Fire*
> We are, we are we are *Stardust*
> We are *Love!*" ©

I immediately began singing the chant aloud. I laughed and told Tenanche that I imagined this as the song Venus was singing as she transited the Sun. Tenanche agreed, and we sang another round. Then Tenanche reminded me of another chant, an Indigenous Taino song:

"The women have within them
The rhythm of the Universe."

A beautiful tribute from Divine Feminine Venus to the women of this Earth, I mused. We honored the message of that chant as well singing it joyously.

We fell silent, each tracking our inner attention in a flow of awareness. I next became absorbed by the image of another one of the Transit photos: the vast disc of the Sun as a backdrop to the tiny dot of Venus conjunct within it.

That particular image reminded me of the illustration on the *Sacred Path* card I had pulled for this second day of the Venus Transit. It was called The Great Smoking Mirror: Reflections. It showed a human sitting below, looking up at the Great Mirror disc above. The human was doing a Sacred Pipe ceremony of unity, honoring All Our Relations, and was offering the smoke up to the huge disc-Mirror in the sky. This heavenly disc above showed another human face within it, mirroring the human in ceremony below. My photo image of Venus reminded me of that card.

I showed the card image to Tenanche. The image of The Great Smoking Mirror: Reflections, was instructing me to see the vast Sun and the tiny Venus conjunct within it as a mirror, a reminder, that we are each a unique localized expression of that Infinite Divinity. The Universe is expressing as each unique one of us.

And with that realization, the core teaching of that Great Smoking Mirror card was emphasized: We are all reflections of the Infinite One. As the Maya say, "In Lak'esh." It means "I am another one of yourself." This phrase also translates as "We are different faces of each other." I smiled, recognizing more Cosmic Language of Unity and Love.

My version of that same Cosmic message, given to me from the Spirit of the Serpent at my adventure at the Serpent Mound was:

I am in you.
You are in me.
We belong to Each Other.

Chapter 25 - Dreamtime
Messages: Unlimited Vision

. . . .

I WAS ON HIGH ALERT AGAIN.

My *Sacred Path* card for the day was Dreamtime: Unlimited Vision. This card teaches about the Indigenous understanding of dreams as offering access into parallel realities, which sounds more like quantum Superstring theory than ancient wisdom. *Maybe someday science would finally catch up to Indigenous Shamanic knowledge,* I thought.

I also pulled an animal *Medicine Card* and received Porcupine, expressing the innocence of Faith, and trust in a Divine Plan guiding Creation.

As I picked up Jamie Sams' two books to re-read the text and listen for which parts of the teachings would emerge as most relevant for the day, something interrupted my attention. I was stunned.

Underneath the two books, lying on the floor, was an ankle bracelet.

"What? What in the world is this doing here?" I exclaimed aloud to myself. I had not thought about this ankle bracelet in years. I had not looked at it. I had not touched it. I had forgotten it even existed. And here it was, showing up underneath two books that

I used every day, in a spot that was visible to me every day. *What was that?*

I picked up the ankle bracelet, examining it. It was made from small yellow round Citrine stone beads. Yellow, the color from my Seneca Medicine Wheel studies that represented LOVE—as the Lover/Conquerer, conquering obstacles with LOVE. And the ankle bracelet had a silver charm of a dragonfly. I recalled that the Dragonfly was one of the four creatures serving as guardians to the Dreamtime. My hair prickled. Dreamtime was my guidance card for the day. And Dragonfly Medicine also served as a Buster of the Illusions of physical reality.

Ah, yes, Dragonfly was sure bursting MY illusions of physical reality by manifesting this ankle bracelet underneath my books, where Spirit knew I could not fail to notice it.

Like I said, I was on high alert again.

My hair continued prickling and my goose-bumps were vibing. That Dragonfly was underlining the need to pay attention to the Dreamtime card message.

I read from Sams' book:

"The parallel Dreamtime reality is where your soul or spirit is operating on a continual basis to send you information. The waking dreams of the Dreamtime can overlay into the sleeptime reality if the need to know is strong enough. The Dreamtime reality is as ancient as our universe and holds all possible doors to every level of awareness."

"[Dreamtime] abilities can be achieved through contacting the four animal Allies who are most strongly connected to the Dreamtime. The Dragonfly is the Doorkeeper who allows the gates to the other dimensions to be opened, through the breaking of the physical illusion."

Wow. The Dragonfly apparently was not waiting for me to contact it. It was contacting ME. Go Dragonfly! Open that Dreamtime door for me, Honey! I was cheering inwardly as I read on.

"The Dreamtime is asking you to see with unlimited vision; pay attention to the messages that you are receiving from the parallel universe. You are a co-creator in the Two Worlds and will be given unlimited sight and knowing if you ask for it."

Thank you, once again, Jamie Sams. And Great Spirit.

Okey-dokey. I was now honoring Dragonfly, polishing up the silver charm, and putting the bracelet onto my left ankle, making literal contact. And I was now sending out the intention for unlimited sight; *another way of being a Sacred Seer,* I chuckled.

I invoked grandmother Dona's favorite practice: S-T-A-R:

"I **SURRENDER** to the highest guidance. I stand in **TRUST**. I **ALLOW**. I **RECEIVE!**

I immediately recalled two other recent Dreamtime transmissions that had each crossed over from sleep into waking attention.

The first of these two Dreamtime experiences was the phenomenon I already described, that awoke me on the day of my first trip to meet Grandmother Dona and collaborate with her at the Great Serpent Mound. That was when I was wakened from my sleep by the commanding Cosmic Voice penetrating into my awareness by articulating the single word, "ECSTATIC!" just preceding the 7:32 AM moment that my alarm sounded, in a cosmic punctuation of that message. And that 7:32 had appeared a total of five times since then, further punctuating other profound moments. Five, the number of the star-pentagram embodied in the divine human form, the human star.

Synchronistically, I had also been led to material on numerology that finally illuminated the significance of the recurring 7:32 phenomenon. The numerology of seven represents Spirit or the Spiritual realm. Three represents catalytic energy and joy. And two represents duality, especially human duality. So taken together, the numerology of 7:32 was translatable into the Cosmic Language message, "Spirit using the catalytic energy of joy to transform humanity."

I would certainly characterize my adventures with my Kindred Spirits at the Serpent Mound and in Pittsburgh this way. Better to have the catalyst be joy than suffering, I always say! And I recalled Mayan spiritual teacher Ac Tah being adamant that joy—not fear— was the needed catalyst for our collective 2012 Shift, facilitating our emergence into the New Earth and humanity's Golden Age beyond that timeframe.

The other Dreamtime message I now recalled had occurred a few months ago. I had awakened from a disturbing dream where Grandmother Dona and I were crouching behind a hedge, witnessing predatory males operating with hate and aggression. After I awoke to recall that vivid, repellant image, I lay quietly pondering *why—with all of my experiences of the accelerating frequencies of 2012—was I being shown that image of predatory consciousness, especially since I knew that it was dissipating from our planet as Earth ascended into higher Love frequencies?*

While I lay pondering this question—awake, but with my eyes still closed—I witnessed another vivid visual. As if I were dreaming again, but I wasn't, I saw a room where the dust-infused air was being streamed with a shaft of light that made all the dust particles suddenly visible. As I watched these dust particles randomly floating in the air, I was startled to observe that a whole group of the dust particles were suddenly re-arranging themselves into the constellation of the Big Dipper.

As I watched this stunning nocturnal revelation in amazement, I heard that now-familiar Cosmic Voice declaring, in a calm and authoritative manner: "Rest assured, no matter what the appearance of your reality currently looks like, know that everything in

Creation—even the specks of dust—are aligning with the frequencies of Oneness. REST ASSURED."

That voice carried such a calm and magnificent ring of authority that I was truly resting, assured. However, I remained curious as to why the constellation depicted in my waking Dreamtime transmission was the Big Dipper, of all the possible constellations rather than, say, the Pleiades, which repeatedly kept coming up in connection with Mayan material and ascension material as well.

My answer to that question had also shown up with a rapid synchronistic reassurance.

A day later, scanning through David Tresemer's book *The Venus Eclipse of the Sun 2012,* I was stunned to read that the Hindu and Vedic texts referred to Seven Rishis or Sages, who have overseen humanity's development since its inception, and who were often identified with the seven stars of the Big Dipper, as the great seven above, in heavenly counterpart to the seven earthly sages below.

You could have knocked me over with a feather.

So I had already learned to deeply trust (which was today's teaching from Porcupine) the messages from the Dreamtime; that a Divine Plan was being overseen, and that, while humanity still must do our part, all was well. "As above, so below," indeed.

After properly noting this stunning stream of Divine Dot Connection within my own musings, I continued on high alert to see where my attention wanted to be directed next.

I noticed feeling quite drawn to go find the new book I had just gotten from the recent Evolver Pittsburgh conference: *Manifesto for the Noosphere,* by the late Jose Arguelles, which was highly recommended by Evolver co-founder and author, Daniel Pinchbeck. I hadn't had a chance to look at it, but it was definitely calling to me now. As I searched for my copy of the book, I recalled the quadruple rainbow that had appeared just following the Evolver Pittsburgh weekend's closing group ceremony. And I recalled that Pinchbeck had said something about Arguelles' material; about a Rainbow Bridge, and humans manifesting rainbows.

The Evolver attendees had flooded outside to marvel together at the quadruple rainbow. Daniel Pinchbeck and many others of us agreed that we had played a part in manifesting this quadruple rainbow. All weekend long, we had been in a heart-field together. We had assembled as Rainbow Warriors of all races, ages and sizes, heart-fully focused on expressing our highest visions of a more beautiful future, that would be brought into being through expressing the gifts of our highest Essence Selves—our unique Original Medicine. Now the Cloud Beings were sending validating Sky Language as an agreement from the Universe of our successful Evolver weekend—a message in the quadruple rainbows, as if to say: "As below in Pittsburgh, so above in these rainbows. You made it so good, we are producing four rainbows!" Some even commented that the four rainbows mirrored Pittsburgh's four converging rivers.

I smiled with this memory as I opened up the small book and casually flipped through its opening pages, until author Jose Arguelles' words on page 11 literally leapt off the page at me and riveted my attention:

"Like the Dreamtime known to our aboriginal ancestors, the noosphere is the collective unconscious impelled into conscious awareness."

I felt a confirming electrical shock jolt through me. I was in awe. As experienced as I was in the appearance and the workings of synchronicity, this phenomenon was still overwhelming when it showed up with this degree of perfection and profound impact.

How amazing was this: *I pull the Dreamtime guidance card, with teachings from ancient Indigenous wisdom. Then, my own immediate reality is shape-shifted by the manifestation of a Dreamtime phenomenon, connected to the inexplicable appearance of a forgotten ankle bracelet with a Dragonfly charm; the Dragonfly being the dreamtime guardian. Next, I recall previous Dreamtime events that have taught me to trust the strange intrusion of Dreamtime messages.*

And then I am led to instructions in a book about the modern reincarnation of the Dreamtime appearing as the Noosphere.

I kept shaking my head, as if to make sure this wasn't a dream. Then I burst out laughing. *It isn't a dream. It is the Dreamtime! Here I am, being given Divine instruction, through the medium of the Dreamtime itself, about the Dreamtime's own reappearance in modern incarnation as the Noosphere. Hilarious.*

I recalled that Barbara Marx Hubbard and her impressive group of collaborators communicating from the pages of her newly released book *Birth 2012 And Beyond: Humanity's Great Shift Into the Age of Conscious Evolution* also highly endorsed Jose Arguelles' *Manifesto for the Noosphere*. I followed that Trail of Guidance and found Hubbard's reference to the Noosphere described as "knitting together our global brain/mind/heart, synchronized by cosmic mind." Awesome.

I took a deep breath and returned to reading Arguelles' book.

"Human beings, as agents of the noosphere, would eventually lead to a new state of collective planetary wholeness. Humanity is now going through its final preparation to enter, as a harmonized collective, into this *new conscious dreamtime.*" [Italics mine]

I had to stand up and walk around to reground myself. A big energy was filling me. I wanted to cry and to giggle, at the same time. *This was making so much sense. And it was moving; inspiring; breathtaking. Okay, okay, breathe. Now, back to Arguelles:*

"In speaking of it as an entry into a new dreamtime, we are casting the Noosphere into the psycho-mythic framework of a planetary emergence myth—a planetary rite of passage, wiping away the old world into the new creation of the next world."

Wow. Arguelles was fitting all of this neatly into the mythic framework of the Hopi, Mayan and Aztec myths and prophecies. And into a global Rite of Passage. This man was speaking my language.

My thoughts were racing. Go Arguelles! What an ally that guy is. However, he is on the other side now, helping us from his beloved Dreamtime-Noosphere.

Words from my Multi-Dimensional Beings rap song were floating into my thoughts now:

> "The magic of the Earth
> She will Dream through us
> Our hearts so open
> Love will stream through us
> We are multi-dimensional beings."

Of Course. The Earth will Dream through us... if we allow it. The Earth herself wants to participate as a player in this grand Dreamtime Planetary Rite-of-Passage. And why not? Gaia Mother Earth was finally being understood as a conscious Being.

I looked down at the Dragonfly on my ankle bracelet. It seemed that if it had not been attached, it would have soared around the room in jubilation! My whole body felt like it was humming in joyful celebration; in victory.

As if that weren't enough, something else was now tickling my awareness, wanting to capture my attention from this Dreamtime-as-Noosphere. I sat attentive in Sacred Listening. Sure enough, *Dayenu*, another message was clearly emerging. It was the Great Invocation from Starhawk, author and Priestess of the Divine Feminine. This message seemed a perfect summary of our planetary rite-of-passage into the New Earth, our collectively co-created next world. And it was appearing in perfect timing, as if on cue:

> "All began in Love,
> All seeks to return to Love.
> Love is the Law,
> The Teacher of Wisdom,
> The Great Revealor of Mystery."

I was moved to tears now, my Tears of Truth. *Love is the LAW. How perfect is that?* Now I giggled, as another Dreamtime experience from my more distant past crowded in. The dream arising in my memory was an auditory dream of a clear conversation without any visuals. In Dreamtime I had asked, *"How shall we communicate then?"* And that calm, authoritative, now-familiar Cosmic Voice had declared the profound and simple answer that would resolve all obstacles to communication: *"Through only LOVE."*

Of course. Humantity would be learning to communicate in that feeling-language; we would become fluent in the Cosmic Language of Unity and Love.

"The magic of the Earth/She will Dream through us/Our hearts so open/Love will stream through us." I realized that this song, and all of the songs I had received from the New Earth were revealing the same Dreamtime message.

Amen! Awomen! I was being shown that we were not only receiving help *from* the Dreamtime/Cosmic Mind/Noosphere, but we were *co-creating with it*, infusing it with our highest visions! We were conscious *co-creators.*

There was no need to doubt that we were becoming collective Sacred Seers and Sacred Sayers. Our collective power to call forth our own planetary rite-of-passage into the New Earth of Unity, Oneness, Peace and Love was clearly established, supported by the new Dreamtime-as-Noosphere, and synchronized by cosmic mind.

Chapter 26 - The Serpent Speaks

. . . .

THE VIVID PRESENCE OF THESE DREAMTIME lessons continued to accompany me into the next day. I felt an excitement like a young child unleashed with her first experience of blowing bubbles; that sense of pure exhilarating joy. The purity of that joy kept flowing through from the Dreamtime-as-Noosphere. I accepted it as a substantiating feeling-language confirmation of the arriving New Earth.

I kept peeking up at the sky, anticipating a glimpse of that vast Planetary Rainbow Bridge surrounding Earth that Arguelles described was possible for humans to generate from our entrained hearts of loving intention. I wanted to be part of generating such a "planetary work of art," as Arguelles called it.

After a buoyant, playful and celebratory day, bedtime arrived. Still feeling connected to the Dreamtime language, I went to sleep and had an unusually vivid dream. My dreams rarely have significant tactile sensations, but this dream emphasized the tactile dimension quite dramatically.

I dreamed that I was holding a magnificent Python snake in my right hand; my writing hand. I vividly experienced its weight as

I held it, and its muscular, sensual, undulating movements. I could feel the Python's extraordinary skin patterns, and the nuances of its texture and temperature.

As I marveled at the serpent, I noticed that it had a second head on its tail end! And that other head looked like it was talking. Its mouth was moving open and closed as if in conversation. Then I heard the Python emit a high-pitched sound-frequency, that I understood to be a signal of alert, that more was to be communicated. I felt that the Python knew that I understood its unusual language. Then I woke up.

So, the Dreamtime *was* still with me! That dream was so vivid that I truly could not tell I was dreaming, until I saw the serpent's second head. *What was it trying to tell me?*

It was three days before the demands of my work life allowed me to tune in and ask in a process of Sacred Listening, at the Summer Solstice. I opened my connection with my Higher Guidance in my usual way, and surrendered into divine service, offering to be a mouthpiece, asking if there was more for me to receive.

I was stunned as another song immediately arrived. I had not considered that there would ever be another song for me to catch. After all (I was giggling now at the silliness of my own sense of recurring surprise) I was not a musician, nor a singer, nor a songwriter... but sure enough, a song was arriving. This time, the song was from the Spirit of the Serpent.

I captured it in my journal, as the verses arrived. I was completely moved. OF COURSE! It made perfect sense that a song from Serpent would want to arrive.

The song from the Cosmic Serpent was arriving to be a part of the re-balancing and restoring of the Sacred Feminine, so maligned and distorted under millennia of Patriarchy. Its message served to remind humanity that the Serpent in the Garden was embodying the Life Force of the Ancient Great Goddess at the Ancient Tree of Life, not Satan.

Of course the Serpent herself would want to assert her voice, as the creative Life Force of Love returns to its proper place of power in the arriving New Earth.

I read over the verses of the Song from the Cosmic Serpent. It had verses that gave instruction of right relationship and reverent understanding of Serpent Medicine. And it incorporated the information of the *inner* Cosmic Serpent, a la Jeremy Narby's anthropological documentation of the Serpent in our DNA. And it had a refrain that sounded celebratory. I found myself singing a playful, catchy melody to the words:

Song from the Cosmic Serpent
Summer Solstice, 2012

"There is a secret; and it's hidden in plain sight.
If you are ready, you can learn it with delight
For once you know it, you will hold the Sacred Key
To transform Reality.

So thank the Serpent, Ancient Teacher to behold.
She shows the process: Shedding skin of the Old
Through grounded movement, in communion with the Earth.
What a glorious re-birth!

Sacred Serpent: Symbol of Ancient Mother
Sacred Serpent: Living in our DNA
Sacred Serpent: New Life Bringer
Sacred Serpent: Revealer of Mystery.

The Sacred Serpent, living in our DNA
Is activating humanity's templates.
An inner blessing, from the Serpent in our cells
Shifts us into our Highest Selves.

232

Her Kundalini, arising in our spines:
Her Life Force Essence, awakening our minds.
A Transformation—the Prophecy foretold—
Earth's Golden Age to behold!

Sacred Serpent: Symbol of Ancient Mother
Sacred Serpent: Living in our DNA
Sacred Serpent: New Life Bringer
Sacred Serpent: Revealer of Mystery."

I called Grandmother Dona in excitement, and shared the song with her, and the dream preceding its arrival. She was ecstatic. "Oh, Victoria, how perfect! What incredible words. That Python was calling to you through the Dreamtime's parallel reality. You did an amazing job catching the Song in your sacred listening. I need to sing it at the Serpent Mound. I wish you were here to sing it with me."

"Well," I offered, "as I am listening to you now, I am seeing a visual of you singing the Serpent song at the Serpent Mound sacred site, while I sing the Serpent song at the Four Rivers sacred site. And since the two sites are now vibrantly connected, through the serpent force activated in the underground waters, we can just consider this a simultaneous bi-location ceremony."

Grandmother Dona's voice nearly jumped through the phone, "That's it! That's what we need to do; a synchronized, bi-local ceremony." Then we both began musing about what else wanted to occur as a part of this ceremony.

"You know," Grandmother Dona pondered, "I have these Trail of Tears beads from my Spider Medicine necklace that broke repeatedly this week. It broke three times. There's that cosmic signal, "three," again. I think that I am supposed to offer those beads to the Spirit of the Serpent. Those beads are the symbol of the grief of the Native peoples as they were forcibly removed from their ancestral lands by government soldiers. The routes that they were made to walk are called The Trail of Tears. The beads symbolize their tears that fell to Earth as they waked their Trail of Tears leaving their beloved homelands. It is said that where each of their tears fell as they cried along that trail, a corn-like plant grew up. It is the seeds of this plant, called corn beads, that are called the Trail of Tears beads.

She paused a bit to gather her thoughts further. "What sorrow and grief that Trail of Tears recorded. Those beads of suffering are not going to hold my power necklace together any longer. They must be given to Mother Earth and the Serpent, who will transmute their suffering."

I was completely moved by the potent synchronicities of what was unfolding. Before I could reply, Grandmother Dona interrupted our musings. "Victoria!" she called out through the phone.

"What is it?" I asked, my hair already prickling.

Grandmother Dona's voice was hushed now, reverent, "I just realized something… something very holy and miraculous…"

"Well… tell me!"

"I recall just reading about this online. At this very time, Grandmother Margaret of the 13 Grandmothers—called Grandmother Red Spider Woman of the Cheyenne—is re-enacting the Cheyenne Trail of Tears! She is leading a group of Cheyenne on horseback, from Oklahoma to Lame Deer, Montana, for the next gathering there of the International Council of 13 Indigenous Grandmothers. As the Cheyenne recreate their Trail of Tears to heal their history in current time, we will simultaneously be doing the meta-ceremony in our two locations, to infuse it all with the healing and transmuting energies of the Serpent and Divine Mother!

I was so moved that I could barely speak. We both sat in awed silence, in recognition of the magnitude of this synchronistically-guided and inspired process.

"Wow." I replied, "I get it. I am so moved. The synchronicity of our ceremony is timed to perfection. And I have a bottle of 'Mary's Tears' that was created as a vibratory water essence from the tears caught from a weeping statue of Mother Mary in Italy. I will sprinkle her loving tears of compassion over the Earth at the Four Rivers site in Pittsburgh, as you release the tears of suffering at the Serpent Mound. Both the Sacred Serpent and Divine Mother's love will dissolve and transmute that path of suffering imposed by separation consciousness that is ending now on our planet. May the Trail of Tears end for the Indigenous peoples and for all people. May the Trail we walk now be on the Trail of Love."

"Oh, that is so beautiful, so perfect," Grandmother Dona agreed. "We will embody "holographic resonance," by symbolically enacting the transformation that we intend. We will project that highest vision into the Noosphere; into humanity's upgraded Dreamtime consciousness. As Sacred Seers and Sacred Sayers, we will energize the intention that humanity is now freed from being hostage to separation, domination, greed and suffering. And that symbolic enactment of healing is also what Grandmother Margaret will be doing simultaneously on her end, as the Cheyenne complete their journey on horseback in Lame Deer, Montana. Oh, Victoria, this is all happening with such aligned perfection!"

My goosebumps were in arriving in waves. "Wow. Well spoken. I guess we need to acknowledge that our ceremony is actually a TRI-local ceremony! The Serpent Mound, Ohio, The Point of the Four Rivers in Pittsburgh, Pennsylvania, and culminating in Lame Deer, Montana."

"That is so magnificent," Grandmother Dona acknowledged.

I continued, "Well, for the Love part of the ceremony, I also have a vase full of beautiful miniature rosebuds—maybe five dozen—that suddenly wilted and dried on their stems yesterday. Roses are the symbol of love, and of Divine Mother. I was so astonished and disappointed when they wilted, but now I see that they must have been readying themselves for this ceremony. How did they know?" I laughed. "They have dried themselves so perfectly. I will harvest them for our ceremony."

I added, "Let's intend to synchronize our bi-local parts of the ceremonies. As you drop the Trail of Tears beads at the Serpent Mound, I will replace the Trail of Suffering with the Trail of Love represented by dropping a Trail of Rosebuds, as a symbol of Divine Mother's love. I will drop rosebuds as I walk at the converging Four Rivers site, after sprinkling the purifying Mother Mary Tears."

"Yes!" Grandmother Dona declared. "We are reclaiming this planet as the Home of Love." Her voice sounded triumphant.

"Yes!" I declared in response, "because we say so! We are HOME. It is BEAUTIFUL. It is COMPLETE."

"BECAUSE WE SAY SO!" we both declared in unison, laughing.

We now had our ceremonial plan for our synchronized bi-location ceremony that we would enact tomorrow. And it felt ECSTATIC.

I said goodnight to Grandmother Dona and hung up. I was glowing. I returned to my musings about the Python dream and the profound Song from the Cosmic Serpent.

So THAT is what the Python in my dream wanted me to stay alert for: its song. And how moving that this song from the Cosmic Serpent arrived on the Summer Solstice; the time when the warmth of summer enlivens all creatures with the longest day of vibrant light. And in perfect timing to ceremonially support the real-time historic enactment of transmuting the Trail of Tears into the Trail of Love.

But why the Python, I wondered, *of all the snakes I could have dreamed about?* I reached into the neurons of my brain to recall my Greek mythology lessons. I vaguely recalled that the Python was connected to the Oracle of Delphi. I checked out the Python online and in some of my personal library's references.

Wow, sure enough. Python was the Earth-dragon who guarded the Oracle of Delphi of ancient history, and was typically portrayed as a serpent. This made sense to me, since the two animals were so interchangeable; the dragon being the celestial serpent.

Python's mother was Gaia, Mother Earth herself. And the Oracle of Delphi originally was the domain of the Earth Goddess and her priestesses, who channeled the wisdom and prophesies of the future, receiving their revelations through the earth-opening at the sacred navel stone of Omphalos, considered to be the umbilicus to the womb-center of the Earth.

The priestess who channeled the Oracle at Delphi was named after its guardian, Python, and was called Pythia. In some accounts, the original Oracle was the Python itself. *Hmmm,* I mused. *Python is another version of the Cosmic Serpent as bringer of the Life Force and bringer of knowledge that all the ancient Indigenous Shamanic traditions acknowledge and respect.* I sent out a blessing of gratitude to my Dreamtime Python.

I resumed my research.

As Patriarchy increasingly took over, the Oracle of Delphi was corrupted. The Oracle's fate mirrored the fate of all the non-violent, non-warring Goddess-based cultures previously pervasive on the Earth. After sufficient time under Patriarchal domination, the Oracle closed, and Goddess-based cultures faded from existence, barely noted in Patriarchal records of history.

Mother Earth, it seemed, was not willing to offer prophetic wisdom under Patriarchal domination. And, as we have seen, the intuitive, interconnected right-brain of Oneness atrophied with the over-development of the linear, logical, left-brain of separation-consciousness, employed by male-dominated Patriarchal perspectives. What a tragic loss.

The original power and meaning of the Serpent was disguised, debased and demonized. Women's status was likewise denigrated.

But that important interconnection and attunement with Mother Earth—the Sacred Feminine and her Serpent Wisdom—was once again being restored in many ways on the planet during this historic timeframe. And now, it was being restored by this amazing song from the Spirit of the Cosmic Serpent herself. Reclaimed. Remembered. Revered once again. Released from hostage-status, after 5,125 or so years of being demonized, defiled and degraded, along with women, and the Ancient Great Goddess.

Finally, the Serpent and her Medicine—her Life Force—were being recognized and revalued once again. I recalled the Mayan glyph that Grandmother Flordemayo showed me in 2008. It was the final Mayan glyph from the Dresden Codex of the Maya, depicting the current timeframe we are now living. This final glyph showed the Spirit of the Feminine holding the Staff of Power that was being transferred from the Spirit of the Masculine. That Staff of Power resembled a serpent.

On the same synchronistic page as that Mayan glyph, Ross Hamilton had recently shared with me his spiritually-guided plans to create a modern version of the ancient Mystery School in the Serpent Mound area of Ohio. This Mystery College would restore the nearly-lost knowledge and arts of deep spiritual initiation of humanity, in service to our own transformation. It would educate its students to participate in deep service to humankind, animal kind, and perhaps most urgently at this time, to the Earth herself. And the first project of this vision would be to establish "The Oracle of the Grandmothers." That Oracle would follow the original guidelines and resurrected technology of the ancient Oracle of Delphi, and would be owned and operated entirely by women, dedicated to the service of all.

This was stunning, to reflect on all of this....

And now my thoughts meandered to the various psychics over the years who had told me that I had lived multiple lives serving as a Priestess for the Great Goddess, including lifetimes as an Oracle at Delphi.

I recalled how, since my early 20's, I had resonated with the psychological archetype of the High Priestess as my inner Soul-archetype; how I had spontaneously created "working altars" for over 30 years; how I had marked my 50th birthday with a collaboratively-created Priestess Ordination Ceremony as a public celebration of my inner Priestess.

And I smiled as I remembered that two summers ago—just before Grandmother Flordemayo had facilitated my introduction to Grandmother Dona—I had done a ceremony at my Sacred Tree, offering myself as a mouthpiece in service to Mother Earth and Divine Mother.

Then shortly after that consecration, I was given the gift of the taxidermy-preserved baby rattlesnake and I created my Altar of Surrender. I shed the skin of my limited self. I called Grandmother Dona the next day, and one month later the two of us made our first collaborative journey to the Great Serpent Mound in Ohio.

Chapter 27 - The Final Revelation

· ·

THE MAGIC CONTINUED. I RECEIVED ONGOING confirmations that I truly have returned Home to a sacred world. My ongoing experience fit with the description from Jamie Sams' *Sacred Path* card, Shawl: Returning Home—"coming home to the magic you once believed in; honoring the beauty in each unique expression of Creation; coming home to the embrace of Mother Earth and being loved and loving." This described how I live now.

I was still working on the final edits of this story, before sending them off to my editor. As I did so, something Big happened.

I was proofreading the Dreamtime chapter. While immersed in the editing, an even deeper, fuller impact of the meaning of that chapter lit me up and I began weeping my Tears of Truth. I was so filled with awe. I had to stop and make an immediate pilgrimage of gratitude to my Sacred Tree in my personal Power Place. It was late, already a bit after 7 PM; I knew the cemetery gates would be locked at 8 PM.

Still teary upon my arrival, I walked toward my Tree singing the five sacred songs given to me throughout the timeframe of this story, feeling radiant. I was stopped in my tracks by two lively groundhogs frisking around the graves nearby. I wondered, *What are they doing still out and about at dusk? They are usually safe in their lairs by this time, ready to bed down.* Their behavior was so unusual. They were actually climbing up on large headstones of three different graves. I had watched groundhogs here on many occasions, but had never seen them do this. It took quite an effort for them to hoist their plump bodies up onto these sizeable elaborate family grave markers. I continued watching.

The two groundhogs were playing repeatedly upon three particular headstones. The names on the gravestones were Rote, Wright and Priddy. The larger groundhog hoisted his body up onto the Wright headstone again. This time he pulled himself upright to a standing position upon the headstone, which was situated between Rote and Priddy. He focused his gaze directly to me. I bowed to honor him. The second groundhog scampered out of sight.

The larger groundhog remained in stillness, fully upright, gazing at me. That is when the groundhogs' message hit me. Rote, Wright, Priddy.

Oh my Goddess! The groundhogs are communicating to me, "you rote it wright priddy, Honey!" They are speaking to me using the words on the gravestones! They want me to know they think that I wrote my story right pretty! That I made it GOOD, Honey! I broke out in a big grin, bowing to them and letting them know that I got their communication. I recalled the words of my Multi-dimensional Beings song: "The animals, they will speak to us/Nature Spirits will be real to us." I giggled realizing that they were quite resourceful in finding effective ways to speak to us.

I became aware of the sun setting in the darkening clouds, mindful that the cemetery gates would be locked soon. *Here I am again,* I thought, *in a spontaneous co-creative ceremony with Nature on behalf of the New Earth, at the closing of the day. There really IS something important about this time of dusk.*

I looked at my watch. It was 7:32 PM.

Electricity shot through my being, in recognition of yet another confirmation from the Dreamtime. I recalled the numerology of 7:32, translated as "Spirit using joy to catalyze humanity's transformation." I bowed again to my groundhog ceremonial partners. This certainly was a joyful collaborative celebration of the Spirit-guided messages of my book, and the Dreamtime chapter in particular that I had just been focused upon editing.

The larger groundhog now climbed off the large headstone and came even closer to me, between two of the flat cement block casket markers lying in front of the huge family headstone. His eyes were still focused on mine. He was so close that I could see each of his whiskers. We gazed at each other in a sweet communion of connection and appreciation, until he disappeared into his borrow hole right there, between the two cement casket markers.

Sweet dreams, dear Friend, I thought in silent blessing and goodnight. I continued on with my walk, after a brief visit to my Sacred Tree. I returned home to complete my edit review of the final pages of my last chapter, and sent the document to my editor. I was still basking in the energies of oneness and miracles I had experienced at the cemetery.

Before going to bed, I consulted Ted Andrews' *Animal Speak* book, to remind myself about the groundhog's medicine. All that I could recall was that groundhogs were connected to Shamanism, trance states, and the mystery of "death without dying," due to their ability to alter their body temperature and hibernate through the winter months.

When I re-read the groundhog section, a passage jumped off the pages and I bolted up out of my chair: the groundhog is also the symbol of opening fully to the *Dreamtime!* And its medicine allows the individual to use the Dreamtime more powerfully, including altered states of awareness. My thoughts were racing so intensely now. I had to pace around my room and ground my energy in order to settle down.

The dots connected so powerfully now: The Dreamtime chapter was what had propelled me to the cemetery! And I came home from there with the 7:32 Dreamtime message delivered by its ally, the groundhog, that I wrote it right pretty, Honey!

Wow.

It took me a while to wind down from all of that. Once I finally went to bed, I was so tired. But I could not fall asleep. I was still feeling flooded with the power and the magnitude of the revelations of this story, *The Seer and The Sayer*. I was feeling such deep gratitude that I had served as its mouthpiece. And to think, I had almost refused to write the story.

I tossed and turned. I realized that, as stunning as all this was, I did not quite know how to talk about my book to people. Describing it did not lend itself to sound-bites and elevator speeches. Then I realized that I myself needed to open more fully, to understand the magnitude of my own story's message—*for myself.* That understanding would allow me to be a better mouthpiece for my story's mega-message.

After some deep musing, the mega-message that I became clear about is this:

We are living in an aware Universe that wants us to be co-creators with it at this time in history. This aware and loving Universe is inviting us, along with all of Life, to write the story of Creation together.

And it is through becoming Sacred Seers and Sacred Sayers that humanity is empowered to collaborate—with the Intelligence of Nature and Creation Itself—to write this next story of Creation together: the story of the New Earth and a fulfilled future of the next Golden Age of Peace.

243

I knew for sure that the magic would continue. The New Earth is here. We ARE Home now. Many are learning how to live as Sacred Seers and Sacred Sayers. And many, many more will join us.

Afterword

REMEMBER.

Remember not to identify with the toxic appearances of the dissipating Old World as it transforms. REST ASSURED. Everything is aligning with the frequencies of Oneness.

Remember that challenges are best dealt with as disguised blessings for growth and mastery.

Remember to surrender your ego, allowing it to be in service to your Soul- essence and its Original Medicine gifts of your unique puzzle piece that you are here to contribute.

Remember to cultivate and catalyze joy, not fear, to become a Sacred Seer and a Sacred Sayer of the New Earth consciousness.

Remember to keep adding to the Dreamtime/Noosphere's collective brain/mind/heart by participating with your own acts of Sacred Seeing and Sacred Saying.

Remember to trace the New Earth from the Future back to the Present. Live from the inspiration of this highest vision.

Remember to learn the Cosmic Language of Unity and Love. It appears in the dialects of synchronicity, alignments, resonance, intuition, telepathy, ceremony, communion and revelation.

Remember that we are multi-dimensional, Divine Beings.

Remember to honor Indigenous wisdom, and to reclaim your own Original Whole Indigenous Soul, through honoring the Shamanic consciousness of interconnection with all of Creation.

Remember: "I am Another One of Yourself." We are different faces of each other.

Remember that the Cosmic Serpent is alive within you, too, in your DNA. We all have Serpent Medicine. The Serpent is the Life Force, the bringer of knowledge and wisdom.

Remember to listen to—and collaborate with—the spiritual intelligence of All of Creation: animals, stones, trees, rivers and bones, and even the Fairy Folk, the Cloud Beings, the Ancestors and the Star-Nations.

Remember that Gaia, this New Earth consciousness, wants an intimate, ongoing relationship with you. Find your own Power Place to love, and allow it to teach you reverent engagement.

Remember to practice aligned living, mirroring the wisdom "as above, so below."

Remember that all sites on Earth are to become Sacred Sites. Earth is becoming the Home of Love.

Remember that, as much as Life keeps revealing and bestowing blessings (sometimes disguised as challenges), there will be even more blessings. Dayenu! Stay in gratitude.

Remember that as Sacred Seers and Sacred Sayers, we are writing the next story of Creation together, with all Life. It is the story of the New Earth of Love, and our Golden Age of Peace.

Remember to Make it GOOD, Honey!

WE ARE HOME NOW! IT IS BEAUTIFUL! IT IS COMPLETE!

Remember, Remember, Remember!

Ecstatic!

Appendix I

NOTE: I received these powerful words during a meditation transmission, words of instruction from Gaia, Mother Earth, on 6/3/2006. I now understand them as preparation for all the New Earth songs that I received in *The Seer and The Sayer* story's two-year timeframe. And I know that other "song-catchers" are out there, too, singing the songs of the New Earth.

The Birthing of the New Earth

I am Gaia, Mother Earth. I come in the name of Truth and Oneness.

Each of you is so dear to me. I love you. I honor you. And I need each of you urgently at this cycle of our co-evolution. The intensity of my birthing pains are arriving in waves of cleansing that you experience as "Earth Changes," or natural disasters, of increasing frequency and intensity.

Our new life must come forth on Earth.

You who are aware, you who are willing, you who are aligned with love... you are my designated birth attendants. I call upon you now to sing with me our songs of the New Earth being birthed in radiance and grace.

You are my birth attendants. This means that you do not fear the pain that brings forth the new life. This means that you have the understanding of this process, of laboring into Being this New Energy for our planet.

Hold me gently in your awareness, with each contraction of earthquake; hurricane; tsunami. Stay focused on the miracle in process, rather than the contraction of pain. Pour your love into me. Sing to me the sounds of transformation with your mantras, chants, and tonings. Sing to me the sacred songs that open my birthing in joy.

You are my sacred midwives, bringing forth the New World. Trust. Trust yourselves as I trust you. I know you. You are who I want with me at my birthing process. You are Holy.

Be grounded in deep joy that we are bringing forth this new Life Force on Earth.

Trust. You are a portal, an opening for the Infinite Presence of Wholeness to pour into finite form. This assists the process of our ascension. Creation needs your open hearts. I need your open hearts.

These vessels of your hearts are filling with the purest, holiest love in creation. Each of your hearts, filling with this holy love, is like a well—a moving well—moving across a thirsty earth. Your hearts are giving drinks of love to all those who thirst.

Keep filling your hearts from the Source. Keep offering this drink of Divine Love to all who thirst, that their hearts may become filled. The Truth is that we are Whole and One with Mother/Father God, with all Creation.

As each heart fills with this Divine Love, the new Life Force becomes established as a Living Presence, anchored within each person. And we create Heaven on Earth. You are here to assist this sacred purpose. Thank you for your assistance.

New Earth Songs

Song from the Fairies, Serpent Mound, Ohio
© Victoria A. Hanchin 11/01/2010

Come weave a web with me,
A Rainbow web of Harmony
Come weave a web with me.

Come weave a web with me,
Beauty for all to see,
Come weave a web with me.

Weaving, weaving, weaving a New Earth Dream,
Weaving, weaving, weaving a New Earth Dream.

Come weave a web with me,
Fulfillment, joy and ecstasy!
Come weave a web with me.

Come weave a web with me,
All Life expressing Unity!
Come weave a web with me.

Weaving, weaving, weaving a New Earth Dream,
Weaving, weaving, weaving a New Earth Dream.

First Song from the Sacred White Buffalo

© Victoria A. Hanchin 11/06/2010

White Thunder, Black Lightning, flowing underground.
What was rent apart, now restored, within sacred sound.

A time of separation, holding in protection, Earth's final gestation,
Birthing Holy Ground.

The song within arising, Light and Dark uniting:
Humanity, Divinity
Forever re-bound.

Second Song from the Sacred White Buffalo

© Victoria A. Hanchin, 11/19/2010

(For the rap version of this song go to KelleeMaize.com/Music)

Indigenous Soul: Original Whole
Seeing with Sacred Eyes
Life's interconnection, speaking as Blessing
Divinity realized.

In a Sacred way, creative as play
Offering our self-expressions
As gifts freely given, joyously living
Abundance the lesson.

A new way to listen: Oneness the mission
Listening to Creation:
Animals, stones, trees, rivers and bones
Honoring All Our Relations.

Releasing the lies of shallow eyes,
Beholding each other's beauty.
Freed from the chatter, speaking what matters:
Heart, Soul, Community.

No more separation, now co-creation.
Relating essence-to-essence.
Original Blessing: joy, peace and sharing.
A New Earth expressing Love's presence.

We Are Multi-dimensional Beings—
Interweave With Fairy Song
© Victoria Hanchin 1/23/2011

We are multi-dimensional beings
It's through our hearts that we are seeing.

The animals—they will speak to us
Nature Spirits will be real to us
The magic of the Earth—She will dream through us
Our hearts so open love will stream through us

We are multi-dimensional beings
It's through our hearts that we are seeing.

The songs of the angels—they will sing through us
The Rivers' flow of oneness—they will bring to us
Power stones—they will reveal to us
Ancestors' Wisdom—it will heal through us

We are multi-dimensional beings
It's through our hearts that we are seeing.

The animals—they will speak to us
Nature Spirits will be real to us

Come weave a Web with me, a rainbow Web of Harmony….

The magic of the Earth—She will dream through us
Our hearts so open love will stream through us

Come weave a Web with me, Beauty for all to see.

The songs of the angels—they will sing through us
The Rivers' flow of oneness—they will bring to us

Come weave a Web with me, fulfillment, joy and ecstasy.

Power stones—they will reveal to us
Ancestors' Wisdom—it will heal through us

Come weave a Web with me, All Life expressing unity.

We are multi-dimensional beings
It's through our hearts that we are seeing.

Weaving, weaving, weaving a New Earth Dream
Weaving, weaving, weaving a New Earth Dream

We are multi-dimensional beings
It's through our hearts that we are seeing.

Weaving, weaving, weaving a New Earth Dream
Weaving, weaving, weaving a New Earth Dream.

We Are Multi-dimensional Beings (without Fairy Song)

© Victoria Hanchin 1/23/2011

We are multi-dimensional Beings
It's through our hearts that we are seeing

The animals—they will speak to us
Nature Spirits will be real to us
The magic of the Earth—She will dream through us
Our hearts so open love will stream through us

We are multi-dimensional Beings
It's through our hearts that we are seeing

The songs of the Angels—they will sing through us
The Rivers' flow of Oneness—they will bring to us
Power stones—they will reveal to us
Ancestors' Wisdom—it will heal through us

We are multi-dimensional Beings
It's through our hearts that we are seeing.

Song from the Cosmic Serpent
© Victoria Hanchin Summer Solstice, 2012

There is a secret; and it's hidden in plain sight.
If you are ready, you can learn it with delight.
For once you know it, you will hold the Sacred Key
To transform Reality.

So thank the Serpent, Ancient Teacher to behold
She shows the process: Shedding skin of the Old
Through grounded movement, in communion with the Earth—
What a glorious re-birth!

Sacred Serpent: Symbol of Ancient Mother
Sacred Serpent: Living in our DNA
Sacred Serpent: New Life Bringer
Sacred Serpent: Revealer of Mystery.

The Sacred Serpent, living in our DNA
Is activating humanity's templates.
An inner blessing, from the Serpent in our cells
Shifts us into our Highest Selves.

Her Kundalini, arising in our spines:
Her Life Force Essence, awakening our minds.
A Transformation—the Prophecy foretold—
Earth's Golden Age to behold!

Sacred Serpent: Symbol of Ancient Mother
Sacred Serpent: Living in our DNA
Sacred Serpent: New Life Bringer
Sacred Serpent: Revealer of Mystery.

Appendix II

Victoria's Original Articles as Context for *The Seer and The Sayer*

To read the original articles that were the catalysts for *The Seer and The Sayer*, Go to www.WholePersonWholePlanet.com and select <Articles>

You may then select from these titles:

We Are The Ones We Have Been Waiting For: The Mayan Calendar and Pittsburgh's Role in the Coming 2012 Transformation (Integrating the teachings of the Mayan Calendar prophecies, the Shift of the Ages, and the predictions about Pittsburgh's Mayan 2012 prophetic link that were later confirmed.)

Confluence of Miracles (The report on the Mayan Elders 2007 visit to Pittsburgh, confirming the Pittsburgh three rivers/Mayan 2012 prophetic link. This article includes the full text of Mayan Elder Don Alejandro's "Statement of Revelations and Prophecies" and his "T'zite Oracle Forecast.")

Rivers Alive in Us (The article about the Indigenous Chinese wisdom of poet-artist Huang Xiang, related to the four rivers of Pittsburgh.)

About the Author

Victoria (Vikki) Hanchin, is a Licensed Clinical Social Worker (LCSW), Wholistic Psychotherapist, transformational writer, and visionary activist. Her writings are found at www. WholePersonWholePlanet.com.

Victoria lives in Pittsburgh, Pennsylvania, where she raised her two sons. She offers wholistic psychotherapy in her private practice of over 25 years. She has become quite a fan of "Peaceburgh" and its sacred geography of the converging three rivers and the fourth underground river, which her research revealed are connected to the ancient Mayan 2012 prophetic teachings.

Contact Victoria at: vikki@wholepersonwholeplanet.com